1. 174 Avenue Road - The Village Corner Club
2. 202 Davenport Road - Joso's (second and present location)
3. 169 Avenue Road - The Cellar (first location)
4. 102 Avenue Road - The Night Owl
5. 89 Avenue Road - Le Spot Discotheque (in Regency Towers)
6. 44 Avenue Road - The Place
7. 32 Avenue Road - The Concertino Cafe/La Coterie
8. 53 Avenue Road - The Avenue Road Club/Devil's Den/The In Crowd
9. 51 Avenue Road - The Hamburger Joint
10. 49 Avenue Road - Sammi's Pizza
11. 47 Avenue Road - Half Beat/El Matador
12. 45 Avenue Road - New Gate of Cleve/Boris'/The Red Gas Room
13. 35 Avenue Road - The Purple Onion
14. 134 Yorkville Avenue - The Riverboat
15. 132 Yorkville Avenue - Jacque's Place/The Psychedelic Discotheque
16. 183 Cumberland Street - Half Beat (first location)
17. 158 Cumberland Street - The House of Hambourg (third location)
18. 159 Cumberland Street - The Inn on the Parking Lot/Charlie Brown's/The Booby Hatch
19. 119 Yorkville Avenue - The Golden Gate Discotheque
20. 116 Yorkville Avenue - The Upper Crust
21. 115 Yorkville Avenue - El Patio
22. 114 Yorkville Avenue - The Mynah Bird
23. 138 Cumberland Street - Kiki Rouge
24. 110-112 Yorkville Avenue - The Penny Farthing
25. 106 Yorkville Avenue - The Mousehole
26. 107 Yorkville Avenue - The Macabre/Rive Gauche/The Home of the Blues/The Strawberry Patch
27. 109 Bloor Street West - The Green Door
28. 90 Yorkville Avenue - The Flick
29. 88 Yorkville Avenue - Chez Monique
30. 84 Yorkville Avenue - Picasso Key Club
31. 71 Yorkville Avenue - 71 Coffee House/Act One Scene One/The Continental Caffe/Joso's (first location)
32. 89 Bloor Street West - The Concerto Cafe
33. 40 Scollard Street - The Clef Club/The Cave/Le Chat Noir

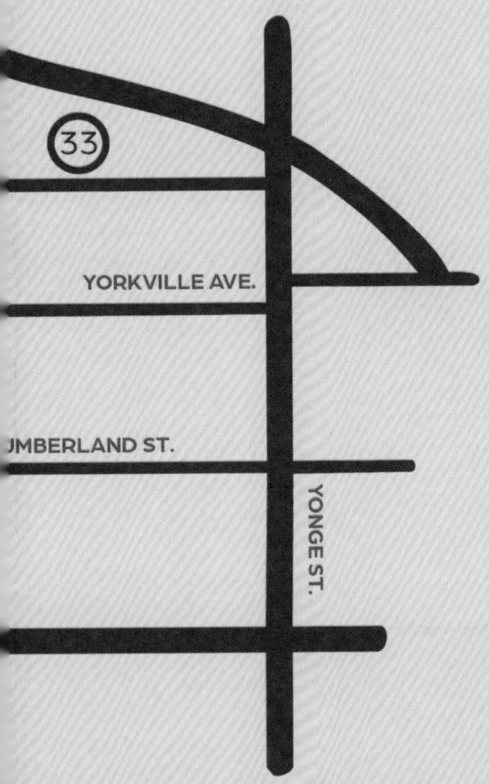

YORKVILLE

YORKVILLE

HOW A 1960S COFFEEHOUSE SCENE REWROTE POPULAR MUSIC

MIKE DALEY

sh.
SUTHERLAND HOUSE

TORONTO, 2026

Sutherland House
416 Moore Ave., Suite 304
Toronto, ON M4G 1C9

First edition, September 2026

If you are interested in inviting one of our authors to a live event or media appearance, please contact sranasinghe@sutherlandhousebooks.com and visit our website at sutherlandhousebooks.com for more information about our authors and their schedules.

We acknowledge the support of the Government of Canada.

Manufactured in China
Cover designed by Lena Yang
Book composed by Karl Hunt

Library and Archives Canada Cataloguing in Publication
Title: Yorkville : how a 1960s coffeehouse scene rewrote popular music / Mike Daley.
Other titles: How a 1960s coffeehouse scene rewrote popular music
Names: Daley, Mike, author.
Description: Includes bibliographical references and index.
Identifiers: Canadiana (print) 20260198188 | Canadiana (ebook) 2026019901X | ISBN 9781997701569 (hardcover) | ISBN 9781997701712 (EPUB)
Subjects: LCSH: Popular music—Ontario—Toronto—1951-1960—History and criticism. | LCSH: Popular music—Ontario—Toronto—1961-1970—History and criticism. | LCSH: Yorkville (Toronto, Ont.)—Social life and customs.
Classification: LCC ML3484.8.T686 D14 2026 | DDC 781.6409713/541—dc23

ISBN 978-1-997701-56-9
eBook 978-1-997701-71-2

Contents

Introduction

POPULAR MUSIC IN THE last fifty years has been transformed by the contributions of Joni Mitchell, whose sublime work took songwriting and record production to new heights; by Neil Young, whose unique approach to composition and performance set the tone for a generation of songwriters and presaged the grunge genre; by Gordon Lightfoot, whose songs helped to define Canadian identity; by Steppenwolf, who laid a foundation for heavy metal music while literally naming the genre.

All these seminal artists spent their formative years in a tiny enclave of coffeehouses in the heart of Toronto, called Yorkville. It was a former village of crumbling Victorian houses, bohemian life, creative ferment, collaboration, and competition. A veritable who's who of 1960s folk rock, R&B, and jazz passed through its smoky, liquor-free venues: Leonard Cohen, Jimi Hendrix, Judy Collins, David Crosby, Ian and Sylvia, Murray McLauchlan, Lenny Breau, and Sonny Greenwich are among them. Others made Yorkville their home without becoming household names: the Paupers, Kensington Market, Luke and the Apostles, Klaas VanGraft, Malka and Joso, and many more.

The venues where the music rang out were for the most part tiny, undercapitalized, poorly policed, and often fly-by-night coffeehouses run by a rogues' gallery of eccentric, determined, creative proprietors who made it up as they went along. They faced a hostile city government that let the scene develop through a bylaw loophole, and then clumsily scrambled to put the genie back in the bottle. In the end, they succeeded in turning Yorkville into an upscale, if sanitized, shopping destination, the live music venues nothing but a fond memory. This is the story of the coffeehouses of Yorkville between 1954 and 1968, a brief time and a small place that rewrote popular music.

I wasn't there, and in fact was born in 1968, the year that closes out this history. I've always loved the music of this era. I began working as a professional guitarist and singer as a teenager in the 1980s, with a turn into academia in my twenties. I studied popular music history at York University in Toronto and eventually earned a PhD in ethnomusicology. After a few years of adjunct lecturing at various Ontario universities, I moved toward adult education, especially for retirees. It was in 2017, while developing a course on the Toronto Sound of the 1950s and '60s, when my interest in this history was sparked.

As I pieced together the material for the course, I realized that these stories were being lost, as the principal participants were now in their seventies, eighties, and nineties. Beginning with Ronnie Hawkins, I conducted more than a hundred interviews with musicians, club owners, managers, go-go dancers, fans, and others, while delving into archives, directories, and other primary sources to reconstruct the built infrastructure of the scene. After delivering the course, I continued my research part-time. My question was always, "Why Yorkville?" What was it about this tiny scene that gave it such an outsized impact on music history?

This book is a combination of narrative and oral history; my aim is to foreground the voices of those who were there, and their sometimes conflicting versions of what happened. Wherever possible, I've tried to step out of the way when my informants had something to say about the subject at hand. Unless otherwise noted, all block quotations in the book are from my own interviews and have been edited for clarity. For conversions into 2025 dollar amounts, I've relied on the Bank of Canada's Inflation Calculator at https://www.bankofcanada.ca/rates/related/inflation-calculator/.

Researching and writing this book over the last eight years has been a labour of love. There have been moments when I felt like I was somehow back there, listening to the music in a smoky club. It is my hope that you can gain the same feeling from the stories and insights contained here, and that, like me, you will marvel at how it happened: the unlikeliness of it all, the triumphs and disappointments, the idealism and the ugly underbelly, the tragedies, and the magic of Yorkville.

For Klaas

Chapter One: A place apart

ON A WARM SUMMER night, Yorkville Avenue was empty, its coffeehouses deserted, its once-thronged sidewalks clear. Where once the street teemed with crowds, and music resonated, now only a stony silence prevailed. It was the sound of fear, fear of contracting a catastrophic airborne disease that was hospitalizing young people that summer, the worrying statistics trumpeted by the three daily Toronto newspapers. "An atmosphere of siege has descended on Yorkville," William Johnson wrote in the *Globe and Mail.* He interviewed a waitress at the Penny Farthing identified only as "Maggie" as she sat alone at a table on the club's capacious patio. "I haven't worked all week," she complained. "It's going to take the whole street months to recover." John McHugh, the Penny Farthing's co-owner, told Johnson, "Just like that nobody came. It was like a pandemic."[1]

Yorkville's coffeehouse live music scene was already in decline in 1968, with licensing hassles and rising rents being the most obvious factors. But the so-called "hippie hepatitis," a public health scare propagated by the local media and abetted by local merchants, would strike the death blow. The scare cleared the streets of the old Village long enough to wipe out almost all of the coffeehouses that were left.

By then, injectable amphetamines were increasingly popular among Yorkville hippies. A few cases of hepatitis, an infectious and sometimes deadly disease, were found among young residents of Yorkville's rooming houses. Even though the total number of cases in Toronto was 135 compared to 220 at the same time in 1967, the localization of the occurrences in Yorkville caused concern. In May 1968, Women's College Hospital proposed that a testing site be opened in the Village. A medical trailer was parked in a vacant lot at the southeast corner of Avenue Road and Yorkville Avenue, where blood samples were taken and analyzed.

By July, an unusual number of patients suffering from hepatitis—fifteen in all—had been admitted to hospital. Most of the patients were suffering from hepatitis B, transmitted through dirty needles. But two were infected with the more communicable hepatitis A, which caused concern of an outbreak. Women's College Hospital tried to keep the information under wraps, but the newspapers were tipped off by the chief pharmacologist at Queen Street Mental Health Centre.[2]

An emergency meeting of the city health board was called. Suggestions that the entire neighbourhood should be quarantined were dismissed, though housing inspectors were sent to Yorkville to check on unsanitary conditions. On August 8, the *Toronto Daily Star* front page reported that two police constables had been felled by the "hippie hepatitis." As Anne Keyl from Women's College Hospital told the paper, "There is a danger to the whole city."[3]

Bruce Cockburn (singer-songwriter): It was ridiculous. At first, we did believe it. But nobody was that scared of it except for suburban parents. It was sort of exotic. They had a mobile health clinic and it was all about hepatitis and getting checked out and everything. It's reminiscent of the Covid experience, but without the governmental dictates, because

> they didn't need it. The audiences didn't come to the clubs. At that point it all kind of fell apart, it died, and it was intentional, obviously. The developers had their way. There were certain members of the city government who were embarrassed by [Yorkville].

In the end, the threatened hepatitis epidemic never came to pass. As acknowledged in a tiny *Star* article buried on page 28 in February 1969, what was touted as a major public health disaster turned out to be a minor hepatitis B outbreak, with all but two of the cases being the result of dirty needles.[4] But the damage was done.

* * *

The area of Toronto known as Yorkville has always been a place apart from the city at large, which was founded as the town of York in 1793. The main north-south artery connecting York with the farmland to the north was Yonge Street. To finance the paving of the road, a toll gate was built in 1820 at the intersection of Yonge Street and the First Concession Road, about three kilometres north of the town. An inn and tavern, the Red Lion Inn, was built at the intersection to serve farmers travelling back and forth; this would be the nucleus around which Yorkville grew.

To the west of the toll gate, the York General Burying Ground was opened after 1826 and known to all as the Potter's Field, though it was not, as the nickname suggested, exclusively a pauper's graveyard. At the time only Anglican and Catholic churches had their own cemeteries, so the Potter's Field was a place for anyone of a different faith, or no faith at all, to have a dignified burial for a reasonable five shillings.[5] With Toronto's ballooning population and frequent cholera outbreaks, the Potter's Field was sorely needed.

In 1834, the town of York was reincorporated as the city of Toronto, its new name an Anglicized version of the old Haudenosaunee name for the area. The northern limit of the new city was the First Concession Road, and just outside of that border, Yorkville was about to appear as Toronto's first suburb. From the beginning, it was imagined as a quiet, bucolic respite from the thrum and bustle of the growing city, a bastion of the old ways.

* * *

Joseph Bloor,[6] born in England in 1789, immigrated to Canada in 1818 or 1819 and opened an inn, the Farmer's Arms, on King Street.[7] He sold the Farmer's Arms in 1830 and used the profits to purchase tracts of land just north of the First Concession Road, including a property in the Rosedale ravine, where he built a brewery. Bloor's beer venture was successful, but by the 1840s he had converted to Methodism, a Christian sect that preached abstinence from alcohol. He sold the brewery in 1843 and embarked on a new career as a real estate speculator and urban planner.[8] Along with fellow speculator Sheriff William Botsford Jarvis, Bloor divided some of his land into lots along two new east-west streets: Sydenham Street (later Cumberland Street) and William Street (later Yorkville Avenue).

The next step was the incorporation of an independent village on the site of Bloor and Jarvis's new land development. Twenty years after the establishment of the city of Toronto to replace the town of York, the name Yorkville harkened back to what must have seemed like a more innocent time. Just as children sometimes do, Yorkville grew into its name, becoming an enclave of nostalgia with a tendency to resist change.

The village of Yorkville was incorporated in the first month of 1853. The borders of the 557-acre village were defined at that time as comprising Sherbourne Street to the east, the First Concession Road (by now renamed Bloor Street) to the south, present-day Walker Avenue to the north, and present-day Bedford Road to the west. One of the first orders of business was to "restrain the running at large of Pigs and Swine and Poultry"; Sydenham Street already had the unfortunate nickname of "Pig Street."[9] Another priority was to get rid of the Potter's Field, which was officially closed in 1856. Most of the bodies in the cemetery were moved to the Necropolis and Mount Pleasant cemeteries, but not all; an auto garage owner told a *Globe and Mail* reporter in 1958 that he'd found human bones on his property while excavating for a building on the south side of Cumberland Street.[10]

One of the chief attractions of Yorkville was significantly lower property taxes than in the city proper. But with the village well established as a bedroom community to Toronto, the population had outgrown its ability to be self-sufficient in needed services like water supply, sewage, road maintenance, and police and fire protection. After a request by the Yorkville councillors, the City of Toronto annexed Yorkville on February 1, 1883. Thereafter the old village boundaries would be officially called St. Paul's Ward, though no one since has seemingly called it anything but Yorkville. Sydenham Street was renamed Cumberland Street (after the English birthplace of James Wallis, one of the Village of Yorkville's first councillors) and William Street was renamed Yorkville Avenue.[11]

By the 1950s, the once proud bay-and-gable houses along Yorkville Avenue and Cumberland Street were a little worse for wear; a city council report described Yorkville Avenue as "an old residential street in relatively poor condition."[12] Some of the owners had moved out to more distant suburbs and subdivided their homes into rooming houses. Students from nearby University of Toronto, artists, actors, musicians, and writers filled these spartan flats on the upper floors of the old houses. Below, high-end boutiques offered dressmaking, furs, and jewellery just a block or two from Bloor Street's "Mink Mile" of upscale shops.

The target demographic was called "the carriage trade," women from the nearby affluent Forest Hill and Rosedale neighbourhoods who came to Yorkville to shop and lunch along the shabby but quaint old avenues. The high-fashion emporium Helmar of London abutted L'Oiseau Bleu, a boutique specializing in ladies' hats. Stanley Arculus at 111 Yorkville was your man for heraldic art, and fine antique furniture could be secured at Adam House. As Jane Tiel described in a 1958 article for the *Globe and Mail*, Cumberland was "a street in transition. Old homes stand; some of them crumble and sag: others, remodelled and face-lifted, house shops and studios. An art gallery here, a milliner's there."[13]

* * *

In the years following World War II, Canada began finally to relax its famously draconian liquor laws. With bipartisan government support, Ontario's Conservative government passed the 1946 Liquor Control Act, with a new type of legal tavern: the cocktail lounge. Now patrons, as long as they were over twenty-one, could purchase beer in bottles, wine, or hard liquor. Food could be served with drinks, and live entertainment was now allowed. The bars stopped serving at midnight.

Cocktail taverns then opened all over Toronto but were particularly concentrated on lower Yonge Street, the traditional entertainment district. Beginning with the sumptuous Silver Rail at Shuter in 1947, taverns featuring live music six nights a week proliferated along Yonge: the Brown Derby at Dundas, the Colonial Tavern just north of Queen, Le Coq D'Or at Gould, and the Edison Hotel next door, and just north of those the Brass Rail and the Zanzibar. Yorkville got its own cocktail tavern with the Embassy Tavern at the corner of Bloor Street and Bellair Street, a short street that runs from Bloor to Yorkville.

Inevitably, the easy availability of hard liquor in the Yonge Street taverns led to a more public, visible drunkenness than had been seen since before Prohibition (1916 to 1927 in Ontario). The activist citizens of Yorkville were well aware of this and decided to do something to prevent it from happening in their neighbourhood. Their efforts would have unintended consequences; while they kept the taverns out, they let the coffeehouses in.

* * *

On April 4, 1949, in Toronto City Hall's ornately decorated council chambers, Mayor H. E. McCallum pounded his gavel to pass bylaw 17544, soon to be nicknamed the Fishleigh bylaw.

Harold Fishleigh was a forty-five-year-old pharmacist and Toronto alderman when he sponsored a new bylaw aimed at severely restricting the types of businesses that could legally open within Yorkville. The borders of the affected area were both sides of Avenue Road, extending from Bloor Street to Roxborough Street, then back south to Davenport Road and east, then down the west side of Bay Street, and then west along the north side of Bloor Street. Essentially the western half of the old Yorkville Village boundaries was covered by the bylaw, which allowed only listed uses, including boarding houses, nursery schools, bowling alleys, public halls, and retail stores. Unlisted, and thus forbidden, were dance halls, private clubs, "places of amusement," meaning any kind of entertainment venue with an admission charge—and coffeehouses.

But the real target of the Fishleigh bylaw was taverns. Earlier in 1949, a cocktail tavern had been proposed to be built on Davenport Road, and the good people of Yorkville did not want a repeat of what was happening on Yonge Street; the Fishleigh bylaw was introduced as an attempt to prevent the Davenport tavern's approval. The bylaw was on shaky ground; a similar one had been recently proposed for Roncesvalles Avenue, but rejected on the basis that it would be a "usurpation of the functions of the Liquor Control Board," according to the city solicitor.[14] By the time the Fishleigh bylaw was submitted to the Ontario Municipal Board for ratification, the cocktail tavern proposal had been abandoned. The bylaw passed unopposed.[15]

Despite frequent challenges and amendments, the bylaw was durable. It survived as an exception to more general citywide zoning passed in 1955 and 1959; when the city property committee recommended that it be repealed in 1956, Alderman Harold Orliffe, supported by a petition from the Annex Ratepayers Association, succeeded in having the recommendation stricken from the report, telling the *Globe* that a repeal would "load up the area with beer taverns and clubs."[16]

* * *

Born in the tiny English town of Leighton Buzzard, Claude Hector Dewhurst (1908–1976) would soon see the world. He joined the British army at twenty-one and served until 1954, including military attaché posts in Greece, Crete, Syria, and Iraq. His friend Alistair Horne remembered Dewhurst as "a truly brilliant intelligence officer. Always wearing an unconventional silk foulard [neck scarf], Claude was unabashedly gay . . . Claude delighted in eighteenth-century usages; people were either 'most agreeable' or 'entirely preposterous' . . . However outrageous, he was always fun to be with."[17]

After retiring from the military at the age of forty-six, Dewhurst emigrated to Toronto, where he made an immediate impression. His urbane wit and charm, combined with his vast knowledge of international relations, made him a popular hired speaker at clubs and associations around the city. Newly landed in 1954, this world traveller found a grey, quiet city with little nightlife after the bars closed at midnight. Toronto in those days is remembered as a kind of buttoned-up, grey place, still overwhelmingly English, with all the restraint and reticence associated with that culture. Canadian-born British writer Wyndham Lewis went further, calling postwar Toronto "a sanctimonious ice-box . . . a kind of hell of dullness."[18] Dewhurst felt that Toronto needed a European-style café that catered to the daytime shopping crowd as well as the night owls.[19] As he told the *Vancouver News-Herald*, "It is so difficult to find a quiet rendezvous in Canada . . . [where one can] go in an evening for a cup of coffee, good music and a quiet spot for conversation."[20]

Partnering with Ervin Bolgar (1912–1988), a Hungarian-born former chemist, Dewhurst leased a narrow bay-and-gable brick house at 89 Bloor Street West, on the south side facing Bellair Street and the Embassy Tavern. Because this location was just outside of the area affected by the Fishleigh bylaw, Dewhurst and Bolgar were not impeded in seeking to open a café/restaurant. Named after a musical format where a virtuoso solo instrument is paired with a full orchestra, the Concerto Café promised elegance in an upscale atmosphere. Dewhurst and Bolgar spared little expense with the decor, installing flower-print silk curtains, covering the square tables with high-quality white linen, and commissioning wall frescoes depicting long-necked tropical birds. Eighteen varieties of coffee were offered, along with pastries from two chefs hired from Germany and a variety of entrées.

Launched in April 1955, the Concerto Café was open six days a week[21] and was an immediate hit. At first, musical entertainment was provided in the form of long-playing records, but soon enough Dewhurst and Bolgar decided to engage a professional folk singer to perform. So it was that on June 3, 1955, Toronto's coffeehouse folk music scene began, along with the almost forgotten career of its first full-time professional folksinger, Greg Curtis.[22]

Greg Curtis was born George William Curtis on September 3, 1928, in Vancouver, British Columbia, along with his twin brother Allan. He grew up in the former gold-rush town of Barkerville in the Cariboo Mountains. George was one of five children, all boys. He left home for Toronto in 1948, not long after high school graduation. Once he arrived, he changed his professional name to Greg Curtis and began to take acting lessons. He appeared in a few small dramatic roles but the jobs were few and his acting career was foundering.[23] Not long after, he began to take voice and piano lessons.[24] Two years later, Greg made a brief appearance at the Casino Theatre at 87 Queen Street West singing "pop ballad and jump tunes" but he was already recasting himself as a folksinger, accompanying himself on guitar and singing traditional songs.[25] It was 1951, the second year of the folk revival.

* * *

In 1950, the Weavers, a folk quartet headed by Pete Seeger, scored the surprise #1 pop hit of the year with their version of Huddie "Lead Belly" Ledbetter's "Goodnight, Irene." A plaintive song performed with informal rough-hewn vocal harmony (but lush orchestrations from arranger Gordon Jenkins), it invited participation. It was also dead simple and could be played with a rudimentary understanding of the guitar or banjo. This participatory, you-can-do-it-too spirit suffused a genuine movement of amateur musicmaking that took hold in the '50s, the folk revival.

The folk revival, in its early stages, was remarkably noncommercial, less a popular music trend than a grassroots knowledge economy of personal repertoires and styles, with songs learned and shared orally. Those songs were often in the public domain, drawn from the traditional repertoires of specific regions. The American southeast supplied a rich vein of material through the Weavers and their many imitators. British and Scottish ballads, many preserved in books and anthologies, were another source. Canadian folksingers sought out Canadian songs, which were supplied by the song-collecting work of Helen Creighton on the East Coast and Edith Fowke in Ontario.

The Almanac Singers, Pete Seeger's pre-Weavers group, had first named and defined the "hootenanny," or "hoot." The term originally referred to an unnameable gadget, like a "doo-hickey," and then came to describe an informal folk music gathering, non-hierarchical and not oriented as a performance, but more as what Newfoundlanders call a song circle. There was no cover charge and no money was exchanged. It was the platonic ideal of the folk music experience, and an ideal way to learn new songs and make connections.

* * *

The first hootenannies in Toronto were private parties, often in the home of Edith Fowke (1913–1996), who, in addition to her work as a song collector, hosted a long-running show, *Folk Song Time*, on CBC Radio. Greg Curtis, newbie folk singer, needed to build up his repertoire and began to attend. He picked up songs from other singers and shared the ones he knew. All joined in to sing along.[26] Greg learned centuries-old British ballads like "Barbara Allen" and African-American spirituals like "Michael, Row the Boat Ashore."

In May 1955, Greg got his big break as a folksinger, a steady engagement at the Concerto Café. He would have likely been paid musicians' union scale as dictated by the Toronto Musicians' Association, which at that point was $125 a week ($1,449 in 2025[27]) for six nights of three one-hour sets.[28] Wandering among the candlelit tables, Greg sang "Jamaica Farewell," a Caribbean standard soon to be a hit for Harry Belafonte, and "She's Like the Swallow," a Newfoundland ballad, in a strong, tremulous baritone, accompanying himself with simple chords on his gut-strung guitar. With his growing repertoire, movie-star good looks, and brawny physique, Greg Curtis was a hit with the Concerto clientele.

* * *

With the Concerto a clear success, Claude Dewhurst and Ervin Bolgar looked to open a satellite location: 32 Avenue Road was another bay-and-gable house, this one on the west side of the street just north of Prince Arthur Avenue and facing the corner of Yorkville Avenue. With its close proximity to the boutiques along Cumberland Street and Yorkville Avenue and the Park Plaza Hotel a block south, the property was ideally located. The Concertino Café was, like its predecessor, named after a classical music format: a concertino is a simpler and shorter concerto.

When they had opened the Concerto on Bloor Street, there were no licensing issues with the city, since the south side of Bloor was not covered by the Fishleigh bylaw. But now with this expansion to 32 Avenue Road, they were in Fishleigh territory. On January 26, 1955, a few months before opening the Concerto, Dewhurst and Bolgar's lawyers had appeared before city council to request an amendment to the bylaw. They were rejected, and promptly mounted an appeal with the Ontario Municipal Board, which granted their request. Their hand forced by the OMB, the city passed bylaw 19443 on June 5 to allow for the operation of a "coffee shop" at 32 Avenue Road.[29] This would be the Concertino.

The day-to-day management of the Concertino was handled by Bob and Denyse Sterio, a young couple who were acquaintances of Dewhurst and Bolgar.[30] While coffee was brewed in-house, the food preparation was done at the larger Concerto Café and brought the short distance on foot. Despite Dewhurst's stated plans for "a fabulous design along Roman Forum lines,"[31] a grainy photograph of the Concertino interior from December 1955 shows a room that is decidedly more spartan and rustic than the Concerto, with small, bare tables and what appear to be bamboo chairs.[32]

In the spring of 1956, not even a year into their ownership of the Concerto and Concertino, Dewhurst and Bolgar sold their cafés and parted ways. Ervin Bolgar left Canada for the United States and died in Miami, Florida, in 1988. Claude Dewhurst ran a public relations firm before finally retiring for good in the 1960s. He died in Toronto in 1976.

The St. Regis Hotel, located a few blocks east on Sherbourne, purchased the Concerto to use as a satellite restaurant, and Bob and Denyse Sterio bought the Concertino, renaming it La Coterie, a French phrase for an intimate group of people with shared interests. With a facade of whitewashed brick and an overhanging neon sign in diagonal cursive, La Coterie projected low-key elegance. Just one block north of the Park Plaza Hotel, it was an immediate hit with night-owl hotel guests after the bars closed at midnight.

La Coterie had an underground quality after hours. Decades later, Denyse Sterio remembered sneaking shots of cognac into the coffees of trusted clients and the smell of cannabis smoke.[33] Greg Curtis, now splitting his time between La Coterie and the Concerto, wandered among the tables with his guitar. Other performers at La Coterie included

Mexican-Canadian guitarist Rafael Nunez and a Trinidadian calypso singer whom Denyse remembered only as "José" who "would make up songs about people." After hours on weekends, La Coterie turned into a jazz venue, with frequent appearances by the jazz pianist and fine artist Michael Snow.

On Thursday evenings, the back room of La Coterie was the site of an informal public hootenanny, seemingly Toronto's first. This was a momentous step in the development of the Yorkville folk scene, as it opened up a window to the world. Open stages, jams, and the like are important parts of any healthy music scene, since they create opportunities for unestablished, unknown talent to get stage experience and make connections. While the Concerto employed professional, union-affiliated singers, the back room at La Coterie was open to all, professional or amateur.

In the fall of 1957, the Sterios sold their interest in La Coterie to new owners who stopped the musical entertainment altogether. By that time, Greg Curtis was already gone. After a stint at a summer resort in the Muskoka Lakes district, he left for London, England, on July 27, 1957, to fulfill a year-long contract at the Dorchester Hotel. Chronic digestive problems—possibly Crohn's disease—forced him to end the contract six months early. Back in Toronto in February 1958, he returned to the Concerto, now managed by Otto Day on behalf of the St. Regis Hotel. Often too ill to perform, Greg brought in a substitute, a folk singer seven years his junior named Klaas VanGraft.

Klaas VanGraft (1935–2020) grew up on a tulip farm in the Netherlands and emigrated to Canada in 1955 to avoid military conscription. His family had sung folk songs but a formative high school experience with a multilingual Dutch folk singer made a big impression, shaping his interest in music.

Shortly after arriving in Toronto, Klaas met Dawn Blackstock, an art student who was involved in the local folk scene. They soon married and she brought Klaas to some of the hootenannies around town, where he picked up songs and made connections with more established performers like Greg Curtis. As Greg had done, Klaas soaked in songs for his growing repertoire. He filled five thick notebooks with 359 different songs in eighteen languages, from standards like "Kisses Sweeter Than Wine" to obscurities like "Wicked Alexandria," the bawdy "Cosher Bailey's Engine" and local Toronto ballads like "On the Banks of the Don."

Back at the Concerto, a steady rotation of singers performed, including Greg Curtis, Noreen St. Pierre (possibly accompanied by Ian Tyson), and actor-singer Igors Gavon. Upstairs, Klaas played calypso songs in a trio with percussionist Dick Smith (later a co-founder of the Caribana Festival) and future civil rights lawyer Charles Roach. But after a catastrophic fire on December 14, 1959, which injured two firemen, the Concerto closed for good.[34] Improbably enough, 89 Bloor Street West still stands in 2025, rebuilt internally but externally intact. It currently hosts two high-end jewellery stores.

In the 1960s, Greg Curtis's live appearances became more sporadic. Sometimes billed as "Toronto's first folk singer," he played brief engagements at the Fifth Peg, a folk club on Church Street, and the Gate of Cleve, a Dupont Street venue discussed below. By January 1964, Greg was back at La Coterie, appearing on Fridays and Saturdays from 9 p.m. to 2 a.m. This extended engagement ended a year later in January 1965, after which all references to Greg Curtis disappear from the three Toronto daily newspapers. He seems to have given up music at this time. After a career as a freelance model and actor, Greg died on July 3, 2000, at his home in Toronto at the age of seventy-two. Apart from a handful of brief appearances on CBC Television in the '50s, he left no known recordings.[35]

* * *

Around the same time that the Concerto and La Coterie were seeding Yorkville's folk music scene, the House of Hambourg was its first standard bearer for modern jazz. Clement Theodore Hambourg was born on July 31, 1900, in London, England, the youngest of seven children. His parents, Michael and Catherine Hambourg, had brought their young family from Moscow, where pogroms were making life intolerable, even for a distinguished musician and educator like Michael. His and Catherine's four sons were trained from early childhood to be high-level classical musicians: Jan a violinist, Boris a cellist, and Mark and Clement as pianists.

The family, minus eldest son Mark and daughter Galia, moved to Toronto in 1910, where they found a nascent classical music scene that was hospitable to European-style musical instruction. By 1914, the Hambourg Conservatory of Music at 100 Gloucester Street employed fifty-seven teachers instructing over five hundred students a week. Amid this success, the Hambourg Conservatory was often mired in scandal and persistent debt. "It was a characteristic of all four Hambourg brothers, and their father, that they often, perhaps usually, lived beyond their means," wrote Hambourg family biographer Eric Koch.[36]

Clem, like his older brothers, was trained to be a concert musician, but his 1925 debut at Massey Hall generated little interest. The youngest Hambourg was, in his own estimation, the black sheep of the family, with eccentric interests and unusual ambitions. He married and soon had a son, Klemi, in 1929. At the Hambourg Conservatory, Clem taught piano as well as microphone technique to singers and headed the radio department, which sparked his interest in recording. He married for a second time to Helen Oram. When war broke out in 1939, Clem enlisted at the age of thirty-nine but was given a clerical role because of his poor eyesight.

After leaving the army three years later, Clem didn't return to his room at the Conservatory, but to a rented basement at 1184 Bay Street, just south of Bloor. In this cramped space, he opened Echo Recording Studio to the public. Echo Recording Studio was later renamed Hambourg Recording Studios, the plural more aspirational than real. The facility was spartan, with not much more than a microphone and an RCA record-cutting machine. Surviving recordings evince predictably low audio fidelity. By 1946 the studio and Clem's piano teaching practice were being advertised under the name the House of Hambourg, putting the proud family surname front and centre.[37] Clem embraced his black sheep status within the family while at the same time trying to create his own legacy to match that of his father and brothers.

Journalist McKenzie Porter described Clem with "tawny hair hanging about his shoulders, a rumpled suit, a tie all awry, and the sort of expression you see on absent-minded professors in comic strips."[38] He lived in the recording studio with his third wife, Ruth-Nadine, also known as Ruth or Ruthie. Ruthie had grown up in the deep south of the United States and emigrated to Toronto in 1920. She was a talented dress designer and artist, with a penchant for making dolls and reading up on occult subjects. She was also a jazz lover, having heard it as a young girl. Clem credited her for seeing "the plight of musicians at that time, and drew my attention to it. There were some very good ones in very bad surroundings."[39] He referred to them as "the ragged orphans,"[40] adding, "We gave them a place to breathe. We got to know them intimately, we fathered and mothered them. They played on and on and we had no place to sleep."[41]

After hours, 1184 Bay was fast becoming a hangout and jamming space for Toronto's young jazz modernists. Clem and Ruthie were fascinated with modern jazz. It was complex, angular music, demanding on both listeners and musicians, who put in untold hours of practice. The retinue that attended early gatherings at the Hambourgs' Bay Street apartment reads like a who's who of mid-twentieth-century Toronto jazz: saxophonist/flautist Moe Koffman (1928–2001), guitarist Ed Bickert (1932–2019), saxophonist Don "D. T." Thompson (1932–2004), and vibraphonist Hagood Hardy (1937–1997), among others.

Clem and Ruthie began by simply making coffee and sandwiches for the starving young musicians. Word got out and soon there were more jam sessions. Nonmusicians started dropping by just to listen, and Clem and Ruthie fed them, too.

Ruth-Nadine Hambourg: We at first charged nothing, because we just liked to have the musicians come to our place. Then, when they . . . insisted on paying, we accepted and I became the cook.[42]

In the fall of 1951, Clem and his brother Boris opened a new music conservatory, also to be called the House of Hambourg, to replace the Hambourg Conservatory, which had folded that year. Along with Ruthie, and Boris's wife, Maria, they signed a ten-year lease on a fourteen-room Victorian mansion owned by Creed Furs at 144–146 Bloor Street West, just east of Avenue Road, for $500 a month (around $6,000 in 2025), increasing to $700 ($8,400 in 2025) within five years. This would be a new base of operations for the two brothers, who lived on the premises with their wives.

Music teachers renting studios in the building helped to defray the considerable rent and expenses, but the Hambourgs were struggling financially, with Clem reporting his 1953 income as $1,934.05 ($22,513.98 in 2025). The ambitious new House of Hambourg, it turned out, was a money pit. But even as Clem filed that sobering tax return, he and Ruthie were planning their first real venue, a modern jazz club in the basement of 142 Bloor.

Clem Hambourg: With the aid of the Bloor Street tycoons, we knocked together two houses. We smiled on Bloor Street at the front and kept our guns trained on Cumberland Street at the back . . . Then we dug a cellar and invited the public to hear what we had been hearing.[43]

The House of Hambourg jazz club opened around February 1954. It was not affected by the restrictions of the Fishleigh bylaw, since the south side of Cumberland had been excluded with an amendment in 1949. Patrons walked from Cumberland Street through a dark parking lot to a door lit by a single bulb. At the bottom of the stairs, Clem collected the one-dollar cover charge. A *Star* reporter described the scene: "Bespectacled, cigar-smoking Clement Hambourg, with his mane of white hair, scholarly manner and classical reputation easily fills the conception of a middle-aged, Old World music teacher. That is, until he greets you . . . 'Come on in, man. Check your coat. Things are cool.'"[44]

The House of Hambourg was a brick-walled cellar, seating between one hundred and fifty and two hundred, with a small stage.[45] Patrons sat at round wooden tables, closely crowded together under blue and orange light bulbs and abstract paintings.[46] Spaghetti, chili, shrimp, and salad were transported from the upstairs kitchen to the basement via a dumbwaiter nicknamed "the Monster." With its arched columns, alcoves, and subterranean smoky ambience, the House of Hambourg recalled Le Caveau de la Huchette, already legendary Paris jazz cellar opened in 1946.

The House of Hambourg was a treasured home base for the young musicians that Clem booked. "It's the greatest," pianist Norm Amadio

(1928–2020) told the *Ottawa Citizen* in 1957. "We play the kind of music we like. And we get paid for it." Ed Bickert added, "No commercial stuff, man . . . not even 'Lullaby of Birdland' . . . We just swing the way we want to."[47] Underground no longer, the club was a member in good stead of the Toronto Musicians' Association. The House of Hambourg paid union scale, $36 ($389 in 2025) for three hours per musician, and in the words of trumpeter Herbie Spanier, was "one of the only places in town for improvised jazz."[48]

"By charging admission I just break even," Clem admitted to the *Ottawa Citizen*.[49] But in fact Clem and Ruth were not quite breaking even. Their accountants determined that the House of Hambourg lost $300.15 ($3,494 in 2025) in its first year.[50] By early 1960 the club had moved once more, to a former CBC studio space at 23 Grenville Street. There they presented jazz and occasional folk music seven nights a week in the basement. But just as at Cumberland Street, the Grenville location could not turn a profit. In June 1962, Clem tried unsuccessfully to sell the business. As he told the *Globe*, "It's been getting a little too much for me recently . . . Ruth, my wife, is my only old age pension."[51] Not long after, the prominent tailor and jazz booker Dave Caplan told the *Star* that Clem's savings were gone and Ruth's personal nest-egg of $3,000 ($30,993 in 2025) was depleted as well. Caplan organized a three-day benefit concert beginning July 20 that raised $2,200 ($22,728 in 2025)[52] but the House of Hambourg was closed by March 9, 1963.

The House of Hambourg, along with the Concerto and La Coterie's folk music, laid the foundation for Yorkville's '60s music scene. At one end of the spectrum, improvised jazz brought musicianship and dedication to the scene. At the other, the folk clubs brought tradition and participation and accessibility. The pillars thus in place, 1960 was the year that the Yorkville coffeehouse era sprang to life.

Chapter Two: "We had no idea exactly what we were doing."

As some of my younger readers know, this city is in the grip of a new craze. It has become the fourth-largest folk-singing centre on the continent. The folkniks, as they are now called, are akin to the beatniks. They share an affinity for espresso coffee, non-representational art and off-beat poetry. They congregate in smoky, candle-lit clubs scattered in attics and cellars about the downtown area.

Pierre Berton, "With Notebook and Pencil Through the Land of the Folkniks," *Toronto Daily Star*, November 23, 1960

WHEN THE KINGSTON TRIO'S 1958 version of the old American murder ballad "Tom Dooley" hit #1 on the Billboard pop charts, something shifted in the folk revival. Just as television was capturing the eyes and ears of the masses, folk music offered a kind of countermovement. It promised all of television's opposites: tradition, permanence, honesty, and the pleasures of in-person experience. Folk music was interactive and participatory. Singing along was almost required.

More than the Weavers' "Goodnight Irene," "Tom Dooley" connected with the kids. It might have helped that the Kingston Trio had a casual but clean-cut image and didn't seem to be much older than teenagers themselves. Soon the Kingston Trio, the Limelighters, and the New Christy Minstrels were racking up respectable album sales. Harry Belafonte's 1956 *Calypso* album opened a space in commercial folk music for Caribbean styles. Joan Baez debuted to acclaim at the 1959 Newport Folk Festival, and folk venues sprang up in Greenwich Village in New York City; in Cambridge, Massachusetts; in San Francisco—and in Yorkville.

* * *

The first of the new crop of Yorkville folk coffeehouses was a narrow L-shaped room on the ground floor of 174 Avenue Road. Calling it the Village Corner Club was a trifle disingenuous, since the club wasn't actually within the boundaries of the old Village; it was a block north of Yorkville's northwest corner. The room sat sixty and was described by the University of Toronto student paper the *Varsity* as "small, smokey, dark, cramped and bizarrely decorated with potpourri of paintings, murals, photos, candles and travel posters."[1]

The Village Corner was first opened in February 1960 by John Morley and Roy Davies. Their landlord, John Conforzi, provided seed money. Morley and Davies were thirty-year-old English expats and part-time actors, fond of regaling the Corner crowd with satirical songs by the British music-hall duo Flanders and Swann. The *Varsity* described Morley as "a dark-haired, reticent young man who gives the impression of a high degree of literacy."[2] He preferred the relaxed atmosphere of the coffeehouse to the pressurized atmosphere of his former job, copywriting at a large downtown department store. "Unlike jazz or the classics, a few sweet chords on the guitar, a familiar melody, can make all the worries of a work-a-day week disappear," he rhapsodized to the *Star*'s Sid Adilman.[3]

Despite their sympathies for the therapeutic properties of guitar chords, Morley and Davies were decidedly not folkies themselves. They entrusted the talent booking to Ted Schafer, a banjoist-singer in the Pete Seeger mold, and David Wiffen, a talented blues guitarist-singer and budding songwriter. The weekend the Corner first opened, Schafer played Friday and Sunday nights, with Damiano, a calypso singer whose real name was David Campbell, performing on Saturdays.[4] Later, Klaas VanGraft and his friend Jake Banki took over Sunday nights to present a parody of evangelical preachers, "the Prophets." Wearing long, flowing tunics created by Klaas's wife, Dawn, they performed mock faith healings and sang gospel songs while Banki held up a sign that read "Repent."

The Village Corner operated within the boundaries covered by the Fishleigh bylaw, but it skirted its restrictions by operating as a private club. Back in 1956, Gerald Peters, owner of the Piccadilly Club (137 Avenue Road), a private club for British expats, had petitioned city council for an amendment to Fishleigh to allow him to operate. Council approved his request, passing bylaw 19527, which was in turn rejected by the Ontario Municipal Board (OMB).[5] Later that year, council tried to get Fishleigh deleted from the books and was again rebuffed by the OMB.

When a new city zoning bylaw, 20623, was passed in 1959, Fishleigh remained as a region-specific exception to the regular zoning rules (which allowed private clubs in commercial zones like Avenue Road and Yorkville Avenue), but from this point private clubs were tolerated by the city as "non-conforming uses."[6] The upshot was that the Fishleigh bylaw continued to prohibit taverns, in keeping with its original intent, but private clubs were now allowed to open, even though they technically violated the bylaw. For this reason, many of the Yorkville coffeehouses from this point were private clubs, with nominal membership dues. The first of these was the Village Corner.

Fifty cents ($5.13 in 2025) bought an off-white membership card, good for one year. It entitled the bearer to attend any session for a further one dollar. No membership card, no entry. This policy had a double purpose: it allowed the club to work around the Fishleigh restrictions (which allowed private clubs), and it helped to keep the late-night drunks and rowdies out. Six months after opening, the Corner had 2,600 members. By the end of the year, the number was up to 4,200.[7]

* * *

Bonnie Dobson was born in Toronto on November 13, 1940. She grew up listening to the Weavers with her union organizer father, and began to play and sing folk music at summer camp.

Bonnie Dobson: I really got interested when I went to Camp Beaver in Quebec when I was thirteen. Pete Seeger and Leon Bibb and Earl Robinson used to come up to sing at our camp. The following two years I went to Camp Kinderland, which was run by the United Jewish People's Order. I think I was the only non-Jew. Again, Seeger came up and did concerts. I hadn't planned on singing professionally at all. I was going to be an English teacher. When I hit university, I wasn't very happy with my course. I decided to take a year out. I was doing loads of Canadian songs, like "She's Like the Swallow." I was very traditional. Lots of French-Canadian songs, songs from the Maritimes.

Bonnie began hanging around the Village Corner, occasionally singing at hoots but not actually doing any paid bookings there. But she was a star on the rise. Helped by Edith Fowke's assistant Vivienne Stenson and local concert promoter Martin Bochner, she joined a tour in May 1960 with

Sonny Terry and Brownie McGhee in the United States, and ended up moving there for five years.

Bonnie Dobson: When I got this offer to go on tour with Brownie and Sonny, in order to work in the States at that time it was really quite difficult, because you had to have a visa stating that you had a special talent. Vivienne, bless her, wrote a [support] letter for me, because I hadn't ever done any professional work. I launched forth without having ever sung professionally at all. I did my first tour with Brownie and Sonny in the States, and that was it.

Bonnie was Yorkville's first breakout star. Building on her increased visibility with the Sonny Terry and Brownie McGhee tour, she signed with Prestige Records and released her first album, *Bonnie Dobson Sings "She's Like a Swallow" and Other Folk Songs*, in 1961.[8] She is best remembered today for her original song "Morning Dew," which has been recorded by more than seventy artists including Robert Plant, the Jeff Beck Group, and the Grateful Dead. She moved to England in 1969 and has recently returned to performing after a long retirement.

One night before she left for the United States, Bonnie was sitting in the Village Corner when Ian Tyson walked in for the first time and sang some cowboy songs and blues. "He sounded bloody good," she remembers. "It was obvious."

Born in Victoria, British Columbia, on September 25, 1933, and raised in nearby Duncan, Ian Tyson developed his guitar skills while recovering from a rodeo riding accident. He moved to Toronto in 1958 and worked as a graphic artist. He performed solo at the First Floor Club on Asquith Avenue, and duetted with Noreen St. Pierre, possibly at the Concerto in 1958. He began to appear regularly at the Village Corner in 1960, mostly as a solo act.

Sid Adilman, writing for the *Star*, described Ian at the Corner in those days: "A clean-shaven 24-year-old Vancouverite who makes folk singing his career. Performing on Saturday nights in tight-fitting blue jeans and a freshly laundered sports shirt open at the neck, he sings about feudal England, the Great Depression and prison blues with a relaxed easy manner."[9]

In 1959, Ian was introduced to Sylvia Fricker (1940–), an aspiring folk singer from Chatham, Ontario. Sylvia was statuesque and icy, with large brown eyes, a steady alto voice, and a songbag full of ancient British ballads learned from library books.

Sylvia Tyson: [My interest in folk music] really came about through an interest in English literature. *Grass of Parnassus* was the standard textbook for poetry. In it were a couple of old English ballads, and someone had had the forethought to include lines of music with them. It was a revelation to me that these were actually songs that people had sung. There weren't really that many recordings available at that time. There were a couple of CBC Radio shows, as well as Ed McCurdy and Alan Mills. It was a pretty isolated situation. Folk music was not generally known in Chatham at that time. Ian's boss [from] where he was working as a commercial artist connected the two of us.

Ian and Sylvia began to work up a duo act. Their commitment to precise vocal arrangements and consistent, professional presentation marked them as the act to watch on the Toronto scene. "We did something that nobody else on the local folk scene did—we rehearsed," Sylvia told Nicholas Jennings.[10] They also played to their strengths. Ian couldn't sing harmony, so he always sang the melody while Sylvia harmonized. Her vocal lines did not move in lockstep with Ian's, but seemed to float above, with independent countermelodies of their own. She often strummed an autoharp, its metallic zing lending an extra layer of rhythm to Ian's guitar.

Beginning with an advertised Village Corner engagement on November 28, 1960, Ian and Sylvia made the club their home base, honing their act and building an audience. But with their distinctive sound and good looks, they were not long for Toronto. Within six months the duo signed a management contract with Albert Grossman, who already handled Odetta's career and would soon draw Gordon Lightfoot, Bob Dylan, and Peter, Paul and Mary into his stable. Grossman quickly placed the duo with Vanguard Records who released their first album, *Ian & Sylvia*, in 1962.

Albert Grossman understood the profitability of songwriting and publishing royalties, and he encouraged his clients, who tended to sing traditional songs and not original compositions, to try their hands as songwriters. As Village Corner denizen and guitar virtuoso Amos Garrett remembered, Ian and Sylvia's success with their first efforts influenced the priorities of local Toronto folk singers.

Amos Garrett: I remember Ian coming into the Village Corner club. There were a bunch of us folkies sitting in there and he had just come back from New York. He sat down at the table and he said, "Boys, it's all changing now. You're either going to be with it, or you're going to have to find some kind of path, you know, but it's all changing. It's going to be all about songwriting and publishing."

* * *

In the first half of 1961, the Village Corner only listed "folk singing" in its newspaper listings, which suggests that the club was running informal hoots only, and was no longer hiring and paying singers. But beginning on August 20, John Morley and Roy Davies took a new tack with their year-old folk club: they booked a jazz band. Mike White's Imperial Jazz Band was a traditional group playing in the strict New Orleans style. In the late 1950s, this precise, professional unit had done a long residency at the Westover Hotel near Jarvis and Dundas, playing six nights a week. Now they were part-timers, playing a one-nighter at a folk club with sawdust on the floor. It was no doubt an odd fit, and after a single rebooking in October, the jazz experiment was dropped.

Dave Campbell—a.k.a. Damiano—returned in late September, trading sets with Jim McCarthy, a talented twelve-string guitarist-singer in the mold of the influential but now almost forgotten Bob Gibson. But by October 1961, the Village Corner was closed for renovations and a rethink.

* * *

Three months after the Village Corner opened just outside of Yorkville proper, it was bookended by the Clef Club.[11] The address was 40 Scollard Street, one block north of Yorkville Avenue, midway between Bay and Yonge, on the north side. This took it outside of the area covered by the Fishleigh bylaw, but it was a private club anyway, with a relatively steep membership cost of $1.50 ($15.38 in 2025) and $1 ($10.53 in 2025) per show after. Three months after opening, the Clef Club had a membership of nine hundred.

Peter Ellis, a twenty-one-year-old former factory worker, was the proprietor. He saw the Clef as a place to take a break from mainstream popular culture. As he told the *Star*'s Sid Adilman, "The spontaneous atmosphere in the clubs is ten times better than the stilted one in night club or television."[12]

Billed as a "folk and jazz centre," the Clef seated one hundred people, nearly twice the capacity of the Village Corner. With the walls, ceiling, and even the tables painted a sombre flat black, the Clef is remembered by Sylvia Tyson only as "dark." At some point a semi-abstract mural of a uniformly dressed, seemingly male folk-singing trio, faceless but for their circular mouths in mid-sing, was painted behind the stage.[13] The atmosphere, according to Ted Schafer, was that of "a bohemianly decorated mine shaft."[14] Pierre Berton similarly noted an "authentic Springhill mine shaft effect."[15]

Mary Jane and Winston Young, a husband-and-wife duo, performed on Friday nights from 10 p.m. to 12:30 a.m.

Mary Jane Young: I was born in 1933 in Owen Sound, one of five sisters, and we moved to St. Catharines where we went to the Catholic school, though my father was an atheist and a socialist, a union rep. We sang in the choir there, in Latin. Of all the sisters, I was the only one that did anything with singing afterwards. I sang in a group called the Garden City Singers with Lenny Dolgoy and Adam Timoon.[16] In 1955, I went to a socialist folk music festival in Warsaw [Poland] and that's where I met Winston. When I saw him on the bus, I said, "Who's that guy with the horn-rimmed glasses?" He looked sort of intellectual.

Winston Young, born to an Irish-Canadian family in 1933 in Pembroke, Ontario, was raised in Val-D'Or, Quebec. His Catholic family converted to Jehovah's Witnesses and Winston spent his teenage years knocking on doors for the church. He broke with the community after hitchhiking to the American southwest, and after returning home to finish high school was turfed from his parents' house at nineteen. When Winston met Mary Jane, he was working in construction, operating heavy equipment.

Mary Jane Young: When we got back [from Poland], we were all interviewed by the RCMP because we had been to a socialist country. I went back to my old job [in St. Catharines]. I was working at City Hall in the works department, and the woman there said, "The RCMP were around and they said not to hire you back." I was just disgusted with the idea that they'd go around and do that to people who had been at a festival. I moved to Toronto and I started singing with different people. We had a socialist choir and we sang labour songs. I learned songs in Yiddish, Persian, and Spanish. If somebody was willing to sit down and sing it, I would write it out in phonetics, I'd learn it that way. I prided myself in being good at accents.

After moving to Toronto, I reunited with Winston and we became a couple. We lived together for about a year before we got married in 1957 and had our daughter Michelle in 1958. Shortly after that we formed a little group called the Tamaracks. I don't think we performed anyplace. Shortly after we got married, we got involved in the Farnham folk club and began to perform as a duo.[17] The Village Corner was the first coffeehouse we played, then after that was the Clef Club. I liked that club. The audience there was very enthusiastic. Winston was in the musicians' union but I wasn't, because I didn't play an instrument. We just got paid a very small amount and it wouldn't be union rates for sure, because it was so casual.

Don Cullen [proprietor of the Bohemian Embassy, a coffeehouse near Yonge and Wellesley]: Mary Jane and Winston Young were just wonderful. You know, I feel badly that the world has never really heard Mary Jane and Winston because they were so good and so accessible as performers. And Mary Jane Young was incapable of artifice. She lived so close to her skin that she was magical.

Mary Jane Young: Don was always exaggerating. But at the same time, he

> said that at different times and it made us feel good. He appreciated that our type of songs were a thing that not everybody did. Some of them were pretty raw. People were singing a lot of very pretty things, very acceptable. But we were singing bawdy songs like "The Oak and the Ash" that would be considered a little risqué. And a lot of working-class stories. I think that's what I liked about folk music. It had to tell a story, if we weren't singing kids' songs or nonsense songs. We did a lot of Canadian songs that we learned from Edith Fowke. She lived with her husband around Donlands [Avenue] and she would invite us out [to eastern Toronto]. Each time we went over, she would serve us cinnamon toast and tea and she'd play us a tape. She played us O. J. Abbott singing "On the Banks of the Don," about the Don Jail.

Mary Jane and Winston soon left Toronto to play folk clubs in England and began to wind down their performing career on their return. Winston got a job as a crane operator, notably working on the construction of the CN Tower in the 1970s. He died in 2004.

Aside from being a home for folk singers like Mary Jane and Winston Young, the Clef Club is also remembered as the site of the first meeting to organize the Mariposa Folk Festival in Orillia, Ontario. Founder Ruth Jones and her husband Casey met in February 1961 with Ian Tyson, Sylvia Fricker, and their first manager, Edgar Cowan, there to lay out a plan for the August festival. The performers that first year included the Travellers, Ian & Sylvia and Bonnie Dobson, who premiered her new song "Morning Dew." The clean air and sunshine of the first Mariposa Folk Festival contrasted sharply with the dark, smoky "mineshaft" in which the festival was hatched.[18]

On November 18, 1960, Pierre Berton visited the Clef. Though the club apparently had 1,170 members at the time, only twelve patrons were in the audience that night to see a female duo singing the Irish ballad "Molly Malone." Berton described Peter Ellis, the "youthful manager" as "drowning sorrows in his own espresso."[19] By November 1961, the Clef Club was no more.

***

The Purple Onion was the third Yorkville folk coffeehouse to open in 1960, and over the next five years it established the corner of Avenue Road and Yorkville as the musical centre of the Village. Named after a famous San Francisco club and site of a Kingston Trio live album, the Purple Onion was launched in November by five apprentice accountants from North York: Sam Gutmacher, Al Lastman, Al Tytel, and brothers Art and Barry Witkin, along with Mel Isen, who had no business background but was an aspiring musician. Other investors who came and went included Art Rockert and David Green.

Barry Witkin: We went to high school together [at Vaughan Road Collegiate] and we were club members at the YMHA [Young Men's Hebrew Association] at Bloor and Spadina back in the '50s. So we've known each other as we grew up. Then we all decided that we'd go into accounting. You spent five years working for an accounting firm—it's just like being an apprentice, in effect. We also had an investment group; the [five] of us would throw money into the pot and decide what we would invest it in.

The young accountants incorporated as DEC Investments and each contributed $200 ($2,105 in 2025) for startup costs. They found a main floor and basement at 35 Avenue Road, just north of Yorkville Avenue on the east side. The building was owned by the Rev. Morris Zeidman (1894–1964), a Polish immigrant who converted from Judaism to become a Presbyterian minister and founded the Scott Mission, a prominent soup kitchen still active in 2025. The investors signed a six-month lease at around $750 ($7,896 in 2025) per month with an option to extend up to five years. They saw this as a hedge against being trapped in a money-losing business.

Barry Witkin: We had no idea exactly what we were really doing.

Mel Isen: We were almost closed up because we hadn't followed the rules of the city bylaws and [Rev. Zeidman] really bailed us out and got us going.

Barry Witkin: We found that you can't just have a [music] coffeehouse on Avenue Road. It had to be a club where you had to charge a membership. We said, okay, we'll do that. But then of course that's not going to cover our expenses. So we had an admission charge.

The Purple Onion's membership charge was a nominal 25 cents ($2.63 in 2025) that undercut the Village Corner's 50 cents ($5.26 in 2025) and the Clef Club's $1.25 ($13.16 in 2025). But the club made the money back on the cover charge, which was routinely $1.50 ($15.79 in 2025), 50 cents more than both the Village Corner and the Clef. The membership charge was in any case a token gesture, as the Purple Onion was a private club in name only. It was less a Village Corner-like folk club, with informal hoots featuring amateur club members, than it was a folk concert room, with formal, paid performances by professionals. This was a first in Yorkville, and it presaged the business model for the Riverboat, soon to be the area's dominant folk venue.

The exterior was a standard bay-and-gable front of white-painted brick over a rough stone base. A semicircular stained-glass mosaic sat atop the front window, and seven concrete steps led to the front door. Inside, the original living room and dining room were converted into one long, ninety-seat space on the main floor, with the kitchen at the back and stage in the middle of the long wall. A dressing room for artists in the basement doubled as food storage and a space for the club's mimeograph machine.

Barry Witkin: We were always interested in folk music because that was the nature of what was happening in the music scene at that time. We thought maybe we should consider some jazz, but jazz would have been more expensive for us. With folk music, you can have one person with a guitar singing. With jazz, you sometimes need two or three people. We pretty well concentrated on folk music.

Mel Isen: I can tell you, there were a lot of people who played for us and they got a meal.

The first act known to have played at the Purple Onion was the Sinners, a trio comprised of banjoist Eddie Sokoloff and guitarist Harvey Kotler and Evan "Chick" Roberts (1932–2023).

Chick Roberts: I was born up in the frozen north, Sudbury. My dad and mother came from Wales and my dad worked in the mines. We came to Toronto when I was a baby. We lived on Parliament Street and Ontario Street, and then out in Willowdale. I was totally into jazz when I was a kid. There used to be great noon-hour [radio] concerts out of Chicago, and I would run home to listen to fifteen-minute programmes like that. I learned to play drums with a bunch of guys that I met at an old dance hall on Parliament Street when I was about eighteen. I would lay down a little beat, nothing fancy, "no solos please." That's where I [later] got my nickname, from [jazz drummer] Chick Webb. I studied acting at a place called Theatre 49; it came out of the Toronto Yiddish theatre—hardcore Stanislavski [acting method]. I left Canada and moved to England for about three-and-a-half years; I was going to go to school but I started acting right away. Basically, all the Canadian actors went over there to get film experience, because there were no films here except for the National Film Board. All I wanted to be was in the films. I did my first film on my twenty-third birthday: Charles Chaplin's *A King in New York*. It's not one of his best. I had a couple of scenes. When I was in England, I was doing everything. I was doing a comedy act over there, all the stuff to keep alive. Then I heard that Toronto was getting a lot of stuff done, so I came back in 1959. All they had was background, extra work. I said no. I had my little guitar and my Burl Ives songs and I decided to become a folk singer. Josh White was my first introduction [to folk music]. I used to listen to Alan Mills on the radio, and Ed McCurdy and people like that. Bob Laine, who was the all-night announcer on CHUM radio, had rented a cottage on Lake Simcoe. I went up there and people were playing guitars and ukuleles and singing. I met two guys [Harvey Kotler and Eddie Sokoloff] and we automatically fell into harmony and started singing folk songs that everybody knew. We said, "Hey, this is good." We got together and started playing more and more. We learned all of the Kingston Trio songs, since we were three. We were called the Sinners, and Bob Laine was our so-called manager. We worked about two years. Our first big jobs were at the Purple Onion and we did private parties. We were darlings of the Forest Hill sweet-sixteen type of thing.

Eddie Sokoloff: Between Harvey [Kotler] and me, two Jewish boys. All the boys from the Purple Onion moved in similar circles as we did. They said, "Why don't you come and play?" The first thing is, "How much you paying us?" "Well, we can't pay that much."

It was an informal arrangement at best; the Toronto Musicians' Association was not notified, and no contracts were filed. The first week it opened, the Purple Onion had a total music budget of $30 ($315 in 2025) per night, or $10 per musician, far below union scale, which still stood at $36 ($379 in 2025) per musician per night. To avoid the notice of the union, the Sinners' engagement at the Purple Onion was not advertised in any of the three Toronto daily newspapers.

Like the Village Corner and the Clef Club, the Purple Onion had no sound system, but Sinner Eddie Sokoloff changed that.

Eddie Sokoloff: My father was in the radio and television business, like sales and service. I said to him, "Dad, we could really use a sound system at the Purple Onion." He put together a mic, an amplifier, and a board with about five speakers in it, and he put it at each end of the room.[20] He did it for free. I think it was fun for him.

Any musician will tell you that playing to a crowded room without a sound system can be difficult. Putting in a PA system was a good business move, and necessary. By the end of 1960, the venue had lines around the block. The Purple Onion was the place to be in Yorkville.

Barry Witkin: Everybody would come because there weren't really a lot of places in Toronto at that time that people could go. Somehow it just took off. We realized after six months that we're going to renew for five years and carry on from there. That's how it all started.

* * *

The Half Beat was the last Yorkville coffeehouse to open in that boom year of 1960. It was, in some ways, its most important, since it was the first to be run by a formidable power couple of Yorkville coffeehouse proprietorship, John and Marilyn McHugh.

Born in Brighton, England, in 1934, John McHugh attended prestigious Brighton College. He became an avid jazz fan as a teenager and would remain a "dyed-in-the-wool jazz fanatic," in the words of bandleader Jim McHarg.[21] It was the last years of compulsory National Service in Britain, and John served his military duty at a Singapore supply base. Back home in Brighton in 1957, he hatched a plan with a friend to open a coffee bar with live jazz. Coffee bars were all the rage in London's Soho neighbourhood, so why not Brighton?

John McHugh: [My friend] was twenty-one and I was twenty-two. We went to the bank and they wouldn't even discuss it with us. He had £2,000 [$77,908 CDN in 2025]. I had about £500 [$19,475 CDN in 2025] and I think we wanted to double that; we thought £5,000 [$194,758 CDN in 2025] would open a coffee bar. They told us to get lost. And we couldn't find any money from anywhere else. We went to the town hall and they were unhelpful. So that was it.

This rejection, and John's disillusionment following the Suez Canal incident, spurred him to emigrate to Canada in 1957. He found a one-way flight special to Canada for a hundred pounds ($3,894 CDN in 2025).

In Toronto, John settled in a series of shared flats. In September 1958, John was living at 155 Marlborough Avenue with a vacancy for one more tenant when he met Ian Tyson, newly arrived in Toronto, at a party. They agreed that Ian would move into the shared apartment with McHugh and a potter named Ron Roy.

John McHugh: We had an understanding: he would play folk music on his turntable through his guitar amplifier. I had a beautiful Harman Kardon stereo—I built the speakers myself—but it was jazz only. Nothing else.

John found work as a clerk at the Bank of Commerce and soon met Marilyn Cohen, a bridal consultant. Marilyn was born in London, England, in 1935, the older of two sisters eighteen months apart.

Marilyn McHugh: My mother was studying to be in law, but she got pregnant with me. She had to give it up, so I don't think she was very happy about it. She was secretive, and my father had a secret life. He seemed to be a very nice man, but I didn't know either of them.

When the war started, mothers with young children were evacuated to small villages around the country. Marilyn and her sister went, but their mother didn't. Instead, the girls were raised by a guardian in an Essex village until the end of the war. Back home in London, the sisters were sent to boarding school. One day in 1952, their mother showed up at the school with suitcases.

Marilyn McHugh: My mother left my father, kidnapped the children, and came to Canada, where she had family. I was with my mother, but I met this chap and six weeks later we were married [and moved to Vancouver]. I was only with him a little while. I hitchhiked back from Vancouver to Toronto and left a one-year-old baby. Now I know that child, she's in my life. Not thanks to me, but thanks to her, we have a nice relationship.

I met John McHugh in 1958 on a blind date. He came to pick

me up to take me to a party and I was at my mother's. I said to him, "Have you got a car?" He said, "I've got a ride. Of course." He took me outside and there was a Loblaws [grocery] cart. I was in my sari period, so I was wearing a sari. He was wearing a green suit that made his face even greener. I didn't blink; I got in it. He pushed me all the way up Bathurst Street. Then he brought me home to my mother. The next day we went down to his place on Marlborough, where he lived with Ian, and that's where he and I stayed.

In the summer of 1960, John and Marilyn, now wed, rented a house at 183 Cumberland Street for $120 ($1,263 in 2025) a month with no lease.[22] This was extraordinarily low rent even for the time, which reflected the fact that this was a precarious property. In a few months, the entire south side of Cumberland was to be razed for the construction of the Bay subway station on the new Bloor/Danforth line, or Line 2. The old house was not long for this world. A short time after they moved in, John McHugh's day job hit a snag.

John McHugh: They transferred me to the head office; they had this ledger, and I didn't know what this ledger was. Nobody could tell me what I was doing. It was extraordinary. So I said to my wife, "I want to open a coffeehouse."

Marilyn McHugh: Oh, come on. It sounds very romantic. He worked in the bank, and we used to have all these friends that dropped by. We were supplying the coffee and we really didn't have any money ourselves—I wasn't working. We decided we'd better open a coffeehouse and charge them for their coffee.

John and I went to New York—Greenwich Village—and stayed two weeks. We learned a lot there. Jack Zuccarini sold us our Gaggia machine.[23] He took us under his wing and he taught us how to make coffee. John built the furniture, which was hopeless. And we had a local person make all the lamps.

The original plan was for the McHughs to open a jazz club in the basement, fulfilling John's Brighton coffee bar dream, but this was not to be.

John McHugh: [We] found out that you needed eight-foot clearance in the basement. We had six foot nine. We couldn't afford any construction. That was it. So we put that aside and continued with our lives and then five months later, opened the coffeehouse.

The name—the Half Beat—was suggested by the McHughs' neighbour, designer Sam Smart. The idea was to attract both jazz fans and beatniks.[24] Since the basement couldn't be used as a live music venue, this first location of the Half Beat had no live music other than a one-time appearance by Ian and Sylvia for a private event in March 1961. The only other music heard in the club was recorded jazz from the '20s and '30s from John McHugh's own album collection.

The house was flat-faced, with ornate decoration over the large central arch and a facade of whitewashed brick. To the left of the front door there was seating in the old living room and dining room of the house. Seventeen different coffees, along with hot chocolate, were served.[25] For the interior decor, the McHughs got creative, borrowing a technique that John had seen in a students' bar in Copenhagen, pasting newspaper pages to the ceiling. As rustic as this sounds, John McHugh is still proud of this design touch.

John McHugh: I'll have you know, the newspapers on the ceiling were the front pages of very select Danish and German and French newspapers, with the occasional London *Sunday Times* thrown in. And it was always just the front page, but the headlines showing. It was put up really carefully by me.

Marilyn McHugh: We decorated that old place as if it were our own home, with ceramic ashtrays and fancy crockery. We pasted up signs on the walls and we played the kind of jazz that John liked. And I felt free to throw people out because they had a dirty face or grubby clothes.[26]

From their opening night, a Friday in the middle of December 1960, the club was jammed. As John McHugh would recall five years later, "We had a 80 percent foreign patronage who played chess, talked and listened to good jazz."[27] One of the Half Beat's "foreign patrons" was a German-born chef named Werner Graeber.

Chapter Three: "All we knew was that we liked music."

The immigrant, and especially the foreign-speaking immigrant, views the city differently. He tends to find it cold and unfriendly and he is not dazzled by its size. He is not used to the North American style of community, which is little more than a vast machine for working. He is used to downtown parks and squares, to broad avenues and boulevards, to open spaces of all kinds. He believes aesthetic standards are important and he does not find them in Toronto with its narrow streets, its constricted areas and its hide-bound architecture. He is a downtown man, and in various small ways his influence is being felt. Within a generation he will have changed the face and the feel of the city. The immigrant also wants a freer, easier city . . . Already the bars and coffeehouses and foreign restaurants are blossoming out, and there are even one or two sidewalk cafés straining to bloom, like roses in a desert.

Pierre Berton, *The New City*, 1961[1]

LIKE A SHOT OF hot espresso at an afternoon tea, Werner Graeber hit Yorkville Avenue in 1961. No one did more to tie together Yorkville's coffeehouses into a cohesive scene than the man who contemporaries called the visionary of Yorkville.

Jutta Maue Kay (Yorkville coffeehouse waitress): He was a crazy hippie who loved to challenge the establishment. He was the beatnik, the real deal. He lived by his own rules.

Marilyn McHugh: The nutty one. Well, he wasn't really nutty. In today's world, he would be, but in those days he wasn't.

Werner Graeber was born on May 30, 1930, in Dresden, Germany. He later told friends that he lived on the streets of Berlin from the age of fifteen, having lost his home, and his parents, to an Allied bomb. He was one of nine million Germans bombed out of their homes during the war, in what journalist Kurt Kusenberg called a "starving, tattered, shivering, poverty-stricken, dangerous time."[2] Homeless and alone, Graeber stole vegetables from farmers' fields and slept in boxcars to stay warm. He eventually found a lifeline in a mess-hall job at an American army base, where he trained as a chef. Classified as a displaced person, Graeber emigrated to Toronto in July 1953.[3]

By 1961, he was married to a woman named Edith, who is remembered only as being German as well.[4] They both worked for Frank McEachern and his wife, Florence, an heiress to the Eaton's department store fortune. Edith was a servant, and Werner a chef. The Graebers lived in the McEacherns' Rosedale house, but seem to have left their employ that summer, taking a parting gift for themselves. On June 23, 1961, Edith and Werner were arrested for jewel theft. When they were apprehended, they were holding $2,000 ($21,057 in 2025) in jewellery stolen from Mrs. McEachern.[5] The charges were soon dropped, and the Graebers moved into a row house at 71 Yorkville Avenue, just east of Bellair on the south side.

A forty-man police division charged with regulating nighttime activity, the Toronto Morality Squad kept a watchful eye on sex workers, drug dealers, and after-hours speakeasies. Not long after moving into 71 Yorkville Avenue, they became aware of Werner and Edith. The couple had a party, during which a noise complaint led police to conclude that the Graebers were running an illegal speakeasy. On July 22, 1961, the Morality Squad raided the house and arrested all twenty-two of the occupants. Werner was charged with keeping liquor for sale and for "permitting drunkenness," while Edith and twenty more were booked as "found-ins," a lesser charge reserved for those merely present when the raid occurred. The group was taken to the notorious Don Jail at 6:30 a.m., where the women were ordered to strip and subjected to vaginal examinations (to determine if they were virgins) while the men were sprayed for fleas. Werner spent two days in jail after being interrogated by police about his "beatnik" connections.[6] The case was dropped for lack of evidence within the week, leaving $570 ($6,001 in 2025) in legal fees for the people charged and at least one lost job because of the publicity.

On July 30, Pierre Berton wrote a searing column on the front page of the *Star* that detailed the police harassment and abuse. He suggested that the group was targeted because some of them were foreign-born and had German, Estonian, and Macedonian accents. Berton seethed: "Had this party occurred in one of those solid homes in Forest Hill or Bayview or Don Mills; had the citizens been native-born pillars of society—stockbrokers, say—then is anyone so naive as to suppose that, complaints or no complaints, the police would have carted the whole kaboodle off to the reeking cells of the Don?"[7]

The negative publicity generated by the case spurred the Metro Police Commission to open an investigation. The commission, which included then-mayor Nathan Phillips, found that the raid was essentially an escalation of a noise bylaw infraction, and concluded that police should have issued summonses rather than arresting the partygoers. As Mayor

Phillips told the commission, such raids "bring disrepute to the police force . . . After all, the liberty of citizens comes first."[8]

The Graebers opened 71 Coffee House in September 1961 on the main floor of 71 Yorkville Avenue.[9] The whitewashed brick house was set a few feet back from the sidewalk, with three steps leading to the front door. Under a single lamp, "71 Coffee House" was painted on the white brick in block letters.[10] The café itself was bare white drywall, with rudimentary wainscoting around the walls surrounding unframed paintings: rough-hewn abstract pieces, impressionist landscapes, and a portrait of a sunbaked matron wearing a wide-brimmed hat.

A cup of strong coffee was ten cents ($1.05 in 2025). This was extraordinarily low—a quarter ($2.63 in 2025) was more common—but making it easy and inexpensive for patrons to spend long hours in the club was the Graebers' intent. Coffee was a loss leader; the goal was to build a clientele, to spark a scene. In a photograph taken around 1962, a light bulb hangs from a thin wire, a terracotta flowerpot serving as an ersatz shade. A half-played chess board abuts a glass sugar container. The young, fashionable patrons look to be in their twenties, the men wearing ties and the women patterned dresses. The scene is convivial and casual, the conversation no doubt lively as the patrons of the 71 cram together on mismatched benches and couches.

It was not lost on Werner Graeber that the Morality Squad had it in for him. He had prevailed in court, and worse yet, embarrassed the police department in the eyes of City Hall and the public. From the day it opened, Graeber suspected that plainclothes cops were frequenting the 71, gathering evidence.[11] He didn't have to wait long for his suspicions to be confirmed.

At around midnight on September 24, 1961, a twelve-man contingent of the Morality Squad, accompanied by RCMP officers, took up observation posts in the parking lot across the street from the 71. After two hours they had seen enough and entered the coffeehouse with a search warrant. This time the Squad wasn't looking to bust a speakeasy. This was far bigger game: cannabis. Pot was still classified as a narcotic in 1961, with long prison sentences for simple possession.[12]

"Tear the place apart!" Werner yelled, according to police testimony. Edith escaped out of a rear window, but was quickly captured. Police found four joints: two were hidden on the tops of door frames, one in a false ceiling in the bathroom, and another on the floor just inside a bedroom that was "stocked with contraceptives," according to a breathless *Globe* report, "considerably more than might be considered average." Werner and Edith were charged with narcotics possession.[13]

As part of the investigation, the Graebers agreed to be injected with sodium amytal, a now discredited barbiturate and "truth serum," and questioned. Dr. Michael Tuchtle, the psychiatrist who conducted the interviews, would conclude that neither Werner nor Edith knew about the cannabis. They also undertook lie detector tests with favourable results. Furthermore, because the joints on the doorframe were hidden in common areas, it couldn't be determined that they belonged to the Graebers; they could have been planted by anyone.[14] After eight months and $1,500 ($15,496 in 2025) in legal fees, Werner and Edith were acquitted on April 27, 1962.[15]

* * *

Toronto has become North America's most important folk music city outside New York. Americans imported here report the word is out, 'Go to Toronto' . . . No other city offers folk singers so much opportunity on TV. Wealthy Forest Hill Village residents hire them to perform at parties. Five after-hours spots offer folk singers only.[16]

Morris Duff, "Jazz Declines and Folk Music Soars,"

Toronto Star, December 30, 1961

As the popularity of folk music was growing, there was money to be made. Because of its uncomplicated production needs—a folk singer didn't even need a microphone if the club was small enough—it was easy for a coffeehouse owner to hire an amateur folk singer, stick them in a corner, and pay them a few dollars and all the coffee they could drink. If they didn't advertise the live music, they could fly under the radar of the Toronto Musicians' Association, with its expectations of a $36-per-engagement minimum wage and contracts. To some observers, the coffeehouse folk music economy could be downright exploitative.

Estelle Klein (born Estelle Cohen, 1930–2004) was a natural organizer and leader, with a deep love of folk music rooted in her time at the University of Toronto, where she took part in Settlement House hootenannies in the late '50s. Married at twenty to a successful architect, Jack Klein, Estelle welcomed local folkies into their home on Prince Arthur Avenue just west of Yorkville.

Moved by the plight of folk musicians in securing good-paying work in the coffeehouses, Estelle founded the Guild of Canadian Folk Artists with Travellers mandocellist Sid Dolgay in April 1961.[17] The Folk Guild, as it was known to all, was a nonprofit association of performers and aficionados whose goal was to advance folk music as a performing art; promote public interest and improve standards of folk music performance; and finally to serve as an information centre on Canadian folk music. To this end, the Folk Guild began to publish a high-quality magazine, *Hoot*, in early 1963. Edited in the style of *Sing Out!*, the long-running US folk periodical, *Hoot* was a stapled booklet combining interviews, editorials, instrumental tips, and simple notations of newly written folk songs.

The Folk Guild and Estelle Klein were a powerful presence through Yorkville's folk music heyday, pushing for fair wages, providing performance opportunities through its popular Monday night hootenannies, and generally labouring to bring professional stability to the burgeoning scene.

* * *

In the summer of 1961, John and Marilyn McHugh set up six tables with chairs in front of the Half Beat, their coffeehouse at 183 Cumberland Street. Soon, as John McHugh told the *Star*, "Nobody wanted to sit inside. They would rather sit on the house's front steps or stand to drink their coffee and talk, if there weren't enough chairs."[18]

When the McHughs opened the Half Beat in December 1960, they understood that they had twenty months in the house before it was to be razed as part of the Bloor subway line construction. But the work went faster than expected, and they now had to be out after just eight months. Around August 1961, the Half Beat moved to 47 Avenue Road, a long and narrow room on the main floor of an old house, around the corner and up the street a block. A larger space out front allowed the McHughs to expand their popular patio. Rent was $250 ($2,632 in 2025) a month, more than double their Cumberland Street rent. To cover the added expense, the McHughs raised the price of their coffee by a nickel.[19]

Star writer Morris Duff described the Half Beat clientele as sixty percent European,[20] and John McHugh remembers that chess-playing Hungarians made up a large part of that contingent. As John told the *Telegram* in 1964, "From the day we opened on Avenue Road I knew we would be successful. Traffic slowed down every day to see our place. Then the drivers would come around on foot and stop for an expresso [sic]."[21]

The homemade tables covered in red-checked tablecloth were surrounded by black-painted iron chairs, described by Morris Duff as "ice cream parlour stools," with modern paintings provided by Dorothy

Cameron's nearby Here and Now Gallery adorning the walls—though John doesn't remember any paintings actually selling out of the café. In any case, when Dorothy Cameron moved her gallery to Yonge Street in September 1962, the agreement was terminated. Works by John Gould and Albert Franck (who had moved from Gerrard Village to a nearby house on Hazelton Avenue) were still hanging in the café in November 1962, but this was by direct arrangement with the artists.[22]

In June 1962, Pierre Berton reported that the club was getting unwelcome attention from the Toronto Department of Health, which was insisting that their fare of coffee, tea, sandwiches, and pastries be protected from the elements with metal covers. Berton would sarcastically remark, "How very sanitary! How remarkably healthy! How charmingly Canadian!"[23]

That summer, the McHughs returned from a month-long English vacation to discover that their building, 47 Avenue Road, was for sale. Working with a lawyer friend and customer, they bought the building.

Marilyn McHugh: We'd gone and done it proper, we had. We had become property owners. So, of course we had to have new menus and prices rose another nickel.[24]

* * *

Like the Half Beat, the Gate of Cleve was run by a married couple. Carl Noylander worked for a textbook publisher and his wife, Mary (1920–2017), was a schoolteacher. The club's name was seemingly borrowed from a similarly named restaurant in New York's Sheraton-Atlantic Hotel, itself a replica of an Amsterdam hotel restaurant called Die Port van Cleve. At 161 Dupont Street, the club was just outside of the boundaries of Yorkville, in a house formerly occupied by a long-running steakhouse, the Sign of the Steer. The decor was Tudor, designed to resemble an old English pub with "heavy beams stained to an aged hue, a polished bar from which [non-alcoholic] cider is dispensed, and family escutcheons [coats-of-arms] as colour accents."[25]

The club opened on November 3, 1961, with a performance by Mary Jane and Winston Young. Morris Duff, writing for the *Star*, described the Gate of Cleve as "brightly lit" with "stage lighting and top-notch sound system."[26] The Gate of Cleve was a part-time concern for the Noylanders, who kept their day jobs; it was open only on weekends: Friday and Saturday 9 p.m. to 3 a.m., with Sunday 8:30 p.m. to 12:30 a.m. added by the end of the first month. Advertised performers in the Gate's first couple of months include Sharon Trostin, later of popular children's act Sharon, Lois and Bram; banjoist Ted Schafer; and Greg Curtis, now billed as an "internationally known balladeer and folk singer."[27]

Compared to the Village Corner, Clef Club, and Purple Onion, the Gate of Cleve was elegantly decorated and slightly upscale, even "highly respectable," according to Mary Noylander at the time.[28] Membership was a relatively steep $1.50 ($15.79 in 2025), and, as proclaimed on the Gate's opening night poster, "available to all brave and loyal people of Upper Canada! God Save the Queen."

* * *

The new Yorkville coffeehouses were overwhelmingly folk music venues, but in the second half of 1961, two new jazz clubs took up the mantle formerly carried by Clem and Ruthie Hambourg. Both of the new venues were run by Romanian immigrants. One, the Cellar, stayed open long enough to make a mark, while the other, the Cave, was short-lived and is almost forgotten today.

Stefan "Steve" Ciotlos (pronounced "CHOT-loesh") was born in Sighisoara, Romania, in 1920 and raised in the nearby Transylvanian city of Brasov. After moving to the capital city of Bucharest, he worked as a political cartoonist and played jazz saxophone in clubs. The Communist Party's postwar rise to power in Romania made a parodist like Ciotlos a target for arrest, and he soon left the country, travelling through Western Europe for a few years and finally emigrating to Toronto in the early 1950s.

By 1960, forty-year-old Ciotlos was living in the attic of 169 Avenue Road, a three-storey house just south of Davenport, with his wife, Mary Joyce, and their three children. Downstairs was Ciotlos's employer, Gallery Moos, the first of many successful art galleries run by German-born Walter Moos (1926–2013). This first gallery, opened in May 1959, was something new in staid Toronto, a "crisp white triangle" selling works by Picasso, Chagall, and Braque in its first show.[29]

Sam Shirose (1931–) was born in Toronto and grew up on Walton Street, in the heart of the Ward. He and his friends, who included Paul Volpe and his brother Albert, formed a gang that evolved into the notorious Volpe crime family. Sam was in charge of running illegal poker games for the syndicate. He was, in crime historian James Dubro's words, "a first-rate croupier . . . one of the nicest guys you would ever want to meet."[30]

Sam Shirose: I always liked the entertainment business, just as something to do. I was always interested in music. I used to go up [to Moos Gallery] with friends and sit around the art gallery with Steve. We got talking about music and he had the cellar that was empty. I mean, at the time the ceiling wasn't high enough, you couldn't walk into there.

In early 1961, Moos agreed to let Ciotlos and Shirose open a jazz coffee-house in the basement of the gallery. Ciotlos, who was skilled in masonry and framing, designed a labyrinthine cave of grottoes and curved arches that was consistent with his sense of aesthetics.[31] Straight lines were to be avoided at all costs.

Stefan Ciotlos (Steve Ciotlos's son): He had a different way of looking at things. When he was older, I would be helping him through the financial world, which he didn't understand. I'd say, "Okay, you need to sign this cheque." He would purposely sign it through the line. I'm like, "Why are you doing that?" And he goes, "Because people can't draw a straight line. I'm not gonna sign on somebody's straight line." That was kind of the way he viewed the world.

To a *Maclean's* writer, the Cellar was a "dark, low-ceilinged, slightly dank coffeehouse . . . filled with smoke, gloom and the rough, raucous drive of a small band playing hard bop."[32] The jazz band, a resident trio of Michael Massey (piano), Keith Varley (bass), and Derek Collins (drums), joined by either Fred Duligal on saxophone or Ron Peck on vibraphone, was paid well under union scale. The occasional folk singers who sometimes played between the jazz band's set weren't paid at all. As a result, the Cellar appeared regularly in the pages of the Toronto Musicians' Association's monthly magazine, *Crescendo*, on the "unfair" list.

* * *

Opened on December 9, 1961, at 40 Scollard Street—the space recently vacated by the closure of the Clef Club—the Cave was an after-hours jazz venue run by two Romanian-Canadian Holocaust survivors, Imre (1924–1992) and Hedy Bohm (1928–2026). Imre had been confined to a forced labour camp during the war; Hedy was in the Auschwitz concentration camp as a teenager.[33] The young couple emigrated to Toronto in August 1948 to start a new life, and by 1961 were raising two small children and running a shoe store, Yale Shoes, at 575 Bloor Street West. At this point Imre broke the news to Hedy that they were to open an after-hours coffeehouse in Yorkville.

Hedy Bohm: This wasn't the first time when he surprised me with something he thought of doing, and then he told me after he put it into the works. I was a bit stunned. It was something different that neither one of us knew anything about. We found the place on Scollard Street. Then we went to the landlord, who was very nice, and we agreed on the rent. I remember him asking, kind of concerned, looking at two young people, if we knew anything about the nightclub business and did we know what we were doing? We looked very surprised at such a question, and we said, "Of course, yes." [But] we knew not a thing. All we knew was that we liked music. That's it.

The Cave opened with dancing to Don Carrington's Quartet and a one-dollar ($10.53 in 2025) cover charge.[34] No membership fee was necessary, as the Cave was situated outside of the boundaries covered by the Fishleigh bylaw. A cook made Hungarian food, and coffee and pastries were served. Many of the musicians jamming there until 3 a.m. were drawn from Oscar Peterson and Ray Brown's Advanced School of Contemporary Music (21 Park Road, 1960–1964). Hedy and Imre would sleep a few hours and go back to work at Yale Shoes.

It wasn't sustainable, and the Bohms quickly reduced their hours, cutting Thursdays and closing at 1 a.m. instead of 3 a.m. The resident jazz band also downsized quickly. By July 1962, the band had been reduced to a trio led by Charlie Mountford.[35] The Bohms finally sold the business in the summer of 1962. Hedy remembered that they simply could not turn a profit without a liquor licence. They never opened another coffeehouse, and they went on to open two more locations of Yale Shoes. The new management renovated the space and instituted a two-for-one special for the original cover charge of one dollar.[36] A new group dubbed the Jazz Five was quickly scaled down to the Jazz Four, and after a September 29 appearance by "Jazz Combo with Act," the Cave disappeared from the newspaper listings.[37]

* * *

On April 21, 1961, Ian and Sylvia appeared in the Purple Onion, the folk club run by a consortium of young accountants. This marks the beginning of the Onion as a union shop, with contracts filed and union-scale pay minimums respected. Local folkies Karen James, Dave Campbell (as Damiano), Jim McCarthy, David Wiffen, and Klaas VanGraft appeared along with groups the Courriers, the Sinners, and the Pioneers in double bills on Saturdays and Sundays through the spring.

It was time to up the ante. By the end of the year, the Purple Onion's talent booker, co-owner Sam Gutmacher, was contracting American acts. This new policy began rather inauspiciously on November 17 with Les Chandler Jr., an obscure American act whose main distinction was that he could be easily mistaken for the more famous actor and singer Len Chandler.

Barry Witkin: We started with some very local entertainers, and eventually we had to go to the States and bring in others from New York and other places. That's how the reputation of the club came, because we would bring in some really interesting acts. They were people just starting out themselves.

Ramblin' Jack Elliott played the Onion January 5 to 7, 1962 (Friday to Sunday), and Len Chandler (the real one) played February 2 to 4. A pre-fame Judy Collins (1939–) played there from March 8 to 10, 1962.

Judy Collins: I had already met Ian and Sylvia, and I think I saw them at that point in Toronto. I soon recorded "Four Strong Winds." It must've been before I went to Arizona and was diagnosed with tuberculosis, so I must've been a little out of it.

Another then-obscure Purple Onion performer was David Crosby (1941–2023), who is listed in the *Star* as appearing there for one night on May 10, 1962. Long before he found fame with the Byrds and Crosby, Stills and Nash, David Crosby was a twenty-one-year-old aspiring folk singer, playing "basket houses" in Greenwich Village and presumably popping up to Toronto for a one-nighter.

At the Onion, folk music ruled, with the odd exception. Three, a group featuring vocalist Don Francks (1932–2016), guitarist Lenny Breau (1941–1984), and bassist Eon Henstridge (d. 1967), appeared at the Onion a few times in 1962. Three was short-lived but unusually well-documented, with a prominent place in Don Owen's 1963 NFB documentary *Toronto Jazz*, and live recordings from the Village Vanguard in New York and the Purple Onion.[38] The latter recording is a vivid snapshot not just of Breau's budding guitar mastery and Francks's freewheeling theatrical vocal approach but also of the sonic ambience—the clinking coffee cups and low murmur—of the Purple Onion itself.

* * *

[The Village Corner was] about the size of a shoebox. Everyone was jammed in like matchwood . . . It was so dark you could hardly see. The air was hot and sticky, the air conditioner wouldn't work, but the coffee machine was working overtime. The smoke hung over everything like fog.Gordon Lightfoot and Terry Whelan, liner notes, *Two Tones at the Village Corner*, Canatal Records CLP 4026.

On January 20, 1962, Gordon Lightfoot (1938–2023) recorded a live album at the Village Corner with a duo called the Two Tones. Terry Whelan (1938–2004) played baritone ukulele and Gordon the guitar; they sang solo and in harmony, performing traditional folk songs along with recently composed numbers. The Two Tones' tight harmonies and rehearsed jocular patter was reminiscent of the Kingston Trio, the Limeliters and others of the more commercial American folk groups. But those groups, and the Two Tones themselves, were on the way out.

Lightfoot was already a familiar figure on Canadian television screens through his work on CBC's *Country Hoedown*, a country music and dance show where he sang well and danced badly. At this early stage in his career, Lightfoot was still figuring out his sound and image; with his polished musical skills and good looks, he seemed to be bound for stardom whether he was a country singer, a folk singer, or a mainstream pop crooner. But Lightfoot didn't exactly exude folk credibility that night at the Village Corner.

*Pearl Dacks (*Hoot *magazine staffer, sister of Estelle Klein)*: He looked like *Country Hoedown*, that's what he was wearing. Everybody was laughing because he looked like such a hayseed. I don't remember being incredibly impressed, but he was always a wonderful guitar player.

Two Tones at the Village Corner was released later that year to little notice on the tiny Canatal (https://www.discogs.com/label/181972-Canatal-Records?srsltid=AfmBOortCpCN8sd_4AzHYeonOnFoe6RI_RUFhFygAxGmcuGauBvJqy0i) label; the Two Tones soon broke up and Lightfoot, with his new wife, Brita, moved to England to host BBC-TV's *Country and Western Show*. When they returned, he played some solo dates at a now-expanded Village Corner. In June 1962, the Corner had reopened after a renovation that expanded the capacity from sixty to over a hundred; it was a "shoebox" no more.[39] Another change was the return of listed performers, beginning with Greg Curtis and including Mary Jane and Winston Young, and Ian and Sylvia. The venue was now in line with the Toronto Musicians' Association and paid union scale to performers.

In December, John Morley and Roy Davies sold the business to Shelley Abrams, a twenty-five-year-old bookkeeper, along with her boyfriend Michael Cavendish, who is remembered as a tall and strapping bluegrass guitarist. Even as their competitor the Purple Onion was booking American folk acts, Abrams and Cavendish defiantly (and perhaps frugally) instituted an all-Canadian music policy, with rare exceptions like the New York-based Barry Kornfeld. "There has got to be a place," Abrams told the *Star*, "an outlet for Canadians to be heard. They are given far too little chance."[40]

Chapter Four: "That espresso machine was a licence to print money."

When the morality squad finally got their man, it was for a noise violation. Possibly inspired by the McHughs' Half Beat patio, Werner Graeber set up six tables in front of his 71 Coffee House in the summer of 1962.[1] The proprietors of the Antique Tea House next door at 73 Yorkville soon complained to the police that "shouting, singing, and screaming" kept them awake until 3 or 4 a.m., seven nights a week, for three months through the summer.[2] On September 21, Graeber was again charged by police, this time with violating Toronto's anti-noise bylaw.

Pierre Berton weighed in on Graeber's travails, recounting the trial in a sarcasm-drenched *Star* editorial entitled "Let's All Give a Lusty Cheer for the Good Old Morality Squad." Berton made it clear that the police went above and beyond in pursuing a simple noise complaint. Three plainclothes officers—Graeber hadn't been paranoid after all—conducted an investigation over the course of six clandestine visits, with photographs and witness testimony. The police testified that they could hear the noise where they were parked, 180 feet away.

Graeber, an atheist, refused to take the oath on the Bible. He testified that he was making coffee at the far end of the 71, and couldn't always hear the patrons, but had warned them several times not to make noise. He argued to Magistrate P. T. Bolsby that he believed that "more noise than usual was tolerated by neighbours in a commercially zoned area." The judge was unmoved, and after a two-day trial demanded a $10 fine plus court costs of just over $40. As Berton commented ironically, "the wretched Graeber has been given a taste of Canadian justice."[3]

* * *

Part of the noise complaint that brought the Morality Squad to the 71 could be blamed on the 71's new resident folk singer, an operatic tenor and recent arrival. Born in 1929 in a Yugoslavian fishing village off the Dalmatian coast, Josip Špralja (nicknamed Joso, pronounced "YO-so") grew up in the coastal town of Zadar, an area of the country more Italian than Slavic. Young Joso showed an early artistic talent; when he was twelve years old, he was already working as a photographer for the Zadar archeological museum. That same year of 1941, Germany invaded Yugoslavia and the country became an Italian Fascist outpost, with the Ustaše puppet regime keeping a brutal order. From November 1943 to October 1944, Zadar was bombed thirty times by the Allies; 80 percent of the town's buildings were destroyed. Like his soon-to-be-employer Werner Graeber, Joso knew the horrors of war.

Amid the destruction, a local priest recognized the boy's preternatural singing talent and arranged for him to be sent to Zagreb for operatic training with Antonio Salvaro, a retired tenor soloist with the Prague Opera.[4] Back in Zadar, Joso sang roles in local opera productions and on radio, performing with a Klapa male vocal group.[5] He married his childhood sweetheart Angiolina when he was twenty-five and she was nineteen, and they soon welcomed two children, Elena and Leo.

In late November 1961, Joso boarded a ship bound for Canada, leaving his wife and children behind. He had a six-month visa to visit Angiolina's sister and her husband in Toronto, and work in his brother-in-law's photography studio. One night, Joso chanced to walk by the 71. He heard singing coming from inside and walked in. Borrowing a guitar, he sang a few songs in Italian, Spanish, and Croatian, which thrilled the patrons, along with the club's owner, Werner Graeber.[6]

Graeber had welcomed occasional, spontaneous, and unpaid music-making in the 71, but had never gone so far as to actually hire a musician. On the spot, the German entrepreneur offered the Yugoslavian balladeer a steady gig. For $75 ($775 in 2025) a week, Joso would play at the 71 from Monday to Saturday, five hours a night. Though this was far below musicians' union minimum wage, which would have netted him $216 ($2,231 in 2025) a week, it was the most money Joso had ever made. The first money transfer he sent home was received like the family had won the lottery. He decided to stay in Canada, extend his visa, and work as a musician.

At the 71, Joso wandered among the patrons, strumming the cheap, battered acoustic guitar he'd bought in Italy on his way over. The club had no stage or sound system, and as an unamplified, itinerant performer, Joso was more "atmosphere" than featured musician. This jibed with Graeber's vision of the 71 as a quiet club for chess, coffee, and conversation, and not a music venue. Graeber never advertised or listed Joso as performing at the 71 in the entertainment listings of the three Toronto dailies. But Joso was there, performing his songs in Russian, Spanish, Croatian, Italian, French—anything but English. His English was weak, and he avoided English-language song material. It hardly mattered, with Joso's reserved but charming manner, fine tenor voice, and handsome profile. By the winter of 1963, in addition to his regular performances, he was running an informal hootenanny on Wednesday nights in the basement of the 71. One night early that year, he met Malka Himel and a memorable duo was born.

* * *

Malka Stein was born in 1936 near Nowy Wiśnicz, Poland, where her parents lived in a log cabin. Three weeks after her birth, the family moved to Kfar Saba, a kibbutz in British mandate-era Israel, where she grew up a confident, outspoken farm girl, and an avid dancer, singer, and actor. As a preteen, Malka appeared in one of the earliest Israeli feature films, *The Village Tale* (1950), a drama produced by the Women's International Zionist Organization, portraying a Yugoslavian Jewish family settling into an Israeli kibbutz.[7]

At seventeen, Malka took part in a folk dance display at the Maccabiah Games (the so-called "Jewish Olympics") and met Sydney Himel, a basketball player and young Toronto lawyer. The two soon married, and Malka moved to Toronto in 1954. They had two sons. Malka tried to assimilate into the Jewish enclave in North York, a suburb north of the city. But at social gatherings, Malka's outspokenness—"I had the pride of the immigrant," she says today—and strong Israeli accent didn't help her to fit in. She was homesick and needed an outlet.

All that Malka knew of Eli Kassner was that he was a guitarist and he was Israeli. She invited him to get together and work up some Hebrew and Yiddish songs to perform at synagogues. After a series of basement rehearsals, they would play a few concerts, but accompanying folk singing was not in Eli's long-term plan. He wanted to find Malka a more permanent musical partner.

Eli was playing at the Stratford Festival Theatre when an actor told him about the 71 Coffee House, and the remarkable singer-guitarist who performed there. A few weeks later, Eli visited the 71 and met Joso. Here, he thought, was someone who could take over Eli's role as Malka's accompanist. He arranged to bring Malka to the 71 basement one Wednesday night around 11 p.m.[8]

Malka Marom (formerly Malka Himel): It was extremely small, extremely damp, with a long table surrounded by horrible chairs and people sitting on benches around it. And Joso sang with a terrible guitar, the only guitar he could afford. I was floored because he was so very good. He was the best singer in Toronto.

Malka and Eli found a space among the patrons and watched as Joso sang a Croatian fishing song in his strong, trained voice, followed by a succession of others, each performing in their native language. When it was her turn, Malka began to sing a Hebrew folk song to Eli's guitar accompaniment. Malka's voice was strong, with a reedy, penetrating tone. She expected the song to be as unfamiliar to Joso as his Croatian song had been to her. But after she sang a few phrases, Joso began to strum along. Then he joined her in near-perfect vocal harmony singing in a language he didn't understand, watching her lips and intuiting the lyrics. Their vocal blend—Joso's clear tenor voice locked in tandem with Malka's rustic tone—brought a smile to both of their faces. They knew.

Later that night, Joso tried to talk to Malka, finding common linguistic ground in the few words of Italian that Malka knew. He communicated to her that he wanted to learn "Hava Nagila" and asked her to return. The next Wednesday, and the Wednesday after that, Malka and Eli did come back to the 71.

Malka Marom: There was something in our voices, in the combination of our voices that created a sound that was attractive. The word got around that on Wednesday, I was coming there and you could hear us singing a song or two.

Soon the basement was packed on Wednesday nights. Among Malka and Joso's new fans was a local booking agent named Sylvia Train. Train had just been charged with finding talent for the new Flaming Grill Room at the Lord Simcoe Hotel downtown. On hearing Malka and Joso, she coaxed them into leaving the 71 with her to drive immediately to the hotel to audition. They were hired and then panic set in.[9] "We only know three songs," Malka said. "Sing them twice," Sylvia replied.[10]

With only two weeks to go before the start of their first professional gig, Malka got to work phonetically learning the lyrics to the Italian, Portuguese, Spanish, and Slavic songs in Joso's repertoire. In turn, she taught him Yiddish and Hebrew songs, his keen ear helping him master the pronunciations.

Malka and Joso were still unsure of their fifteen-song set when they opened at the Lord Simcoe on April 1, 1963, so they shared a microphone, staying close together but never touching, "each [of us] desperately trying to read the lyrics," Malka recalled, "on the lips of the other."[11] The audience immediately picked up on the intimacy and the palpable sexual tension between these two attractive, tempestuous singers as they sang the roles of a lovesick gondolier and a beautiful girl in the Italian tune "Gondoletta," or sweethearts playing hide-and-seek in the forest in the Byelorussian peasant song "Marfuta." Many assumed that Malka and Joso were married, or at least lovers.

Estelle Klein was by this point the artistic director of the Mariposa Folk Festival, now in its third year of operation as a three-day, all-Canadian folk festival. Estelle heard Malka and Joso at the Lord Simcoe and offered them a booking at the festival. Malka and Joso, still billed in the Mariposa programme as "Malka Himel and Joso Špralja," played their main stage set on the final night, first in a lineup of four acts leading up to Ian and Sylvia, the breakout stars that year.

The reception was warm, if not overwhelming. Some in the folk world felt that Malka and Joso didn't fit Mariposa's definition of Canadian musicians. In his review of the festival in *Hoot*, Ted Schafer sniped, "Malka and Joso, cosmopolitanly witty and well-received as they were, had no place in a format which proudly boasted an all-Canadian bill of fare."[12]

Still, Malka and Joso's Mariposa appearance opened up a number of venues for them, from Yorkville coffeehouses including the Penny Farthing, Purple Onion, and Inn on the Parking Lot, to downtown taverns like the Silver Rail and Castle George. "Mariposa changed everything," Malka remembered. "Every coffeehouse owner could see that we were the hit of the festival."

After a recommendation from Sam Sniderman (proprietor of well-known record retailer Sam the Record Man), the duo signed a recording contract with Paul White of Capitol Records Canada. Malka and Joso released three albums on Capitol between 1964 and 1966: *Introducing Malka and Joso*, *Mostly Love Songs*, and *Autour de Monde*.

* * *

Jutta Maue Kay: I was born and raised in Hamburg, Germany. My home life wasn't the coolest. My stepfather was this domestic fascist. So as soon as I got home from work, I ate and left. You could go out [to clubs] when you're sixteen and you have to be out by ten. These clubs didn't start until after ten, so we'd just hide in the bathroom until the cops were gone and then it went to six in the morning. At the Top Ten Club, the Beatles were backing up Tony Sheridan.

I emigrated October 22, 1962, as an au pair. I worked for a family up in Forest Hill and that didn't work out too well. That's not my kind of job. I just wanted to come over. Solveigh [Schattmann] and I met on New Year's Eve 1962 in Parry Sound, and we just hit it off. She came over as an au pair, too. We were the same age.

Jutta got a job as a waitress at the 71 in the spring of 1963 and then moved a block over to Werner Graeber's second coffeehouse venture. Opened in November 1963, the Inn on the Parking Lot at 158 Cumberland Street was a converted living room in a three-storey Victorian house on the north side of the street. It was, in fact, adjacent to a large parking lot that was later converted into a parking garage. The name of the club was a sly parody of the recently opened Inn on the Park, a ritzy hotel in North York.

The Inn on the Parking Lot was at a disadvantage from the day it opened. While Yorkville Avenue was busy at night with restaurants like the Gaslight and L'Aiglon, not to mention the 71 Coffee House, Cumberland was still rather desolate after dark. The entire south side of the street from Bellair Street to Avenue Road had been razed in preparation for the Bloor subway line, while the north side was dominated by boutiques that were only open during the day. The foot traffic on Cumberland at night was negligible.

Graeber's new place, unlike the 71, would feature more-or-less regular and advertised entertainment, but the entertainment lineup was less than stellar and lacked cohesion. In its first months of operation, the Inn presented folk music, Dixieland jazz, and an April 1964 one-off Pierre

Berton performance, reciting his poetry and singing his own songs backed by Joso Špralja and guitarist Rafael Nunez. After Graeber booked the comedian Eve Law, a *Star* writer described her as "coarse and unfunny," performing to an audience of eight. As Graeber complained to the paper, "I have one lemon: the Inn."[13]

***

In 1963 and 1964, the Purple Onion was the premier folk music room in the city, presenting a mix of American and Canadian acts. Buffy Sainte-Marie wrote her song "Universal Soldier" in Toronto, at least partly in the green room at the Onion.[14] In September, the Simon Sisters, a duo of Carly Simon and her sister Lucy performed. They had recently scored a #20 Canadian hit with their musical arrangement of the poem "Wynken, Blynken, and Nod."

In January 1964, Val Pringle, a Harry Belafonte protégé, performed a week at the Purple Onion with Doug Bush, a local accompanist, on guitar. Aspiring guitarist and couch-surfer Zal Yanovsky remembered meeting John Sebastian at this engagement, presaging the alliance that would blossom as the Lovin' Spoonful, one of the most successful pop groups of the '60s.[15]

Having broken up the Two Tones, Gordon Lightfoot approached the Purple Onion for a job but met resistance.

Gordon Lightfoot: I asked if they could get me in and it was always, "Well no, we don't know if you're ready." Then they called. I got a couple of recordings [of my songs] done by Peter, Paul, and Mary and before that Ian and Sylvia, and that was enough for [Sam Gutmacher] to hire me [to open] for a New Year's Eve artist he brought in.[16]

This was presumably New Year's Eve 1963, when Brock Peters, another Belafonte protege who appeared as an actor in *Porgy and Bess* and *To Kill a Mockingbird*, headlined. Lightfoot returned to the Onion as a solo act the following May, where he did one performance in particular that would have a major impact on his career going forward.

Gordon Lightfoot: The first time I auditioned for the management company that signed me [Albert Grossman and John Court], they came to see me at the Purple Onion. And that's where they sat, on barrels right in front of me.[17]

Lightfoot had entered Albert Grossman's orbit through Ian and Sylvia, Grossman's other Canadian clients. When he signed with Grossman and Court, he made a connection with the highest echelons of the US folk music business and truly began his ascent to fame.

* * *

With the Half Beat doing steady business, John and Marilyn McHugh looked to expand their investments within Yorkville. John McHugh had a good relationship with the realtor Eric Townsend. Though 112 Yorkville, a prime location near the corner of Yorkville and Hazelton on the north side, was available for $5,000 down, he didn't have the money on hand.

John McHugh: I said, "I can't afford it." This is in February [1963] after a hard winter, I mean, winters were hard. So he said, "Well, what have you got?" "I've got $600." "That's okay. You can pay me next year."

The McHughs' original plan was to lease 112 Yorkville to a shop or similar business.

John McHugh: Nine out of ten of the first applications were all for wanting to open a coffeehouse. So we said, "No, no, we'll open our own." We opened a Victorian coffeehouse called the Penny Farthing.

The Victorian theme, complete with a real penny-farthing bicycle mounted on the wall, was inspired by the house decor itself—"flocked wallpaper and bead curtains," says McHugh—which had been little updated since Victorian times.

The Penny Farthing opened in March 1963. Arnold Rockman, writing in the *Star*, described the interior: it was "scrubbed down to the brick wall, painted white, had an arch pushed through one wall and been roughly plastered on other walls. It all looks faintly, quaintly Spanish while the tables and chairs of white-painted iron are all fairly, squarely uncomfortable."[18]

After a few months with recorded music only, John McHugh began to book live entertainment. Margaret Milligan performed folk songs on the main level beginning on November 29, 1963. The basement space, after a brief period as a used-furniture shop run by the McHughs called the Village Bin, was opened up for late-night jazz from December 14, featuring the British-born clarinetist Don Simmons's Jazz Band. John McHugh had finally realized his dream to run a jazz club, but folk music paid the bills.

The McHughs had formed the VYA (Village of Yorkville Association) with two interior designer/antique dealers: Robert Dirstein (1931–2025) and Budd Sugarman (1921–2004), who later called Yorkville a "charming oasis of cultural commercialism."[19] The association's main goal was to control development in the Village, which they felt was possible since most of the properties were still in the hands of single owners, rather than corporations. As the *Globe* reported, "[The VYA] does not want towering buildings. It does not want wider streets (too much traffic) . . . It wants lots of trees—many of its members operate European-style cafés with outdoor service in summer. It is dickering for its own, distinctive style of street lighting."[20] All the same, the VYA wanted to expand Yorkville as a commercial district. The McHughs, Dirstein, and Sugarman managed to get the north side of Yorkville rezoned.

The rezoning went far beyond the north side of Yorkville Avenue. On June 20, 1964, city council and the Ontario Municipal Board approved a bylaw that had a major effect on development in Yorkville's commercial area.[21] While the blocks north of Scollard were designated as low-density residential, Scollard and lower Hazelton were zoned as low-density commercial, with both sides of Yorkville Avenue, the east side of Avenue Road to Davenport, and the north side of Cumberland Street changing from low-density to high-density commercial.[22] This change opened the throttle for new coffeehouses going forward, allowing an influx of new clubs to convert what had been a largely residential area to an almost completely commercial one.

* * *

By 1963, Walter Moos had moved his gallery out of 169 Avenue Road to 136–138 Yorkville. Steve Ciotlos took over the Avenue Road house, keeping a framing and art shop on the main floor and expanding the operations of the Cellar. For the first time, he began to advertise his club in the newspaper entertainment listings.

Open from Thursday to Saturday, the Cellar was home to a generation of Toronto jazz musicians, with resident players like the bebop saxophonist

Fred Duligal, the troubled but brilliant piano prodigy Tony Collacutt and the influential guitarist Sonny Greenwich. Folk singers appeared on occasion, including former Concerto and La Coterie singer-guitarist Klaas VanGraft. The Cellar was now a union shop, and the musicians were paid scale. The exception to this was Wednesday nights, when anyone could get up and perform.

Paul Hoffert (jazz pianist/vibraphonist): There were a lot of heavy-duty drugs going on and pills. There would be, for example, a jar right in the second floor of the Cellar. Somebody would rob a drugstore and they would just take prescription pills, and they're all different colours, and people would just take handfuls of things to see how fucked up they could get as an alternative to doing smack, which some of them did.

Sam Shirose: [Steve Ciotlos] wasn't good with people. He had a few incidents with people that I had to sort of straighten out. I wouldn't have chosen Steve as a partner in any business myself, after I got together with him. The club was very successful, and that seemed to bother him for some reason.

Paul Hoffert: [Ciotlos] was just a very sweet guy to us. Always helped us out. He was one of the European underground that conflated jazz with freedom and democracy and anti-Soviet imperialism and all of that.

The Cellar was in some ways a continuation of Clem and Ruth Hambourg's vision of a sanctuary for modern jazz in Toronto. If there was any doubt that the Cellar was carrying on his legacy, Clem himself began to appear there shortly after the last location of the House of Hambourg closed in early 1963. On and off until August 1965, Clem held forth at the Cellar as the white-haired, wild-eyed music professor, serving as master of ceremonies and playing Chopin etudes on the upright piano between jazz band sets.

Mike McKenna was born in Toronto in 1946 and grew up in his grandmother's Cabbagetown boarding house. He took up the guitar as a teenager and soon fell in love with the blues. With his high school friend Pentti "Whitey" Glan, he heard as much live music as he could, including Ronnie Hawkins and the Hawks' legendary all-ages matinee shows at the Concord Tavern at Bloor and Ossington.[23] Robbie Robertson's fluid lead guitar caught Mike's attention, and he tried to replicate Robbie's licks.

Whitey and Mike formed Whitey and the Roulettes with singer/keyboardist George Olliver, second guitarist Ken Boyington, and bassist Don Elliot. They won a regular gig at Club Bluenote, an after-hours R&B coffeehouse at Yonge and Gerrard. Whitey and the Roulettes played for dancers and backed up guest singers. There was just one problem.

Mike McKenna: Anybody that came in to sing would give us sheet music. Well, I couldn't read. I could read chord charts, but I wasn't a [note] reader. I'm way over my head here. Eventually I said I was gonna go back to school.

Domenic Troiano replaced Mike on guitar, and Whitey and the Roulettes were renamed the Five Rogues, and then the Mandala. Having returned to high school to complete his diploma, Mike formed a new group, Mike's Trio, with Graham Dunsmore on bass and Rick McMurray on drums. They played some of the R&B songs that Mike had done with the Roulettes, along with Jimmy Reed songs like "Baby What You Want Me to Do."

Mike McKenna: Live music was really hard to find. I went to the Cellar Club because it was live jazz. Now, I wasn't a jazz guy. And it was also a very beatnik type of thing. It was a very dark, dingy place with brick walls. Always packed with people. I mean, jam-packed. People with cigarette holders and berets. Sonny Greenwich was the guitar player there. Somehow I had the nerve to go to the guy [Steve Ciotlos] eventually, after I was going there a lot. I said, "I've got a little band that plays the blues. Do you mind if we play between sets?" He said, "Sure, why not?" And the people loved it. They thought it was a nice change between the jazz stuff.

In late 1963 and into early 1964, over five or so months, Mike's Trio played Sunday nights between the sets of the jazz bands, marking the first time that an electric blues or R&B band performed regularly in Yorkville. In Mike's memory, they were paid around five dollars each ($50.79 in 2025) and were never advertised: "We were just happy to be playing."

* * *

Patricia Tancock was born in London, England, on July 30, 1936. When German bombing raids came to London, Patti and her mother were sent to a Welsh village for five years. Intelligent, lively, and attractive, Patti had lost all interest in school by the time the family was reunited in London. She entered the workforce at fourteen.

Sola Fiedler (Patti Tancock): On the weekends, I worked in a department store, Littlewoods, and I ran the record department. I got to play the music throughout the store—I had control of the sound system. In the evenings, I was a ballroom dancer. I went dancing every night.

I came to Canada in '59. I was twenty-three. I'd seen my boyfriend with another woman on the Saturday night and I was so furious that on Monday morning I went to the Cunard office and booked out on the next boat. I thought that it would be snow and mountains and igloos. I was totally surprised to find tall buildings. Coming to Canada was like fresh new territory, and anything you did was okay. There was no class distinction.

Her future husband, Bernd Fiedler, was born December 8, 1938, in Berlin, Germany.

B. C. Fiedler (Bernd Fiedler): My father was a sergeant in the army. In 1940, Hitler said, "Women and children out of Berlin." With my mother, aunt, cousin, and grandmother, I went to the [Baltic] sea, very close to the Polish border for three years.

Back in Berlin after the war, Bernd was a boy soprano in the Berliner Boys Choir, eventually performing for Easter services at the Vatican. In high school, he fell in love with American popular culture.

B. C. Fiedler: We were very influenced by the American Forces Network. I knew about Elvis; I knew all of them. I was heavily into the music. I had a Dixieland jazz club when I was fifteen, sixteen, called the Flat Feet Club in a bar in Berlin. And of course, James Dean. I even had a red jacket made out of silk. I wanted to go to Hollywood no matter what. A friend of mine's brother, Bob King, had moved to Canada. He said to me, "Come to Canada. You will not regret it. You practically find the money on the streets. It's so easy there. The [Canadian] people don't really work as hard as the Germans." I turned eighteen and Canada paid for my trip, $200. I had to pay it back in instalments of $10 a month. I came to Toronto in April 1957. I had five dollars on me and I went to live with [Bob's] family there.

Rather than rendering his nickname in the usual spelling of "Bernie," Fiedler chose the more idiosyncratic "Burnie," its spelling perhaps a nod to his white-hot ambition. He got a job at Dixon Manufacturing making brushes and brooms. The job paid $27 ($274.26 in 2025) a week, five days from 8 a.m. to 6 p.m., and at night school he studied English.

B. C. Fiedler: I hated it [in Toronto]. Toronto was the most boring place in the world in 1957. I went back to Germany in May '58. I got to Berlin, loved it there for a second. I did some kind of construction job removing anti-termite paint from buildings. You can imagine the dust. I called Bob. I said, "Bob, I've got to get out of here. I've got to come back to things. Get us an apartment, you and I, we'll move out of your mother's place. Number one, get me a job." Bob got me a job in a big coffee company, Club Coffee. I just said I was an accountant—I had no idea what I was doing. They had me add up the drivers that were coming in. I was really not that happy, and I really wanted a company car. So I became a salesman. I got a little Chevy and a route all up Yonge Street and over to Bathurst, all the way north into Aurora.

One of Burnie's clients was Marilyn McHugh of the Half Beat, who remembered, "He used to sell that awful coffee until he got educated."

Sola (Patti) Fiedler: When I came to Canada there was virtually nothing. There wasn't anywhere to ballroom dance. I had this suitcase filled with ballroom dancing outfits with the matching satin slippers. I was in the formation dance team at the German Club. They had a beauty competition. There was Miss Toronto and Miss Casa Loma. The people in the German Club persuaded me to enter this competition.

B. C. Fiedler: I had a girlfriend, and she was beautiful. The German Club had a big deal at Casa Loma. My girlfriend won the second prize. She got a salami.

Sola (Patti) Fiedler: Burnie's girlfriend came in ninth. I won first prize.

B. C. Fiedler: It was a big deal because [the contestants] were all German, and [Patti] was English. I just loved that girl, but I didn't see her [for a while] after that.

Patti and Burnie would soon meet again. Bored with her day job doing consumer research at Procter & Gamble, Patti got a waitressing job at the Half Beat that lasted about a week, and then at the Coffee Mill, a café tucked away in the Lothian Mills enclosed courtyard on Cumberland Street. On her time off, she sometimes met with friends at the 71 Coffee House.

B. C. Fiedler: One day I drive through Yorkville; it's about dusk. There she sits with a friend of mine at Werner Graeber's, outside. Well, I stopped the car and went over there. I said hello to him and then he introduced me. I didn't know whether he was dating her or not. I didn't want to say to her, "Can I have your phone number?" But she slipped it to me.

Sola (Patti) Fiedler: Werner looked after Burnie in a way. Burnie came over as a young immigrant and I think Werner was like almost like family to him.

B. C. Fiedler: After going in and selling him espresso coffee, Werner says to me, "Burnie, how much money do you make as a coffee salesman?" He's German; I'm German. I said, "Werner, not enough." "Well, why don't you sell the coffee by the cup instead of by the pound?" "Yeah, I'd like to, but . . . " "I'll help you!" he said. And he did. At that point [Patti] already had a ticket back to England. She had sold her car and she was going to go back and that was the end of it. I just thought, if I keep her here, then it'll be okay. I convinced her to stay. [I said,] "Let's try this coffeehouse." We went up north to this farm. We said, "We're from the school; we're building a [set for a] Christmas thing." He said, "You take as much barnwood as you want, but you've got to invite me for the show," which we never did.

Burnie and Patti rented a basement at 106 Yorkville Avenue for $250 ($2,592 in 2025) a month and set up the Mousehole, their new sixty-seat coffeehouse, in five days. Spending $1,300 ($13,479 in 2025) that Patti had saved for her England trip, they installed the barnboard on the walls, put in some tables and chairs, and hung a distinctive wooden sign at the entrance that portrayed a cartoon mouse lying, dazed, in a coffee cup.

Sola (Patti) Fiedler: I asked a young man to paint it for me. That little mouse drunk from caffeine, lying in the cup, is really exactly what Yorkville was all about. We were all fueled by caffeine.

At first, Patti and Burnie allowed folk singers to drop in and perform in the corner of the room. There was no microphone, and no payment. Traditional singers like Jim McCarthy, Michael Sherman, and Alan MacRae played informal sets into the morning hours.

Sola (Patti) Fiedler: If you stayed open late, you were then faced with the drunks after 2 a.m., but also the shift workers, the musicians, the bartenders. And that's ten percent of the population. You might come off shift in the middle of the night, and then where is there for you to go to socialize and unwind? Burnie kept the Mousehole open till 6 a.m. He's a bit of a night owl, and I'm an early morning person.

B. C. Fiedler: We both worked at the Mousehole, but I was still working in the coffee company. They wouldn't let me go. I had to give three months' notice. I actually left there and went to the coffee company to check in, only to go home and go to sleep.

Sola (Patti) Fiedler: The big expense was the Gaggia machine, which I think was $900 [$9,142 in 2025], and of course we didn't have the money. But that espresso machine was a licence to print money. We paid it off quite quickly. [The Mousehole] was packed from the moment it opened.

B. C. Fiedler: The first year, Patti and I made $58,000 [$589,961 in 2025].

Chapter Five: "Coffee houses could be the ruination of this area."

Yorkville Avenue was fast becoming the hub of the scene, with the 71, Penny Farthing, and now the Mousehole between Bay and Avenue on the one-way street. The next coffeehouse with live music to open on the street in the turbulent year of 1963 was the almost-forgotten Le Macabre Coffeehouse at 107 Yorkville Avenue.

Open daily from 3 p.m. to 3 a.m., Le Macabre was a tiny basement club seating around thirty people. In keeping with the horror theme, the door, found around the back of the building, was marked with a black metal sign, featuring a skull and crossbones; the tables were shaped like coffin lids. The club began with jazz in December 1963; Geordie McDonald's group with guitarist Sonny Greenwich held court for a while.[1] By 1964, Ron Gerston and his friend Erik Budman were playing folk music regularly on Friday and Saturday night.

Ron Gerston: Between sets we would have a hootenanny in the back dressing room, with friends who would drop by. We exchanged some songs, licks, and stories.[2]

Tony Quarrington (1948–) grew up in the Don Mills neighbourhood of Toronto. He picked up the guitar around 1961 at summer camp.

Tony Quarrington: I was doing folk music because that was what was happening at the time. You know, the rock was not that interesting. There wasn't real rock and roll yet. There was just Elvis and some, you know, pop guys, but Peter, Paul and Mary, I found interesting.

Around that time, he took a class in folk music at the North York YMCA led by Sid Dolgay, the mandocellist of the Travellers.

Tony Quarrington: You showed up every week for five weeks and he would play some records. That was the first occasion I ever heard Bob Dylan's "Masters of War."

Tony's first coffeehouse haunt was Le Macabre.

Tony Quarrington: You had to go around the rear of the building and there was a stone stairwell that led down into the basement. It was bare brick, with no windows at all. Tables, tablecloths, and chairs, that's about it. There wasn't ever a stage or a sound system or anything. People just used to take their guitars and hang out.

* * *

Another hybrid folk and jazz club briefly flourished on the south side of Bloor Street, not far from the site of the old Concerto Café. The Green Door, opened in April or May of 1964 at 109 Bloor Street West, was tucked behind the Colonnade, a brutalist fourteen-storey, mixed-use building. The club was, predictably enough, entered through a green door, with modern jazz and folk music on Fridays and Saturdays and traditional jazz on Sundays. Jim McHarg's Vintage Jazz Band held down the trad jazz spot, while the modern jazz rotation included groups led by pianists Wray Downes and Paul Hoffert. The folk offerings included the Twin Tone Four, a high-school-aged ensemble featuring future film director Ivan Reitman (*Stripes*, *Ghostbusters*). The Green Door closed in April 1965.

* * *

With the Penny Farthing up and running, it was time for John and Marilyn McHugh to expand again. They built a large swimming pool in the backyard and now presented live music on two floors, with long-term engagements by folk singers Margaret Milligan and Stan Thomas seven nights a week upstairs, and jazz bands on weekends in the basement: the Black Eagle Jazz Band and Don Simmons's group predominated for the first half of the year. Beginning in August, the bookings changed to one- or two-nighters, with a rotation of folk and blues singers: Doug Brown, Chick Roberts, Greg Winkfield, and Elyse Weinberg, along with jazz bands led by Don Wilson, Art Ayre, and Ron Peck.

Jutta Maue, having waited tables at the 71 Coffee House and the Inn on the Parking Lot, began to work at the Penny along with her friend Solveigh Schattmann.

Jutta Maue Kay: Victorian red curtains, I remember velvet and that beautiful espresso machine. I still have the scars [from the hot steam]. I lived upstairs in the front room. I wanted to go home to Germany after I had been away for two years, and Marilyn thought I would never come back. She took my suitcase! Here I was with the ticket and no suitcase. I eventually got it back.

Solveigh and I didn't make much money, so we doubled up there and handed in the tickets twice to make a little extra at the Penny Farthing. We cheated a little. Let's put it that way.

Marilyn McHugh: Everybody used to keep their money in their pocket. We had all these seats and they had no money coming in, so we [hired] a detective company to see why we were losing all this money. They did a written report and [we found out] it was the ones we trusted who were taking money.

When the jazz bands weren't playing, the basement of 110 Yorkville was an informal performance space, open to amateurs. Future superstar record producer Bob Ezrin played there as a fifteen-year-old aspiring folk singer.

Bob Ezrin: I think Peter, Paul and Mary dragged me into folk music, like they did so many people. They had a hit record, and you heard it and then you went, "wow." Also, we went to summer camps, so we learned "Kumbaya" and other things. There was always somebody with a guitar at summer camp who would play "Sinner Man" or "House of the Rising Sun." That opened up the door to Bob Dylan. I got into Judy Collins, Judy Henske, Theodore Bikel, and Tom Rush.

I would play in the basement as much as I could. The basement was sort of the up-for-grabs room. It was rarely formally booked. I would go down there and play, and people would go down there when they just couldn't take the noise upstairs, or they were looking for, you know, a place to neck or something like that. I would regularly play to [nobody] or two people. I rarely got paid.

By the spring of 1964, the large front and back patios of the Penny Farthing were packed almost every night. The Penny was a success, but running two clubs proved to be too much for the McHughs. Marilyn's mother had remarried in Toronto, to a lawyer named Syd Ezrin. Ezrin, "a modest, quiet man" according to Marilyn, was also Bob Ezrin's uncle, and a serious jazz record collector. A silent partner in the Penny Farthing, he offered to take over the Half Beat so that the McHughs could concentrate their energies on the Penny.

John McHugh: We'd gone in with my stepfather-in-law, work that one out. When we told him that we were putting a swimming pool into the Penny, he said, "Oh my God, you take that and I'll take Avenue Road."

Syd Ezrin ran the Half Beat for around eight months. In late January 1964, with day-to-day management and booking being handled by Bill Klotzhoff, the club began to present live music. A small sound system and single microphone were installed, and local performers were hired for ongoing Friday and Saturday night residencies. Folk singer Mitzi Hurd held a residency from January 31 to March 14, after which Half Beat music listings disappeared for a few months.

As of September, Syd Ezrin was still an investor and part-owner of JMS (John-Marilyn-Syd) Coffeehouses Ltd., but the McHughs were back running the Half Beat. John McHugh was now in charge of the music, and the first thing he did was install one of his favourite local bands, a rough and tumble traditional jazz group called the Black Eagle Jazz Band. In so doing, he planted the seeds for a remarkable Toronto tradition that continues to this day, that of Kid Bastien and the Happy Pals.

Cliff Bastin (1937–2003) was a British expat, a traditional jazz lover, and sign painter who styled himself "Kid Bastien." Cliff played all of the trad jazz instruments—cornet, clarinet, bass, drums, and piano—but in the Black Eagle Jazz Band he played banjo. The Black Eagle Jazz Band, as heard on their Onward LP (recorded at the Naval Veterans' Hall at 14 Hayden Street in Gerrard Village) was, by modern standards of traditional jazz, a raw, pounding unit, with a raucous ensemble sound.[3] They were true to the style, yet played with abandon, with Kid Bastien's steady banjo chops barely audible in the murky mix.

Jack King (Happy Pals banjoist): Cliff's musical philosophy was four strong beats to the bar. "Just play fours . . . We gotta lay that beat down."

Joe Van Rossem (Black Eagle Jazz Band cornetist): Cliff went so far as to call what he did "folk jazz."

After the breakup of the Black Eagle Jazz Band in the mid-'60s, Cliff formed the Camellia Jazz Band, another traditional combo. In 1968, the Camellia Band began a regular Saturday afternoon residency at Grossman's Tavern on Spadina Avenue. Over the next six decades, Cliff's band became a finishing school for young traditional jazz musicians; he is fondly remembered as giving free lessons on any of his instruments to anyone who wanted to play this music. The final incarnation of his band, the Happy Pals, has played Saturday afternoons at Grossman's from 1980 to the present day. After Cliff's death in 2003, trumpeter Patrick Tevlin took over and has continued the tradition of training and nurturing young jazz musicians to keep the music alive.

* * *

Marilyn McHugh: We had this long garden—it was huge. I decided to have a fair with boutiques and let all the artists—the silversmiths and painters—have their stalls.

On May 14, 1964, the Yorkville Festival began, a weeklong event sponsored by the business owners, who contributed $25 ($250 in 2025) each. In keeping with the rustic image of Yorkville that was so much a part of its attraction, entertainment would include folk singing, puppet shows, dancing, and carriage rides. The idea, as gallery owner Stephen Sobot told the *Star*, was "to draw the attention of the public to this area through the arts."[4]

Even before the festival had begun, tensions between the upscale merchants and the coffeehouse owners were coming to the surface. Bob Dirstein, the antique dealer who had helped to get the north side of Yorkville Avenue rezoned, complained, "Coffee houses could be the ruination of this area. They attract a rowdy element." The alderman for the ward, Charles Tidy, added, "I would like to see it developed for the carriage trade, a cultured commercialism." On the side of the coffeehouses, Werner Graeber spoke up. "This street only comes alive at 9 p.m.," he told the *Star* reporter. John McHugh simply said, "We're here and we're not going to move."[5]

Three days before the festival was to begin, Yorkville made the news when an estimated five hundred youths converged on Yorkville Avenue and the police were called in to disperse the crowd. In the melee, Werner Graeber suffered a broken ankle.[6] The Yorkville Festival itself was, predictably, heavily policed. Thirteen uniformed men roamed the streets along with plainclothes officers, and three police vans stood at the ready. But the expected problems failed to materialize, and the crowds were moderate, at least until the Friday.

That night hundreds of young people converged on the Village looking for something to do. Some went to the coffeehouses or the Embassy

Tavern if they were over twenty-one, and others just hung out, sitting on the steps of the businesses along Yorkville, Cumberland, and Avenue Road. The police, not knowing what to do, stayed on the sidelines until Marilyn McHugh, who was spraying down the Penny Farthing patio, turned her hose on an errant youth.[7]

John McHugh: Marilyn was hosing the front patio down and somebody leapt up on the wall. We had just had new tables delivered with glass tops. And she literally held this guy off by spraying the hose in his face.

With this, the cops moved in and arrested four people for creating a disturbance, and then forcibly cleared the street. The incident, along with its predecessor on May 11, formed the basis of the journalistic shorthand known as the Yorkville riots.

On May 30, the *Star* ran an article by Morris Duff entitled "Yorkville: The Sad Village." Describing the goings-on at the Yorkville Festival as "student riots," Duff set the scene:

> An area of gay coffeehouses, shapely girls in tight pants, expensive art galleries, bearded youths, high-priced restaurants, guitar-strumming folkniks, girls in bikinis, noisy motorbike toughs, the unwashed, the unshaven, the rebels without a cause . . . But it's not all as carefree as it looks . . . Pimpley-faced [sic] racists . . . circulating hate literature . . . crumpled men who sit from 9 p.m. till 3 a.m. playing chess . . . Performers continually compliment each other, basking in the reflected glory of Ian and Sylvia and Pierre Berton [Berton had left the *Star* in 1962]. Yorkville is a place where the mediocre can excel.[8]

By the summer of 1964, there were no fewer than twelve coffeehouses offering live music within the old Village boundaries, or just outside of them. In January 1960, there had been zero, with the Concerto closed and La Coterie open but without live music. This was the most striking outward change in the Village, and it was both a symptom and driver of its popularity, along with increasing press coverage in all three daily newspapers, local and national radio, and television, and countless magazine articles. Yorkville's new notoriety and popularity were causing tension, and some of the more established coffeehouse proprietors felt that the situation was getting out of hand.

Speaking to the *Star*, Sam Gutmacher from the Purple Onion placed the blame on the clubs that offered live entertainment without a cover charge. He felt that this attracted a more downscale, volatile element to the area, leading to an increased police presence. "Who wants to come here when there's a lot of toughs hanging around?" he lamented. Presciently, he added, "Many of us in the coffeehouse business are afraid that the same thing that happened in San Diego will happen here. A couple of years ago there were twelve coffeehouses there; now there isn't one.[9] The unsavoury element simply ruined it. We're afraid here that one of these days the city fathers here are going to get up in arms about what's happening in Yorkville and re-zone the place."[10]

That summer of 1964, some observers were noticing that something had changed in the Village. In a *Globe* article entitled "Has the Zest Gone Out of Yorkville Village?" Jurgen Hesse wrote, "The only trouble is that Yorkville Village coffeehouses, by and large, are getting squarer and squarer as prosperity brings fatter bank accounts." Interviewed for the article, Marilyn McHugh complained that, of late, most of the clientele were ordinary people with jobs. She said, "I'd like to see more genuine eccentrics." In the same piece Werner Graeber said, "When we first started, we sat and argued until eight in the morning. Now they're still here but not doing anything. It's commercialized too much."[11]

* * *

Even at the height of the folk boom in April 1963, the Village Corner Club was in dire financial straits, with twenty folk acts performing at a benefit concert for the club that month.[12] Proprietors Abrams and Mike Cavendish raised the membership charge from fifty cents ($5.10) to one dollar ($10.20 in 2025) and the admission to $1.25 ($12.75 in 2025), but three months later the club was behind on their $250-a-month ($2,550 in 2025) rent.[13] At the height of summer heat, a bailiff came to confiscate the air conditioner.[14]

A pharmacist named Jack Devoretsky brought an infusion of cash in the spring of 1964, but there was a catch: the all-Canadian booking policy had to be abandoned.[15] Starting with D.C. bluegrass group the Country Gentlemen, the Corner would feature touring American acts. But the extra expense of the touring acts was not being covered by door receipts. Burnie Fiedler, finding himself on a night off from the Mousehole, dropped in to the Corner in late August or early September to hear Jesse Fuller, a sixty-eight-year-old Georgia-born one-man band best known for his song "San Francisco Bay Blues," perform.

B. C. Fiedler: I walk in there; there's nobody there. The stage is lit. I say, "What the hell is going on?" I thought there must be a waiter somewhere. I sit down and nobody comes. All of a sudden I hear noise behind the stage and who comes out, Jesse Fuller. He sits down and starts playing a set. He played his entire set and I just sat there and nobody was there. I couldn't believe it. I felt so bad about this situation. I felt sorry for

> Shelley Abrams because, you know, when Ian and Sylvia played there and Gordon [Lightfoot] with the Two Tones, that was the good times. It was the wrong place.

To *Star* writer Morris Duff, the Corner had been "the dirtiest, the darkest and the most beatnik" of Toronto's folk venues until Abrams's tenure. Abrams told Duff that "we've got to be clean if we're going to attract adult customers." She retiled the floor and painted the kitchen. Working the door, waiting on tables, and preparing food in the kitchen, Abrams put in eighteen-hour days. She paid musicians out of pocket if the club lost money, and as a result sometimes couldn't afford to feed herself. As she quipped to Duff, "I'm losing weight without dieting."[16]

Abrams and Cavendish soon sold the club to Jack Devoretsky, its angel investor of the previous spring.[17] Devoretsky put together a fifteen-member board to run the venue, but the next months were chaotic, with the venue opening and closing twice.[18] The club also went non-union, which eliminated American acts from the roster and caused a rift with Estelle Klein and the Folk Guild.[19]

* * *

In September 1963, Carl Noylander was publicly musing about selling the Gate of Cleve.[20] By December, *Star* writer Dave Caplan announced that "the Gate of Cleve is still in operation but is on the selling block for a reasonable figure."[21] In late February 1964, a young folksinging group from Oakwood Collegiate high school called the Yorke Singers IV played the Gate. When the nineteen-year-old leader of the group, Warren Haller (1944–2018), heard that it was for sale he told his mother Alyce, who purchased the business from the Noylanders. The Gate of Cleve became the New Gate of Cleve, and was henceforth run by the members of the Yorke Singers IV, with the understanding that they would take over full ownership when they had all reached twenty-one. Their bookings and public relations were handled by Joe Lewis.

Joe Lewis: They were still technically in school. They didn't quite know how to book, or who to book, and I pretended that I did.

I was born December 21, 1941, in the Annex, on Walmer Road. I went to Central Tech [high school]. They were the only school that had a course in broadcasting. They actually had a radio studio there. I knew at that point I wanted to go into radio broadcasting.

I got unofficially involved [with folk music] at the end of the '63 Mariposa Festival. I was working with [folk music radio host] Randy Ferris. He bought the rights to Mariposa [i.e., he purchased the festival name and took over as president]. He said, "I just acquired this, why don't you work with me on it?" It was as simple as that; it could have been Zulu music for all I cared. I had already had some PR experience. He knew that. I guess I became the PR director at that point, because there wasn't one, and somebody had to.

The New Gate of Cleve reduced its membership fee from $1.50 to fifty cents, and raised the regular admission charge to $1.50, with a special one-dollar price for students. The new owners generally continued the booking policy of the Noylanders, with a few wrinkles: introducing standup comedy with Sammy Taft and some newer singers on the scene including members of the Dirty Shames, Greg Winkfield, David Rea, Elyse Weinberg, and Tom Brewer (later of Brewer and Shipley and "One Toke Over the Line"), who played the Gate for two weekends in October 1964. By January 23, 1965, *Globe* writer Michael Hanlon announced that "the New Gate of Cleve is finding itself fed up with booking the same local song-pedlars as the other coffeehouses in the neighbourhood . . . until the end of March, the Cleve will feature only acts imported from the United States, starting with the Greenbriar Boys who arrive January 28."[22]

Joe Lewis: The New York agents I dealt with were treating Toronto almost with the same respect that they treated the New York scene. I think the notoriety that Toronto got in the United States was a result of the American performers who came, performed in our clubs, saw the activity, saw all the action. And of course, Ian and Sylvia, and then Lightfoot, had [a] New York manager. So the word was getting out.

The engagement by the New York-based bluegrass group the Greenbriar Boys was favourably reviewed in the *Globe* by Marvin Schiff, but he noted an audience of thirty-five on the opening night, far below capacity.[23] Joe Lewis worked with New York booking agents to bring in legendary names in American folk and blues: Mississippi John Hurt, Sleepy John Estes, John Hammond Jr., John Lee Hooker, and Sonny Terry and Brownie McGhee. The New Gate of Cleve was now open five nights a week instead of three and featured American acts almost exclusively, with the Allen-Ward Trio, Gordon Lightfoot, and the Travellers among rare exceptions.

* * *

The long arm of the Toronto Musicians' Association had reached into several of the Yorkville-area coffeehouses by 1964: the New Gate of Cleve, the Village Corner Club, the Purple Onion, and the Bohemian

Embassy were all venues in good stead with the union, with performers drawn from the membership, and contracts stipulating that musicians would make scale, the TMA minimum wage.

Joe Lewis: Quite a number of folk singers felt they were forced to join the union. For some, they didn't really want to do it, but in order to get the gigs, they had to, because the union was organized well enough where they were able to put the pressure.

Don Cullen (co-owner of the Bohemian Embassy): Gordie Lightfoot worked for me initially for $15 [$152.81 in 2025] a night. We realized that there was a real problem with the TMA, because I would sign these documents saying that I was going to pay them a lot more than I could. No coffeehouse could, but we would sign these contracts. Finally, a guy by the name of Jim Mitchell, who played the bass in the jazz group that operated every Saturday night, brought a little delegation to the [TMA] and sat down with [TMA secretary-treasurer] Gurney Titmarsh. Jim said, "We've been signing these documents fraudulently. Everybody does."[24] Gurney went ballistic. Jim said, "There has to be a coffeehouse scale. We can't lumber coffeehouses with the same kind of payment that bars are asked to pay. It's ridiculous."

Titmarsh took the idea to the TMA executive, which now included Klaas VanGraft. Klaas knew well the realities of the coffeehouses and became an advocate within the union for the change. "Coffeehouse scale" was approved in September 1964 at a rate of $25 a night ($263.78 in 2025) instead of the usual $36 ($359 in 2025) per musician.

* * *

A month after coffeehouse scale was instituted, Patti Tancock began to book and advertise folk singers at the Mousehole on weekends, beginning in October 1964 with Alan MacRae, a West Coast-born banjoist and guitarist who was part of the Chanteclairs, a popular Toronto folk trio. MacRae held the weekend residency until February 1965, when Greg Winkfield was added to the rotation. Klaas VanGraft, now another member of the Chanteclairs along with Beverlie Sammon, was added on Sundays in April. By July, continuous live folk music rang through the tiny club six nights a week; the Mousehole only closed on Mondays.

Unlike most of the other folk venues, they did not have a cover charge. But overpriced coffee more than made up for it. As strong an influence as Werner Graeber was on the couple, Burnie and Patti did not emulate the 71 Coffee House's pricing of ten cents ($1 in 2025) for a cup of coffee. Coffee and soft drinks at the Mousehole were a flat fifty cents ($5.01 in 2025).

Sola (Patti) Fiedler: I knew nothing about the folk scene. I had two singers who alternated sets. We did fourteen sets a night. And each time the place would empty out at the end of the set and fill up. Everybody was trying to hook up, so they would wander in and out of places and catch a set. People might go to four or five places in one evening.

Yorkville's popularity was exploding, and the Mousehole was making a fortune one cup at a time. Just as the McHughs had done with the Penny Farthing, Burnie and Patti looked to expand their empire with a second coffeehouse; their new venue would be the greatest of them all, the pearl of the Yorkville folk coffeehouse scene, the Riverboat.

Sola (Patti) Fiedler: We went to Germany and we went to this discotheque. In those days they were mostly in basements and they were called

Whiskey-a-Go-Go's. They were very dark, smoky little places. But then in Berlin, on the fourth floor of this warehouse, there was this most elegant discotheque. It had the most beautiful dance floor, with little pieces of copper that moved as you danced on them. It was called the Riverboat. I was so impressed and I loved the name.

B. C. Fiedler: When I visited Berlin, I had a friend; she was a bartender at a place called the Riverboat and it was huge. It was different, and that's where I got the name from.

"The Riverboat" conjured images of the steam-driven paddlewheel vessels that plied the Mississippi River around the turn of the twentieth century, with jazz in the ballroom and high-stakes gambling on the deck. Films like 1953's *The Mississippi Gambler* painted a Technicolor picture of danger and romance on the big river, while the rollicking music of the riverboats was celebrated in songs like Hoagy Carmichael's "Riverboat Shuffle."

It was decided that Burnie, who had by this time left Club Coffee, would manage the Riverboat and Patti would continue to run the Mousehole. The Riverboat, at 134 Yorkville Avenue was, like the Mousehole, a basement. But this basement had room for 117 patrons, nearly twice the Mousehole's capacity. And when it came to decorating the venue, Burnie and Patti had money to spend; there was no more need to wheedle barnboard siding out of credulous farmers. They dropped some $15,000 ($149,582 in 2025) getting the new club in order, constructing much of it themselves.

The room was panelled in lacquered, dark-stained pine, and the booths were red leatherette, framed by floor-to-ceiling brass poles. Heavy brass portholes were installed along the walls, with their windows covered by translucent blue plastic sheets that softened the glare of the light bulbs within. The stage itself was barely ten feet wide. The room was L-shaped, with just a couple of booths in front of the stage and then a long row to the performer's right.

Bruce Cockburn (singer-songwriter): It was a weird venue, physically, because you were playing across the room and most of the audience was down to the right and a few people to the left—and hardly anybody in front of you.

The Riverboat opened on December 8, 1964.[25] From the beginning, the new venue presented live music with both expensive coffee and a cover charge, six nights a week. The emphasis was firmly on music.

B. C. Fiedler: Where would people go, into which [coffeehouse]? They were all quite nice. But what was the big draw? It was whoever played in the corner. I'm going to get the real good ones coming in that are costing me a lot of money, and instead of having a coffeehouse serving music, I'm going to serve music with incidental coffee. Five shows a night and we cleared the house after each one of them. I was going to put a conveyor belt in there. We had the opportunity—we could ask people to leave. Had we had liquor, we couldn't have done that, because you cannot ask somebody to leave if they paid for a drink.

Sola (Patti) Fiedler: We didn't want people hanging around. We wanted fresh people, because we made the money on the coffee. We got to keep that—we shared the cover charge with the performer. The performers got 60 percent of the gate, I think, in most instances.

Burnie and Patti married on Christmas Eve, 1964. After the wedding, Burnie flew home to Berlin for two weeks and, when he returned, he confessed to Patti that he had been unfaithful to her there.

Sola (Patti) Fiedler: We separated two weeks after we got married. We lived under the same roof, but I had nothing more to do with him. I almost didn't know about divorce in those days. And we were totally tied up with our businesses. I was very protective of the Riverboat. That was my idea. The golden handcuffs. We were making so much money. As I've realized since then, money doesn't buy you happiness. It bought me a lot of misery.

B. C. Fiedler: We bought a house, and we did get married, because we made too much money. I said to myself, "I've got to get secure. At least we're in a marriage here." It was the right thing to do.

Sola (Patti) Fiedler: I made about $10,000 in today's money every night at the Mousehole. And Burnie made considerably more at the Riverboat, and it was cash. It was amazing. It was like a giant casino and it attracted a lot of bad guys. They wanted in. Yorkville was an extremely dangerous place toward the end. It was run by the Mafia, Albert Volpe in particular. Their headquarters was across the road from the Mousehole in a sculpture studio.[26]

B. C. Fiedler: Albert Volpe—dear, dear friend of mine. He had a little store above my Riverboat called Asian Imports.[27] He helped me upholster the chairs [in the Riverboat] and he helped me collect some money for some poker games that [I won].

Albert Volpe's mob bona fides are well established: an FBI memo from January 20, 1965, names Volpe, along with his four brothers, as a major Toronto crime family, with ties to the Buffalo mafia.[28] Robbie Robertson, guitarist with the Hawks at this time and later the Band, described his uncle Nathan Klegerman's ties to the Volpe family in his memoir, *Testimony*. And as noted earlier, Cellar co-owner Sam Shirose had documented connections to the Volpes.

Marilyn McHugh: What wiped the Village out is the [Musicians] Union. We weren't unionized. The union came into there and then the Boys [i.e., the Mafia] moved in. The [Supertest] gas station [on the southeast corner of Avenue and Yorkville] was sold overnight. It's very important, that gas station. Everybody's sort of forgotten about it, but when they go, suddenly the whole place changes. Suddenly there were people coming down to the Village and making a visit. And there were three or four of them. What it turned out to be is that the [Musicians'] Union was going to come in and the clubs didn't have the money to pay the acts, because now they're going to have to unionize. So the Boys would loan the money to the coffeehouses. And then the guys would come on a Sunday to collect with interest, and they would go to each club—the Penny, the Riverboat, every one of them.

They tried to buy the Penny Farthing from us. We didn't want to sell it. The guy comes in and he says that he'd like to buy it, just a nice little man. That's all we know about him. He's got several friends that are sitting at the table waiting for him, but he's by himself and he said, "Marilyn, you and John can go off to have a lovely holiday in England. And when you come back, John, you go to school and Marilyn, you'll run it. You'll be the one." And he took hold of my hands and he said, "You see these little short pudgy fingers? If we find them in the till, you'll be missing some of them." John went green. I looked at the guy and said that we didn't want to do this. He said, "That's not a wise choice." We said, "That's what we're gonna do." Then he said, "I tell you what we'll do. When the boys are coming down collecting on Sunday, we sit and we can have our sandwiches and watch the acts."

Everybody said they made loads of money in Yorkville. They never did. They were paying the Boys, and we all struggled, or we gave it away, or they smoked it away. We weren't very businesslike, John and I. I think that might've been a hindrance looking back in today's world, but at the time it was the only place I wanted to be. We wanted to live comfortably, but we wanted everybody else to share it with their stuff too. We never had a licence or anything like that. We didn't really keep proper books. We were very gullible. We believed in our world that we lived in, that we'd worked for. We'd worked jolly hard for it. We didn't make a lot of money. Somehow, at the end of the day, when we added it up, it wasn't there.

Chapter Six: "The Village started to change."

THE TRANSFORMATION OF YORKVILLE from a relatively quiet enclave of folk and jazz clubs to a raucous, teen-driven rock scene began with the emergence of the Beatles in North America in late 1963. By September 7, 1964, Toronto Beatlemania hit a peak when the Beatles played two concerts at Maple Leaf Gardens and 35,000 kids came to scream at them.

Mike McKenna: When the Beatles hit, it was just like, that's it. Everything just changed and we couldn't believe what was going on. It was overwhelming. All the Toronto bands combed their hair down and wore Beatle suits and started looking for Beatle boots.

Over that winter, the Rolling Stones, the Dave Clark Five, and Herman's Hermits joined the Fab Four on the Canadian pop charts. The new demand for electric rock and R&B bands over jazz and folk music, and the younger demographic that came with the change, would have a transformative effect on Yorkville; its first rumblings emanated from a basement club, the El Patio, in the summer of 1964.

* * *

On April 16, 1964, the El Patio opened at 119 Yorkville Avenue as a Spanish restaurant, with live music by flamenco guitarist Juan Serrano. The El Patio was a long, windowless, subterranean room reached by a few stairs descending from the sidewalk.

Neil Merryweather (musician): With that stage down the middle of the club with nothing in front of you but a wall, and the people were at either end of the club. That was interesting.

The first owner was Manuel Sahuquillo, a former waiter at the Gaslight restaurant next door.[1] His Spanish restaurant with flamenco music was a nonstarter, and weeks later, Sahuquillo sold the business to Mike Burak and Tony Fernandez, who turned it into a rhythm and blues room, Yorkville's first.

Mike Burak (1936–2006) was born in Buenos Aires and moved to Canada at age fifteen. Family lore has him working as a teenage bootlegger and then owning a beauty salon at Yonge and St. Clair, before buying the El Patio. He lived above the club with his wife, Eileen. Little is known of Tony Fernandez, who is remembered as also being Argentina-born. He worked in the kitchen while Burak managed the front of house.

Burak walked into the Cellar one night in the spring of 1964 and heard Mike's Trio, Mike McKenna's electric blues group, playing between jazz band sets. He offered the band $15 ($150 in 2025) per night—the same that they were making at the Cellar, but with double the work per week—to play every Friday and Saturday night. The cover charge was a low fifty cents ($5.01 in 2025), and Mike's Trio's appearances at the club were unadvertised to avoid the notice of the Musicians' Union. Advertising was scarcely needed; there were lineups along the sidewalk on weekend nights.

Mike McKenna: [Burak] couldn't believe the reaction we were getting. Neither could we. People were like, "Oh God, there's some rock and roll going on here that's something different." The owners [of the other coffeehouses] all went, "Look at the El Patio, they're packed." The Village started to change.

Mike McKenna was an increasingly adept electric guitarist but he wasn't much of a singer. In McKenna's memory, his drummer Rick McMurray said to him, "Mike, I love you. You're my buddy. But you're not a great singer." Rick knew Luke Gibson and invited him to come down and sit in.

Mike McKenna: He just looked great and he had this charisma about him. And he got up and sang and all the girls in the club were going "holy shit, who is this guy?"

Anni Lissee (fan): The sexiest singer in Yorkville.

Pat Little (later Luke and the Apostles drummer): The babes loved Luke.

Cathy Little (fan): The best-looking guy on the street. He had a little-boy look.

* * *

Luke Gibson was born David Gibson in north Toronto on October 5, 1946, and moved to the suburb of Willowdale with his parents and younger sister when he was five years old. David became "Luke" as a child, his cowboy-like nickname bestowed on him by school friends. Interested in country music at first, he picked up the guitar at eleven years old.

Luke Gibson: We didn't have a TV, but we had a radio. I listened to CHUM and CKEY and sometimes I could get WUFO out of Buffalo.

I started hearing Little Richard and Chuck Berry. My mom said, "That's rock and roll." [I said,] "Oh—well, I have to do that."

Luke's first band, the Castelles, was three guitarists playing Ronnie Hawkins covers in the garage of one of the members, Don Ogilvie. In the summer of 1964, the group ventured south to Yorkville for the first time.

Luke Gibson: We'd heard about this Village place downtown in the mysterious Toronto. We were walking around, and that was when it was just super crowded with people. I couldn't believe what was going on down there. There was nothing in Willowdale—just a bunch of fields. [In Yorkville] we saw weird people, cars and music, music, music. I heard the strains of "Night Train" being played on a guitar somewhere across the road. I followed that sound down into a club called El Patio, down the stairs. There was Mike's Trio. I actually knew Rick McMurray, the drummer, because he lived in Willowdale. I was amazed—I didn't know he was there. When they were on a break I said, "Well, do you need a singer?" I got up with Mike's Trio, sang a few songs, and it seemed to go over well.

Luke was invited to join the group, which now became Mike's Trio Plus Luke.

Luke Gibson: [Mike Burak] hated it, because he didn't want to pay any more money. So the guys decided to each give me a dollar. They were making four dollars, and I made three. We played till three in the morning. Fights would break out in the audience and spread. It was like a Western movie, tables and chairs falling over. The stage was about six inches high, and [the debris] came right over us like a tsunami, and we're swinging microphones at people, trying to get out.

Once Yorkville started to get really big, [the Musicians' Union] figured, *well, these guys are making money, we better get involved.* They ended up sending their reps down, but they were pretty cool. They knew we were doing it under the table, and they just wanted to come in and say, "Hey, remember who we are?" The union [rep] came down and [Mike Burak] would suddenly disappear. "Oh, where's the owner?" "Oh, he just stepped out for a while." [The rep] would check our union cards and say, "Well, you know, you guys need a contract." We'd go, "Yeah, yeah, that's true. We'll get one done."

* * *

In September 1964, Jacque Amoch opened Jacque's Place at 132 Yorkville. Jacque's was a new and different kind of Yorkville venue; it relied on records and a disc jockey rather than live musicians to provide dance music. The discotheque as a viable dance venue had become possible only recently, with the advent of more powerful amplifiers and speakers, capable of putting out enough volume and low-end thump to match the power of a live band.

Jacque's was open on Fridays and Saturdays only, from 9 p.m. to 1:30 a.m. The cover charge was $1.50 ($15.03 in 2025). It was a relatively small space, and soon crowded with patrons delighted to dance to the latest English hits along with French and Italian selections.[2] The club catered to a young clientele; in fact, by the summer of 1966, people over the age of twenty-one were barred from entering.[3]

Anni Lissee (fan): I graduated high school, got a job, and moved into the Yorkville area; I lived on Prince Arthur. A friend told me about a little club called Jacque's Place and she said, "Oh, you have to go here. It's a really nice place to dance." I remember there was a fellow that was a little older than me. I think he was the owner, Jacque. He was in his late thirties, if anything, and he was a really nice person, but he played records. Whatever was a number one in England, he was playing it. Everyone was so happy that he was playing this music. No one else was doing that in the city.

* * *

In late 1964 or early 1965, Yorkville's first discotheque was joined by a second. Located at 138 Cumberland, Kiki Rouge was owned by thirty-one-year-old John Haakman, an industrial designer remembered by Jutta Maue Kay as "a skinny blonde guy." He claimed to have invested $25,000 ($249,303 in 2025) in the club. "We're aiming at the people who want to go live it up after a hockey game or the theatre," Haakman told the *Star*.[4]

Laurel Douglas (Kiki Rouge waitress): There were a fair number of wealthy patrons there. I remember getting a $10 [$100 in 2025] tip for a cup of coffee. My annual living budget in those days was $1,700 [$17,030 in 2025] a year. So that was a lot of money for me.

A CBC news programme called *20/20*, aired on February 16, 1967, offered a brief glimpse of the club on a typical night. The DJ alternated between two turntables, spinning R&B records for patrons on a small dancefloor surrounded by tables. Album covers hung from the ceiling alongside coloured lights. A year earlier, the *Star* described the club:

"Although open at 9 p.m., [it] doesn't start moving until after midnight. For $1.25 weeknights and $2 Friday and Saturday after 12 a.m. you can dance to 3 a.m. on a very slippery floor to all the latest records. Lots of Nordic, slim-boned beautiful men, dim lights, and a waitress that doubles as a go-go girl."[5]

Jutta Maue and Solveigh Schattmann, star waitresses of Yorkville, worked at Kiki Rouge for a time, with a side hustle as surreptitious bootleggers. Bernie Finkelstein, working in the kitchen, was their accomplice.

Jutta Maue Kay: The clientele wanted to have their after-hours drink. So we just did this, put it in the coffee and well, the laws in those days were pretty draconian, you know?

Bernie Finkelstein: They were always saying, "You gotta keep this bottle of whiskey hidden away," or whatever it was. I finally decided, *well, let's see, they're running me ragged and I'm hiding the booze. The better I do for them, the more money they're making, and I'm getting nothing.* You know, I'm getting $1.10 [$10.80 in 2025] an hour or something. These girls were beautiful, by the way. I would've done anything for them.

The Toronto Morality Squad raided Kiki Rouge on June 3, 1966, and John Haakman was charged with keeping liquor in a public place. He was acquitted after arguing that it was leftover cooking wine from a private party.

* * *

In August 1964, the young folksinger who would become Joni Mitchell arrived in Toronto. Her time in the Yorkville coffeehouses—just under a year—set events into motion that ultimately delivered her to the upper reaches of the music business. But in the summer of '64, she was alone and pregnant in a big city, figuring out her next move.

Born in Fort MacLeod, Alberta, on November 7, 1943, Joan Anderson grew up in Alberta and Saskatchewan as a cherished only child of Bill and Myrtle Anderson. Myrtle encouraged Joan to indulge her artistic urges, and after a childhood bout with polio, Joan showed strong promise as a visual artist in high school. This led to a scholarship to study art at the Southern Alberta Institute of Technology in Calgary, beginning in the fall of 1963. In the summer leading up to her first year, Joni—inspired by a high school art teacher named Henry Bonli, she had changed the spelling of her first name—got a job waitressing at the Louis Riel Coffee House in Saskatoon. It was there that she fell in love with folk music.

After moving to Calgary for art school, Joni frequented the Depression Coffee House, where she sang traditional folk songs accompanied by her own baritone ukulele and then guitar. In May 1964, at twenty years old, she got pregnant with a fellow student at the art college, Brad MacMath. As Joni would recall, "That was a terrible thing for a woman, nothing worse. You may as well have killed somebody . . . it was losing face to the max . . . I tried to spare my parents by going to the anonymity of a large city, under the ruse that I wanted to be a musician."[6]

In early August 1964, Joni and Brad boarded a train from Regina to Toronto. Hoping to hear Buffy Sainte-Marie perform at the Mariposa Folk Festival, August 7 to 9, they took a bus from Union Station in Toronto to Orillia, where the festival was scheduled to be held in a farmer's field about 12 miles from town.

The Mariposa festival had been running for three summers by this point with increasing success. The 1963 festival, in fact, was so successful—between 20,000 and 30,000 fans showed up to a town that normally held 15,000—that the scene became chaotic and overwhelming for local authorities. Packs of drunken frat boys roamed the streets after the music ended, and there was widespread vandalism and theft. Local pressure demanded that the 1964 festival be moved out of Orillia proper, and then banned it from the area altogether at the last minute. This forced the organizers to pull up stakes and move the festival to Maple Leaf Stadium in downtown Toronto.

Joni and Brad were drafted by the Mariposa volunteers to help move the staging. In exchange, they got passes to the sparsely attended festival, which that year included folk singer Alan Mills, the Allen-Ward Trio, Gordon Lightfoot, recently "rediscovered" 1920s songster Mississippi John Hurt, and Joni's beloved Buffy.

Not long after the festival, Brad MacMath left Joni in Toronto to go home to Regina, and then to San Francisco. She would not see him again for decades, but Brad and Joni's relationship had always been casual and there was no talk of marriage. She later wrote: "[He] left me three months pregnant in an attic room with no money and winter coming on and only a fireplace for heat. The spindles of the banister were gap-toothed—fuel for last winter's occupants."[7]

That attic room was in a rooming house at 504 Huron Street, an imposing terracotta and brick mansion three blocks from the corner of Yorkville and Avenue Road. Joni's rent was $15 a week ($150 in 2025).

David DePoe (activist): It was starting to become obvious [that she was pregnant]. She wore very loose dresses and stuff like that. She was really poor, and I took a bunch of food over to her. Partly just to be in her presence, but she was extremely grateful for that because she was actually, I think, possibly starving. I took over a bunch of stuff like spaghetti and a jar of spaghetti sauce. Basic food, some bread and peanut butter.

Joni got a part-time job at Simpsons department store selling ladies' coats and by night hit Yorkville.[8] She soon met John "Spolie" Soules, a waiter at the Penny Farthing.

John Soules: Joni had come into town from out west, and she was just hanging around in a rooming house where a lot of us lived. Everybody lived around Lowther and Admiral, and you could rent out rooms pretty cheap. She was hanging out and playing the guitar. She was a beautiful lady with a beautiful voice. Dave [Pirie, a fellow Penny waiter] and I helped get her a job with Werner [Graeber] at the Inn on the Parking Lot.

Soules remembered that her gig at the Inn on the Parking Lot was Joni's first in Toronto. No published listings of the engagement seem to exist, but if true, it would almost certainly have been between Joni's arrival in early August and September 10, when the Inn switched from folk music to R&B and rock 'n' roll.

Along with John Soules, Joni met Vicky Taylor (1944–2023) soon after arriving in Toronto. Born and raised in London, Ontario, Vicky was a year younger than Joni and another aspiring folk singer acclimatizing to a new city. Vicky remembered meeting Joni for the first time among the towering stone walls of Union Station, the transportation hub at Front and Yonge.

Vicky Taylor: [We were] noticing each other with the long blonde hair and the long black hair and carrying the guitars and, you know, "Oh hi, how are you? Who are you?"

Vicky's repertoire tended toward contemporary songs in the folk style. Bob Dylan was a particular favourite, one that she would emulate and parody in her own talking blues, "Birth Control Blues." A few short years after the 1960 introduction of the birth control pill, and ten years before Loretta Lynn's "The Pill," Vicky was singing its praises in a way that combined risqué humour with genuine advocacy. Vicky had a good ear for musical talent, and in those uncertain early days encouraged Joni to audition for gigs.

Vicky Taylor: I dragged her everywhere to audition, because I thought she was just so amazing. I always have rooted for underdogs—not that you can look at Joni as an underdog, but she knew nobody in Toronto. She had a little bit of a hard time at first, so I dragged her from audition to audition. Not even audition—sometimes we just go to a club and I'd say to whoever, "You gotta let this girl get up and sing. You'll be amazed." I really promoted her.

Joni has credited Vicky as being one of the few folk singers who was kind to her in those early days in Yorkville. As she told Cameron Crowe in the liner notes for her 2020 box set *Archives No. 1*, Taylor "was very kind and very generous to me, which I was not used to . . . she wasn't competitive or vicious, like some of them. The folkies were so competitive."[9]

On her website, Joni is listed as appearing at the Purple Onion in October and November of 1964. As she later said, "You had to be in the union to work all the clubs . . . so I worked at a scab club called the Purple Onion till my sixth month [of pregnancy]. We did good business because I was a good scab act."[10] This remark is curious, since the Purple Onion was decidedly not a "scab club," meaning a non-union venue. She may have mixed up the Purple Onion with the Half Beat, a non-union club that nonetheless listed their performers in the *Telegram*.

Joni did not join the TMA until the summer of 1965, and so was limited in her employment opportunities. Joining the union in August 1964 would have cost her $119 ($1,186 in 2025),[11] though she has variously remembered the dues as approximately $150 ($1,540 in 2025).[12] In any case, this was a steep expense for someone making a meagre living in what was already an expensive city. It was, in Joni's remembrance, "a fortune for me, just an impossible goal. And there wasn't much scab work around, and coffeehouse doors slammed in my face, and it was pretty insulting. There were some dues [to be paid] in that town."[13]

* * *

The McHughs took back control of the Half Beat from Syd Ezrin in the fall of 1964, and by early October leased it for what was intended to be one year, at $300 ($2,991 in 2025) a week, to John Soules and Dave Pirie.[14]

John Soules: Dave and I were roommates; he was a friend of mine. We worked in the Penny [Farthing]. I worked in the kitchen and I think Dave did some waitering. Things were getting so busy there. John McHugh asked if we wanted to take [the Half Beat] over. He couldn't do both of them himself. He figured he could trust us. I went to a lawyer and got a legal thing drawn up and everything. One day I was working in the kitchen and [Dave] was waiting and the next day, we were going down College Street looking for bakeries that we could get pastries from, and looking for suppliers.

Soules and Pirie instituted a fifty-cent cover charge and intended to raise the venue's profile as a place to hear live folk music and jazz. The Black Eagle Jazz Band played weekends, with Joe Mendelson (1944–2023) singing and playing the blues after 1 a.m. Mendelson, who later went by the name Mendelson Joe, had been listening to modern blues and R&B on cross-border Buffalo radio since his childhood. He remembered alternating sets with Joni at the Half Beat.

Joni began her first extended engagement at the Half Beat on October 12. She may have played there for up to five weeks, though newspaper listings are spotty.[15]

John Soules: When we took over the Half Beat, she was part of the people I hung around with. So there's the obvious person to have [perform]. We didn't have any big names. We couldn't afford to be bringing in Sonny [Terry] and Brownie [McGhee] or anything like that. At that time, Joni and Dave and I were all living in an apartment on Bloor Street.[16] And then it was just Joni and I after that at Bloor and Walmer.[17]

In April 2025, the legendary journalist and writer-director Cameron Crowe asked Joni, on my behalf, about her time in Yorkville. In her remembrance of events over sixty years before, it's possible that Joni conflated the Half Beat with the Inn on the Parking Lot; the Half Beat was very much in the centre of the action, while the Inn was relatively isolated on Cumberland Street.

Cameron Crowe: She said that the Yorkville scene was booming, but the Half Beat was one street over. It was the only place she could play, because she was non-union. Johnny [Soules] told her she was the biggest draw ever at the club, making about $15 [$149 in 2025] a night toward the end, but when she left, because she was too pregnant to play, the club faltered. However, she remembered leaving the place at night, and feeling like the truly happening crowd wasn't on that street but she could hear them nearby . . . not on the street that she played. She never felt included in the Yorkville scene.

A month and a half before opening the Riverboat, Burnie Fiedler and Patti Tancock (they had not yet married at this point) went to the Half Beat to hear Joni. As Joni later recalled,

Joni Mitchell: They came in one night, sort of snooping. And Burnie's got this great kind of dry wit. We're friends now, but at that time I didn't really understand him. He came up to me and he said, "Trying to achieve the [Joan] Baez sound, are you?" [laughs] That was my introduction to him . . . It was all like his sense of humour, but there was a certain amount of seriousness to it. He wasn't interested. I wasn't going to make him money.[18]

B. C. Fiedler: Joni did hate me. There was a time I was a real prick. She said that I offered her a job as a dishwasher. That's not true. That was a joke I thought I had between her and I, but I guess she forgot about it. There was no sense for the Riverboat to have anybody in there with no name, no draw.

Murray McLauchlan (singer-songwriter): Good move, Burnie. Well, you know, sometimes he was really good about business and he understood when a talent was rising and had a reputation. But I don't think he was particularly knowledgeable about music, or where it was coming from, or that stuff.

If she couldn't get hired at the Riverboat, Joni could at least sub in for other singers, with the added benefit of staying under the radar of the TMA. Another early Toronto Joni appearance, and the first to be supported by a newspaper listing, was Werner Graeber's third coffeehouse, the Place (sometimes rendered as Zee Place, perhaps imitating Graeber's German accent). Back in June 1964, Graeber had sold the 71 Coffee House business to his longtime manager, Franz Wieltschnigg, who reopened it as Act One, Scene One in August. Possibly inspired by the success of his protégés the Fiedlers, Graeber took a two-pronged approach to his evolving coffeehouse empire. After opening the Inn on the Parking Lot in November 1963, he launched the Place in May 1964.

The Place (44 Avenue Road) was a rare upstairs coffeehouse, with a proper stage and advertised appearances by local singers Carol Robinson, Jim McCarthy, and Al Cromwell.[19] David Cooper worked there as a dishwasher at the time and remembered in 2023 that Joni also washed dishes at the Place, perhaps through the winter. "She and Werner were close friends," Cooper recalled. "She always wore a long navy pea jacket. [I'd] see her walking on Yorkville [Avenue] with her guitar."[20]

Graeber brought Joni in as a sub for an ailing Al Cromwell in late September or early October of 1964. She traded sets with a cross-dressing calypso singer known as Peaches, and caught the attention of folk music writer Volkmar Richter, who gave her a backhanded compliment in his column for the University of Toronto newspaper:

> Why is it that Toronto has so many good male folk singers but very few of the other gender? Girl folk singers that are any good are about as scarce as a cheap cup of coffee in the Village. But then there's Joani [sic] Anderson, a young Edmontonian [sic] who just arrived here this summer . . . She performs with a pleasant Baez-like voice, clear and with a natural beauty. Establishments like the Place are not a good showcase for her talent. She'll be quietly singing a soft lyrical number and suddenly the fellow at the

counter will rudely operate the coffee-machine making it sound like a steam boiler blowing off. But Joani's voice charmed the audience even under those conditions.[21]

Joni spent her first Christmas away from home with John Soules's family.

John Soules: We went up to my parents' place in Leaside and had Christmas up there. It was a good time,neighbours coming around and everything. She was visibly pregnant at that time, and my mother said [to me], "That's not your baby, is it?"

In a 1966 letter to Toronto folksinger and organizer Shelley Posen, Joni called John Soules's parents "my family in Toronto."[22]

* * *

Joni gave birth to a daughter at Toronto General Hospital on February 19, 1965. "We just went different ways after that," says Soules. He moved out of their Annex apartment above the Lickin' Chicken restaurant at 400 Bloor Street West, and Vicky Taylor moved in.

Vicky Taylor: When we were living together over the Lickin' Chicken, she would often be up all night long and she would be unable to sleep because a song would be going around in her head, and it wouldn't leave her alone until she got up and wrote it down and finished it. She was definitely hit by the muse, that's for sure.

Joni named her daughter Kelly Dale Anderson, placed her in foster care, and went back to work playing gigs around Yorkville. Chance again played a part in her performance opportunities.

Joe Lewis: I had her perform at the New Gate [of Cleve]. I actually had an American group [Tom Paxton's duo] booked in who got stopped at the border. She was there to see them—the place was packed. Luckily she had an instrument with her. I said, "I've got a problem. Will you go up and sing a few songs and we'll pay you some money at the end of the night?" And she did. The guys never did get through the border.[23]

The basement space of the Penny Farthing was no longer the "up-for-grabs" room that Bob Ezrin played as a teenager, but a regular subvenue within the building. Joni and Vicky Taylor appeared frequently there in the spring of 1965. Marilyn McHugh recalls, "We used to have to bribe people with sandwiches and coffee."

On April 27, Chuck Mitchell began a five-night engagement in the main room upstairs. He was a slick and professional Detroit folksinger, with a songbag of ancient British ballads and Flanders and Swann material. Sometime during that appearance, Joni and Chuck met and were engaged within thirty-six hours.

Vicky Taylor: I introduced Joni to Chuck. One of the worst things I ever did. I thought he was such a fine fellow, so I introduced him to Joni and—well, sometimes things just don't work out, you know?

Joni moved to Detroit in the summer of 1965, where she and Chuck formed a duo, though she would often perform alone as well. Living in Detroit with the Chess Mate coffeehouse as a home base, Joni now found herself connected to the American folk circuit. She and Chuck gradually expanded their reach outside Detroit; Joni played the Mariposa Festival in 1965, and again in 1966. She would finally play the Riverboat in November 1966.

B. C. Fiedler: I was aware of her because all the other people like Tom Rush and Dave Van Ronk always sang her songs after she had left Toronto. The first time anybody heard "Both Sides, Now" was me. I picked her up at the airport and she said, "Burnie, let's go straight to the Riverboat. I want to play you this brand new song." It was called "Clouds" then.[24]

* * *

As 1965 began, Werner Graeber's coffeehouse empire, and life, were in tatters. The Inn on the Parking Lot closed in December 1964, and the Place closed a month later. It had been open barely eight months. His marriage to Edith had ended sometime after the 1962 cannabis bust; according to B. C. Fiedler, she moved back to Germany. By early 1965, Graeber had been seeing twenty-six-year-old Toba Hausman for two years. Toba, a diminutive dark-haired beauty, was married to a dentist named Larry Hausman and lived with him and their baby son on Foxwarren Drive in leafy Bayview Village. Jutta Maue Kay recalls her being at the 71 "just about every night. She liked the scene."

That winter of 1965, Toba broke up with Graeber and went back to her husband. Graeber, perhaps feeling that now he had lost everything, went off the rails. According to his friends, he was an alcoholic, with periods of sobriety interrupted by binges.

Jutta Maue Kay: He never touched alcohol when I knew him, because he couldn't.

B. C. Fiedler: [When he was drinking] he drank a bottle starting in the morning. I think it was vodka.

On February 20, 1965, Graeber broke into the Hausman residence and beat Toba so severely that she was hospitalized with head injuries. Graeber was charged with assault causing bodily harm and released on bail.[25] Two weeks later on March 3, Graeber again visited the house on Foxwarren. After smashing a basement window to gain entry, he cut his arms and feet on the broken glass. While Toba escaped with her mother and infant son to a neighbour's house and called the police, Graeber scrawled "I love you" in his blood on the inside of the front door. As Detective William Ferguson told the *Star*, "The kitchen was like a slaughterhouse."[26]

When a police constable approached the house, Graeber stepped onto the porch with a loaded nine-millimetre automatic handgun and pointed it at the officer's chest. "One more step and I'll shoot—back up," Graeber told him. After this brief encounter, a squad of heavily armed police arrived at the home and a tense hour-long standoff ensued. Finally, the police fired five tear gas shells into the house and entered. When they found Graeber, he was standing in the bathtub in his underwear, wrapped in a shower curtain with the water on to counteract the effects of the tear gas. After what was described as a "fierce struggle," three officers wrestled Graeber to the ground and he was charged with breaking and entering, possessing a dangerous weapon, and pointing it at a police officer.[27]

At the trial, Graeber's defence lawyer called the incident a "crime of passion," and in court testimony, Graeber said, "I was in love with her." He pleaded guilty to the gun charges and the earlier assault, and was sentenced to two prison terms, of nine months and two-and-a-half years, to be served concurrently.[28]

Chapter Seven: "It was a mellower scene."

BURNIE AND PATTI FIEDLER were now romantically separate but still living together. They shared a house in Rosedale and a goldmine in Yorkville with their two clubs, the Riverboat and the Mousehole. But they ran the two sides of their business separately. At her club, the Mousehole, Patti kept folk singing informal for the time being. Singers were invited to drop in to perform after their regular gigs in the Village had ended. Gordon Lightfoot was a frequent drop-in, as was a young Scottish immigrant named Adam Mitchell.

Adam Mitchell: My parents couldn't afford to buy a house in Toronto, so they bought out in Bolton. I went to Brampton High out there and then Central Peel. Iain Rankin was also in Bolton, also a Scottish immigrant. The folk thing came along and we just started learning to play guitar. We went into the city, to the Bohemian Embassy. It was the first place we ever played, in '62 and '63. We started to get a bit of a reputation because we were good songwriters. We had well-constructed, coherent songs, and we were writing original music right away. Somehow we met [bassist] Bruce Whitehead and Doug Bush, a very good guitar player. We started the Common Folk. I was playing around the Village wherever I could, you know, just doing originals. We heard about the Folk Guild thing and started to make connections in the folk scene.

Adam soon joined Estelle Klein's Folk Guild, and as a young folkie with a quick and organized mind, he was quickly drafted into service.

Adam Mitchell: They didn't ask me. They just nominated and voted me president, which was a very bad idea because I was at [the University of Toronto] and eventually after, I don't know, a month or two, I had to tell Estelle, "You know, I can't do this. The workload at U of T is really heavy."

The Common Folk played Mariposa in 1965, and by 1966 Adam had gone solo. The *Telegram* only lists him as playing at the Mousehole May 13 to 14, 1966, but he remembers that he played there regularly.

Another frequent performer at the Mousehole was Vicky Taylor, who brought her friend Joni to sit in.

Vicky Taylor: I think Patti was an absolutely fantastic broad. I really do. She was one tough little lady. She knew what she wanted and she spoke her mind. One night she said, "You better get some new songs, chickie." I guess I was getting a little lazy about learning new songs.

* * *

Burnie Fiedler was determined to have the top folk venue in town, and to that end was poaching the best talent for the Riverboat, whether it was touring acts like Sonny Terry and Brownie McGhee or local acts like Gordon Lightfoot. The club that John McHugh pointedly nicknamed "the U-Boat" was torpedoing the competition.

For the first advertised weeks of music at the Riverboat, Burnie booked a mixture of touring American acts (folk singers Val Pringle and Clyde Williams) and locals (folk groups the Allen-Ward Trio, the Chanteclairs, and jazzers Tony Collacutt and Moe Koffman). But his first great booking coup was Gordon Lightfoot, who was doing an extended gig in the Venetian Lounge at Steele's Tavern (349 Yonge Street) in the heart of the Strip.

In an article for *Hoot* magazine, Estelle Klein described the Venetian Lounge as being a poor venue for folk music, with its "martian red atmosphere . . . boisterous crowds or none at all, indifferent or sometimes hostile waiters, poor sound, and in one case, a T.V. set tuned into a hockey game."[1]

Al Mair (record company rep and later Lightfoot manager): He was working at Steele's Tavern and most times it was quiet. Just him and a guitar and a mic. I don't think the guitar even had a mic.

B. C. Fiedler: Somebody said to me there's a guy down at Steele's Tavern, you should hire him. He should be playing here, not there. So I went down there and I saw Gordon Lightfoot. I listened to a song, and I went up to him and I said to him, "Listen, hi, my name is Burnie Fiedler, I own the Riverboat. I'd love you to come and play at my place. I'll pay you twice what [owner Steele Basil] pays you." I didn't even know what he pays. And [Gordon] said, "All right."

March 9, 1965, was Lightfoot's first night at the Riverboat. In a *Globe* review, Marvin Schiff praised Lightfoot's choice of material, including songs by Hamilton Camp, Bob Dylan, Ewan MacColl, and Ian Tyson, in addition to his own material. Schiff also singled out Lightfoot's singing style for commentary, noting its Western twang and slight yodel, and that he seemed to be moving beyond his "obvious" Bob Dylan influences. On the negative side, Schiff highlighted Lightfoot's self-conscious stage presence, his "inane" and "superfluous" between-song banter, his poorly paced set and the uniformity of his songs and guitar arrangements.[2]

Gordon Lightfoot: I was doing a mostly traditional repertoire at Steele's . . . When I got into the Riverboat, I felt compelled to introduce a lot more of my own stuff. Ultimately, I worked harder at the Riverboat, because I was suddenly working to a very attentive audience. So the Riverboat really pushed me.[3]

Ten months later, another *Globe* reviewer, John Dafoe, unreservedly praised Lightfoot's return engagement at the Riverboat. In contrast to Schiff's review, Dafoe noted the range of Lightfoot's material and the pace and momentum of his set.[4]

When Fiedler tried to schedule Lightfoot again, the singer had signed with Albert Grossman's New York management company, and his fee had almost quadrupled.[5] A Musicians' Union contract dated November 11, 1965, has him playing three shows on weeknights and four on weekends, for $1,000 ($9,734 in 2025) per week.

Murray McLauchlan (singer-songwriter): [The Riverboat] was not only a launchpad; it was a place to arrive. There was a certain cachet to being able to play there; it was a really big deal. The venue had a certain power of its own to legitimize the artist.

* * *

Sometime in 1965, the Le Macabre, the informal basement folk club tucked behind a house at 107 Yorkville, closed. It was replaced by Le Rive Gauche, with Jean-Marie Schram the listed proprietor at first, followed by Peter Hill. The Rive Gauche name seemed to refer both to the Left Bank of the Seine River, the bohemian area of Paris, and to the fact that it was situated on the north side of the street, or on the left as one drove down one-way Yorkville Avenue. Most of the higher-profile clubs—the Riverboat, the Penny Farthing, the Mousehole—were on the right side of the street.[6]

Murray McLauchlan: What drew me into [folk music] was an emerging marriage between a kind of progressive social trend and this ongoing merging of poetry and music. Most importantly, there was a radio show [four times weekly on CKFH], run by a guy named Randy Ferris, and he would play Woody Guthrie Library of Congress recordings, Sonny Terry and Brownie McGhee, Lightnin' Hopkins. The very first Bob Dylan song I ever heard was on that radio show and it was "Don't Think Twice, It's All Right." I'd be rabidly listening to that every night, and my brother had a little Philips reel-to-reel tape recorder, so I started recording stuff.

I was really dumb and totally inexperienced. And I had no cultural experience whatsoever. I mean, I was a Scottish kid that grew up in North York. I really liked Yorkville, I thought it was just cool. I used to go over there 'cause it was a cool little European village-y thing. It was very quiet, actually. Just nice sidewalk cafés with umbrellas. It was really quaint and it felt bohemian to me. I got my first gig there in a club called the Le Rive Gauche, for the princely sum of I think, $25 [$243 in 2025] for the entire weekend. I'd play "I Walk the Line," "Wreck of the Old '97," "Freight Train," "Ramblin' Boy" by Tom

Paxton . . . a lot of songs about the hero vagabond walking down the dusty road and leaving the girl behind.

Over at 32 Avenue Road, La Coterie closed in 1965 just as Le Rive Gauche was opening. La Coterie had been one of the longest lasting of the coffeehouses, having opened in March 1956, but is one of the least remembered today. The entire block of buildings facing Avenue Road was razed in the 1990s, and a 150-unit luxury condo building, the Prince Arthur Condominiums, opened on the site in 1999.[7] La Coterie co-owner Bob Sterio passed away some time ago but Denyse Sterio, in her eighties, is living a quiet life in Blue Mountains, Ontario, in 2025.

* * *

Joe Lewis: The centralized Yorkville scene was the key. When I first took over [the New Gate of Cleve] at Dupont and Davenport, we realized a short time after that we were going to have to move to the Yorkville area.

In May 1965, the New Gate of Cleve moved to 45a Avenue Road, between the Half Beat and the Purple Onion. The new location, situated in the basement below Lena Lascelles's Maison Francaise dress shop, had seating for one hundred inside, and 250 on the patio.[8] Though the Gate was still owned by Warren Haller's mother, Alyce, Joe Lewis had taken over the management. In a crowded field—his direct competition was the Purple Onion, the Village Corner Club, and the Riverboat—Lewis's bookings packed a punch. In its first year at the new location, the New Gate of Cleve hosted Mimi and Richard Fariña, the Country Gentlemen, Doc and Merle Watson, Phil Ochs, the Rooftop Singers, Son House, Eric

Andersen, Bob Gibson, and the first appearance in the city by Lonnie Johnson.

Lonnie Johnson was a pioneering African-American guitarist, violinist, songwriter, and singer. Born Alonzo Johnson in New Orleans into a large musical family sometime in the last decade of the nineteenth century, he was one of the first musicians to play single-note lead guitar in a jazz and blues context. His playing in the 1920s was utterly singular, with frequent bent "blue" notes and fluid runs. He recorded with Louis Armstrong and Duke Ellington in that decade and made a series of classic guitar duet recordings with the white guitarist Eddie Lang. Like many of his contemporaries, Johnson had a career downturn in the 1930s and '40s, but re-emerged in 1948 with "Tomorrow Night," a #1 hit record on *Billboard* magazine's "Juke Box Race Records" chart that also crossed over to #19 on the pop chart.

The rock and roll era left Johnson behind, and by 1960 he was out of the music business and living in Philadelphia, working as a janitor. After being rediscovered by radio announcer Chris Albertson, Johnson resumed his musical career with a vengeance. He now toured as a solo act, plying the folk clubs that dotted the United States and Canada. In May 1965, this included a couple of weeks at the New Gate of Cleve.

The engagement, which jazz historian Mark Miller calls a "turning point" in Johnson's life, began inauspiciously.[9] One reviewer, the *Globe*'s Patrick Scott, counted four people in the audience, but then noted that the audience doubled within an hour. At the end, he wrote, "I had heard a performance so profoundly moving that its memory will haunt me forever."[10] With reviews like this and word of mouth, attendance improved over the course of the run. When it was over, Johnson went home to Philadelphia, but he was soon to return to Yorkville.

* * *

The Folk Guild's Monday night hootenanny moved from the Bohemian Embassy to the New Gate of Cleve on May 15, 1965. This was a hootenanny in name only; all the performers were professionals, hand-picked by Estelle Klein. Only on the second Monday of the month could amateurs and non-union performers get a chance to perform.[11] On occasion, the Monday night hoots featured guest sets by the likes of Phil Ochs and the Greenbriar Boys.[12] This was a far cry from the early hootenannies, with their more open formats. In any case, the Folk Guild hoot only stayed at the Gate for six months; by November 13, it had moved to the Riverboat.

Attendance figures noted at the time did not always match the ambitious scale of the New Gate of Cleve's new location. A week before Lonnie Johnson played to four people, Richard and Mimi Fariña played for a room of six.[13] The new location rendered the club much more visible in the Yorkville scene, which had by now more-or-less centralized at the corner of Avenue Road and Yorkville Avenue. But the transformation of Yorkville's live music from folk and jazz to rock and rhythm and blues was underway, and the Gate would soon fall by the wayside.

* * *

Change was in the air, and the owners of the Purple Onion knew it.

Barry Witkin (Purple Onion co-owner): Oh, yeah, we knew it. I started to bring in a couple of rock groups at the time, just because folk was starting to fade and we thought, *okay, let's just see what it's like*. Very loud and so on. I mean it wasn't our taste; let me put it that way. We were now all graduating from accounting and we're getting married and we're going to have children and so on. We just thought, *enough is enough*. We put it up for sale and this guy from New York actually bought it.

The new owner, Doug Rodway, had no qualms about changing the music policy at the Onion. He immediately poached the hottest rock act in the Village, Mike's Trio Plus Luke, from the El Patio.

Mike McKenna: [Rodway] threw the folksingers out. He saw the crowds we were pulling down at the El Patio, and he said, "I'll pay you 75 bucks a week each [$730 in 2025], but you gotta play Thursday, Friday, Saturday, Sunday." And we went, "75 bucks each? Are you kidding me? When do we start?"

Rodway banned people over twenty-one from entering the Purple Onion, and was considering moving the upper limit of age down to nineteen. "Adults simply ruin teenage dancing," he told the *Star* in July 1966.[14] A reporter for the newspaper described the scene:

> Open Friday through Sunday from 9 p.m. to 3 a.m. $1.50 for members. $2 for non-members . . . Sullen long-haired high school kids crowd the big barn-like room. Sound bounces off the wall and hits you in the stomach. A mad frenzy is sustained for the duration of the music and then dies down 'til the next set. Rather disconcerting to the novice but undoubtedly the most wild place.[15]

Mike McKenna: There were a lot of rumours around about Doug [Rodway], that he was an informant for the FBI and that he was trying to get inside the scene. There was all kind of talk about it. But nobody knew. He was really good to us. He was a nice guy. He let us practise there and four nights we got to play. We became a great band because we were playing all the time. We'd play Thursday nights and there would be three people there. Friday night to Sunday night, you couldn't even breathe.

The frequent audience fights that the band had dealt with at the El Patio were noticeably absent at the Onion. "It was a mellower scene," says Luke Gibson. "People were smoking weed."

A friend of Luke's, Peter Jermyn, joined on keyboards and Jim Jones replaced Graham Dunsmore on bass. It was time for a name change.

Luke Gibson: At the time, you had Little Caesar and the Consuls, Little Anthony and the Imperials, Robbie Lane and the Disciples. "Luke and the Apostles" was a spoof of Robbie Lane and the Disciples. Peter Jermyn thought of that.

The group played James Brown and Jimmy Reed covers and began to write their own songs at the Purple Onion.

Luke Gibson: We changed gears. We were a little bit more into the culture of Yorkville, marijuana, LSD. It was so forbidden, exotic, and dangerous. Dangerous because in those days there were RCMP [Royal Canadian Mounted Police] undercovers wandering around the Village. At the Purple Onion some fans said, "We got this stuff, LSD. You want to try it?" I had no idea. I thought I was going to get drunk or something. That was pretty mind-blowing.

If drug use in the Village was suspected by the public before, it was about to be assumed. A front-page article in the Star of July 2, 1965, trumpeted that cannabis busts had quadrupled year-over-year and made the baseless and illogical claim that hippies were growing pot around the Village in something called "Yorkville patches." The article also introduced much of the readership to LSD, which had been illegal to sell and possess in Canada since 1962. The chief of Toronto's drug squad warned that one drop of LSD would "send a person crawling right up the wall."[16]

The *Star*'s Ralph Thomas described the scene in the Purple Onion when Luke and the Apostles played: "Luke and his group . . . a pallid group of youths . . . somehow managed to sound like a squadron of Sabre jets, a group of Indian snakecharmers and a holy roller group all at once. And were they LOUD! (I could still hear them an hour after I left the place.)"[17]

Keith McKie (singer-songwriter): They were like a British blues band. They really had it. Luke was amazing—he was like electricity.

Elektra was an American record label founded in 1950 with roots in folk music. By the mid-'60s, the label was making the transition into blues-rock and psychedelia; its new signings included the Paul Butterfield Blues Band from Chicago and, from Los Angeles, the Doors and Love. News of a thriving Toronto music scene had reached Elektra house producer Paul Rothschild. One evening in September 1965, he dropped into the Purple Onion. "He really liked us," says Gibson. "The next day he came around at a rehearsal."

Rothschild asked the band to audition for his boss, Jac Holzman, over the phone and was cleared to sign the band to Elektra. "We were Paul Rothschild's personal project," says Gibson.

The band flew to New York and recorded a single, "Been Burnt"/"Don't Know Why" and played a two-month residency at the Café Au Go Go in Greenwich Village, opening for the Grateful Dead. The single was ready for release when disaster struck; Paul Rothschild was arrested for cannabis possession and the single was delayed while he served a prison sentence.

Luke Gibson: He was gone for eight months. And when he came back, the momentum was gone. And [by that time] the Doors were happening. It was not to be.

Rothschild later called the Luke and the Apostles record "the greatest album I never got to make."[18]

* * *

Steppenwolf, one of the biggest rock groups of the late '60s and early '70s, started out as a Yorkville-based band riding the wave of the Beatles-led British invasion. In their earliest incarnation, they were known as Jack London and the Sparrows, the "Jack London" pseudonym a stage name for British-born Dave Marden.

Dave Marden was born on February 16, 1944. His family lived in a small row house in the Edmonton section of North London, but since the city was being bombed by German planes, his mother travelled to Burnley, Lancashire, to give birth. Dave grew up with a love of music.

Dave Marden: My father used to play a ukulele banjo like [comedic singer-actor] George Formby. I enjoyed that. And then when [skiffle star] Lonnie Donegan came along playing his guitar, I thought, *wow, one of those would be great*. I got my first guitar when I was about twelve.

Dave grew into a mischievous teenager, and when his parents broke up, he fell afoul of his father and was sent to a group home. When he was sixteen years old in 1960, Dave's mother gained custody and sent him to live in Canada. A planned residency with his grandmother didn't work out, so he rented a room in Toronto while studying architectural drafting at Ryerson Polytechnical Institute (now Toronto Metropolitan University). Already writing songs, Dave travelled to New York after completing his course of study and attempted without success to interest music publishers. Now living in Oshawa, he looked for a band to join but found few takers. "I tried to get into a number of bands but most didn't like my accent," he says. "I wasn't bluesy."

In the spring or summer of 1964, Dave met Dennis McCrohan while Dennis was home from his first year at the University of Waterloo, where he was studying psychology. Dennis (born April 21, 1943) and his brother Jerry (October 24, 1946–November 28, 1993) were the sons of Margaret and Owen McCrohan, who owned and managed a dance hall in Oshawa called the Jubilee Pavilion. Since the late '60s, Dennis McCrohan has gone by the name Mars Bonfire.

Mars Bonfire: [Owen] would take me down there every so often with him and I'd hear the bands live. Initially it was all big bands and jazz, but when rock and roll came along he started to move in that direction. Then I got to hear all kinds of early rock and roll. On the radio I heard Little Richard, Chuck Berry, Elvis, and others. At the Coq D'Or where Ronnie Hawkins and the Hawks played, on Sunday they would do a matinee with the bar closed so that people under the drinking age could go in. Because my dad was getting into the rock and roll field, he wanted to see local rock and roll acts. So he took me to their Sunday matinee and I was knocked out by that group. Robbie Robertson on the [Fender]

Telecaster guitar was actually the first guitar player I ever heard that had the distorted, overwhelming guitar sound that became the norm of hard rock.

Dennis was already playing an acoustic guitar, inspired by country singer Hank Snow. Now he would purchase a white Telecaster just like Robbie's, and his brother Jerry soon took up the drums. Dennis was interested in forming a Beatles-styled group with vocals when he met Dave Marden.

Mars Bonfire: [Dave] and I developed a rapport. We decided to work together and form a group.

The first version of the group was apparently a trio, with Dave on vocals, Dennis on guitar, and Dave Hare on keyboards. Shortly, Dennis's brother Jerry McCrohan joined on drums along with Brent Maitland on bass guitar. Maitland was soon replaced by Bruce Palmer (1946–2004), and C. J. (Conrad John) Feeny (1943–2016) replaced Dave Hare on keyboards. C. J. was a more experienced musician than the rest of the group, having released a single in 1962 with his group the Spellbinders, the self-penned piano instrumentals "Candy Apple Black" and "Ramby" on Astral Records.

In September 1964, Dennis returned to university but carried on working with the still unnamed band on weekends. Dave Marden had a vision for the group and a plan for success.

Dave Marden: Once I found a band, we were going to get recorded and we were going to go on tour. I had absolutely no doubts, and everything I did and thought was pointed in that direction. I kept bringing over a little tape recorder and trying to assess what was going on. I played one of those tapes for one of the DJs in the Oshawa radio station, who said, "Well, this is good, but if you want to make it, you've got to have original material."

Dave and Dennis began to collaborate on writing songs, trying to fit in stylistically with the British sound, which was by then ubiquitous on pop radio.

Mars Bonfire: When I understood what he wanted to do, I listened to Gerry and the Pacemakers and all those groups with the melodic sound. After a lot of listening, it was easy to come up with my own versions of those melodies. Once I had it roughed out, [Dave] would sometimes work on the lyric. I'd say it was about a 60–40 collaboration.

The girls were looking for that British accent, so as the front person for our group, Dave, made the group get attention that we otherwise may not have gotten. He wanted the rest of us to pretend to be British! We did it for a while, but it got utterly absurd.

As the group began to book gigs in the area, Dennis and Jerry saw fit to change their surnames to Edmonton. Edmonton, in addition to being a major Canadian city, was the name of Dave Marden's former London neighbourhood.

Mars Bonfire: [We did it] basically for business reasons, [with] our dad being in the music business and running a ballroom. There were one or two other ballrooms in Oshawa, and ballrooms in Toronto and Hamilton that he was competing with to draw customers. We realized that if we wanted to play in any of these other venues, if they knew [the connection], perhaps there would be a little bit of hard feelings.

The next phase in Dave's plan was to get himself and the group, now called the Sparrows (a nod to Ronnie Hawkins's Hawks) a recording contract. Along the way, Dave gained a stage name.

Dave Marden: We recorded our demo tape in the basement of a radio station [in Oshawa]. I presented this demo tape to anybody who would listen. Stan Klees was the guy that said, "I've got a name for you. You should be Jack O'London!"

Stan Klees and his business partner Walter Grealis are remembered today for founding a Canadian music industry trade magazine, *RPM*, in 1964, and creating the precursor to today's Juno Awards. With roots in the nascent Canadian recording business, they did much over the course of the 1960s to build up what was then a mutually disconnected and underfunded homegrown music industry. In the mid-'60s, Klees was a graphic designer and independent record producer, and he brought Jack London (the "O" was quickly forgotten) and the Sparrows to Capitol Records Canada.

With the Beatles' Canadian records being distributed by Capitol, the company was flush with cash in the first half of 1964, which empowered singles promotion manager Paul White (a British expat himself, having arrived in 1957) and president Geoffrey Racine to sign Canadian rock and roll groups to the label. Joining Wes Dakus and the Rebels from Edmonton and Ottawa's Esquires, Jack London and the Sparrows signed with Capitol Records Canada in late 1964. Rather than splitting the royalties equally, the group agreed to an unusual deal. This arrangement would eventually drive a wedge between London and the rest of the group, but at the time he thought it to be proper.

Dave Marden: I said, "Look, there's two parts to the band: Jack London, and the Sparrows. I'm going to get us a record contract come hell or high water. And I want 50 percent of what we do on record. And I want at least 25 percent for all appearances." There's no point in being in a business unless you're making a living.

Stan Klees produced the band's first single, "If You Don't Want My Love/ It's Been One of Those Days" (Capitol 72203), released in December 1964. The record peaked at an impressive #4 on the new *RPM* national chart, no doubt assisted by Klees and Grealis's promotional efforts behind the scenes.

Stan Klees: It worked. It sounded good, it aired well on the radio, and people bought it.

A short time later, keyboardist C. J. Feeny was dismissed from the group, for reasons unremembered. He was replaced by Art Ayre (1940–1994), a capable jazz pianist known for frequent appearances at the House of Hambourg and the Cellar, and the group made their Yorkville debut at a new venue, the Devil's Den.

* * *

Back in April 1956, radio personality Gerald Peters opened the Piccadilly Club at 137 Avenue Road as a kind of social club for recently arrived British immigrants. "We want the English people who come out here to have a place to come to immediately . . . here they are indoctrinated with Canadian propaganda," Peters told the *Globe*.[19] He soon moved the club to larger quarters at 53 Avenue Road, but by the summer of 1963, the Piccadilly Club was closed.

J. W. Wild took over the property, and by January 1964 was operating the Avenue Road Supper Club in the location. The Avenue Road Club, as it soon became known under the subsequent ownership of Murray Campbell, didn't have a liquor licence, but offered dinner and dancing to Jack Bond's Orchestra. Jack Bond, who sometimes billed himself as Jack Bond and his Golden Trumpet, had been leading an English-style society dance band since the 1930s.

In the basement of the Avenue Road Club, an enterprising young German-born musician named Klaus Kussbaum had the idea to open an R&B venue. Klaus Kussbaum was born in 1943 in the lakefront town of Plön, just north of Hamburg, Germany. At the age of nine he emigrated to the Toronto suburb of Scarborough with his family. When he saw Little Richard in *The Girl Can't Help It* (1956), he was entranced by rock and roll, and after seeing Tom Wilson playing bass with local rock and roll band Little Caesar and the Consuls, he gave up the accordion for the bass guitar and began playing in local bands. His stage name was the distinctive Nick St. Nicholas.

Nick St. Nicholas: I never had a lesson in my life but I had ears. I played along with the radio trying to get familiar with songs.

After graduating from Cedarbrae Institute, he attended one year at the Ontario College of Art before dropping out to be a full-time musician.

Nick St. Nicholas: I talked to Murray Campbell, the guy in charge of the Avenue Road Club. It was a big-band dance club upstairs, with polished floors and a twenty-four-piece orchestra. Downstairs, it was a total mess, with rats, mice, boards, fencing, and garbage cans. I said, "Murray, if I cleaned up the basement, would you let me use it as a little club?" [He said,] "Okay. That doesn't sound too bad." I painted the floor blue and made the stage look like a dock, with a little ladder that I put in. We called it the Rat Cellar, and that club would turn into the Devil's Den. I let a lot of people in free. I just wanted people in there. But it was just beatniks sitting around drinking coffee, reading poetry over candlelight, and telling me to shut the fuck up.

Nick St. Nicholas played in the Rat Cellar with his band the Swingin' Doors, soon to become the Mynah Birds. He left the Mynah Birds in early 1965 to join Jack London and the Sparrows, with Bruce Palmer taking his place in an unusual bass player swap. One of his first acts in the Sparrows was to get them booked in the club that he had started, the Devil's Den.

The Devil's Den, active in the newspaper listings by early 1965, appears to have opened in late 1964. Patrons walked along the north wall of the Avenue Road Club to a side door and took a set of stairs to the basement. The small raised stage was decorated with curtains and a painted devil's face. There was a small dance floor in front of the band, with tables and chairs behind. A disc jockey was stationed at stage left to fill in on band breaks.

Linda Shilling (fan): Murray Campbell had a bit of money to throw around. The setup was very much nightclubbish. The crowd was older . . . I'd say twenty to maybe thirty. Certainly the bar crowd. The men wore custom-made suits. The women, too, were spiffy. Full house every night, a large Black contingent. Many of the guys in the Den group were actually pimps who were working the room to add to their coterie, shall we say. The music was terrific. There was the ritual dance circle with guys taking turns strutting their stuff in the middle, always ending with the splits and the James Brown quick step, to the applause of the onlookers.

> I would say there was a little more violence at the Den [than at other clubs], and typically it was some guy smacking his female partner around. There was an undercurrent in Yorkville in those days that, in my experience, people don't like to talk about. There was a lot of violence against women. There were a lot of unwanted pregnancies. There were many, many broken hearts. There was prostitution; there were drug overdoses. In fact, it could be a fairly dangerous place to be if you were female or if you were a vulnerable-looking guy. And that was before the bikers moved in.

On February 5, Jack London and the Sparrows began performing at the Devil's Den, ending a brief jazz policy. By the middle of April, they had captured both weekend nights. But when the run ended, Jack London was fired from the band. The group went on without replacing him, with Dennis Edmonton and Nick St. Nicholas sharing lead vocals. Eventually, they found a new frontman in another German émigré, John Kay, and they found him at the Half Beat.

Chapter Eight: "We smoked all of the profits."

BY DECEMBER 11, 1964, the McHughs had taken the Half Beat back from John Soules and Dave Pirie and they cancelled live music for the time being.[1] They brought in Bill Klotzhoff to manage. Klotzhoff, who had previously worked at his father's bar, the Pilot (then located at 800 Yonge Street just south of Yorkville Avenue), moved into the apartment above the venue at 47 Avenue Road. As 1965 began, the Half Beat was open seven nights a week from 8 p.m. to 3 or 4 a.m. with "a roaring fire, conversation and recorded music."[2] "People want a place where they can talk. Entertainment demands too much attention," Marilyn McHugh told the *Star* in January 1965.[3]

By early June, non-union live music was back with a residency by Victor Garber, later of the Sugar Shoppe, a middle-of-the-road vocal group, and then a long and distinguished career as a film and television actor. The next month, Mike Edmonds was appearing nightly from 9 p.m. to 2 a.m. in the back garden.[4] Soon "Johnny Kay" took over, playing three sets Wednesday to Sunday for $10 ($97 in 2025) a night.

Born Joachim (pronounced "WA-keem") Krauledat in 1944 in Tilsit, East Prussia (now Sovetsk, Russia), John Kay escaped to West Germany with his mother at the age of four; his father had been killed in combat. Growing up in Hanover, he listened to American Forces Radio and developed a love for rock and roll and rhythm and blues. Joachim and his mother, now remarried, emigrated to Canada in March 1958, settling in Toronto. Enrolled at Humberside Collegiate, John was renamed by a gym teacher there who couldn't pronounce "Joachim." Kay feasted on Toronto and Buffalo radio and attended Dick Clark's Caravan of Stars concerts at Maple Leaf Gardens.

By 1963, John had moved to Buffalo, and then to Santa Monica, where he fell in with the local coffeehouse scene, playing acoustic guitar and singing blues. He decided to return to Toronto on his own and to try to make a living as a musician, and naturally headed to Yorkville. As he wrote in his autobiography:

John Kay: Within a day or two of my arrival, I met Bill Klotzhoff, manager of the Half Beat Club . . . I offered my services as a folk singer, and he invited me to come down that evening to audition. I wound up playing there for several weeks . . . I'd play maybe forty minutes, put my guitar away, roam around Yorkville, make some contacts, check out other places to play, then come back and do the next set. I was billed as "John Kay from California." My sets consisted mainly of the country blues material I had been perfecting over the last year or so. I was doing "The Pusher" and "Red, White and Blue" by Hoyt Axton, "C. C. Rider," some Lightnin' Hopkins things, my own "Goin' to California," [blues standard] "Corinna Corinna," [Bob Dylan's] "Girl from the North Country," [Tom Paxton's] "Ramblin' Boy," [traditional folk song] "He Was a Friend of Mine," and a few other things, mostly blues.[5]

Bill Klotzhoff let John sleep on a rollaway bed in the basement boiler room, since he had nowhere to stay. At a party in Klotzhoff's apartment above the Half Beat, John met keyboardist Art Ayre from the Sparrows, who then mentioned John to his bandmates. A few months earlier, the band had fired Jack London and was continuing as a four-piece, though they now lacked a clear frontman.

Nick St. Nicholas and Jerry Edmonton dropped into the Half Beat one night on a break from the Devil's Den—they had returned to play another residency at the club—to check out John Kay. Accustomed to mod English fashions, they were nonplussed by Kay's outfit: tan-coloured jeans with matching jacket and black cowboy boots. And he would need to wash the grease out of his hair. But John Kay had something. Most appealing was his gritty, declamatory singing voice, marinated in blues and lacking even a trace of a German accent. When they spoke, Nick St. Nicholas was surprised to find out that John was also German. "[Then] I figured he was a good man," says St. Nicholas.

Nick and Jerry invited John to sit in with the Sparrows at the Devil's Den. The combination clicked, and he was asked to join on rhythm guitar and harmonica. He was not yet fronting the band, but he soon would.

By this time, Jutta Maue was living in an apartment at 17 Lowther Avenue. Her friend Solveigh was dating Nick St. Nicholas, so she and Jutta went to the Saphire Tavern to hear the Sparrows with their new member, John Kay.[6]

John Kay: [Afterwards] we went to Solveigh's place, which was the corner apartment above the Harlequin House [116 Yorkville Avenue, later the Upper Crust coffeehouse]. We had a little time together there, smoked some weed, which during those days in Canada was basically seeds and stems, and [Jutta] left. I thought, "I'm not going to let her get away." I followed her. This is now one in the morning. She's walking on Yorkville toward Avenue Road to cross to go to Lowther. She hears footsteps and starts walking faster. So I walked faster as well. Obviously, by the time I caught up with her, we were looking at each other. "Want to come upstairs?" I moved in and that was that.

John and Jutta married in February 1967 and remain so in 2025.

Jutta Maue Kay: I hung out with these guys, Art Ayre and Andy Cree. We were shooting up [heroin] together. The jazz musicians, they all did it. I did it for a little while, about six months. Then I met John, and he saw it and he said, "It's that or me." And I quit.

By late July, music listings for the Half Beat had disappeared, and it appears that the McHughs returned to recorded music. In October 1965, *The Varsity* writer Volkmar Richter complained that the Half Beat had become slick and commercial: "The Half Beat, which used to be a small, quaint, unpretentious and well-attended establishment, now has leathered seats, uniform new tables and chairs and piped-in music."[7]

The closing of the Half Beat, soon to follow, was not reported in the press at the time, though former Penny Farthing waitress Kig Vanderleck would remember rather chaotic last days:

Kig Vanderleck: Two of us got control, illegally, of a coffeehouse, the Half Beat, and went bankrupt in six months. Peter the Swede would bring the grass, and we'd put it in the espresso machine and serve all the customers—unbeknownst to them—pot tea. After each set, we'd turn the heat up to about ninety-five degrees, which would empty the place

> fast and make way for a new bunch. "The Kig Special" was $1.50: cappuccino with pot, nutmeg and cinnamon. We ate and smoked all the profits.[8]

Owned and managed by Tony Smith, the El Matador replaced the Half Beat at 47 Avenue Road with Jim McHarg and the Metro Stompers providing traditional jazz through the spring of 1966. The business lasted at least until the spring of 1968, when Smith told the *Globe*: "We accept the kids as people, and don't kick them out . . . mostly we get the tourists, people surging up and down Yorkville. When they get tired, they sit down and watch other people doing it. But at night this place is basically full of Yorkville people. We sell Canadian coffee for only a quarter, which fits the kids' budget."[9]

The east side of Avenue Road was densely packed with coffeehouses in 1965, with the Purple Onion at 35, the New Gate of Cleve at 45a, the El Matador at 47, Pizza a Go Go at 49, soon succeeded by Sammi's Pizza (which may have had informal folk music), and the Hamburger Joint, which likewise seems to have hosted hootenannies led by sometime Rive Gauche denizen Harry Abel, at 51.

* * *

On October 14, 1964, Nathan Cohen reported in the *Star* that after having leased the Half Beat to other proprietors, the McHughs were looking to do the same with the Penny Farthing for $500 ($4,986 in 2025) a week.[10] By December, they had succeeded in leasing the Penny to Brian Walker.[11] Walker at first continued with the music policy instituted by John McHugh, with a mixture of jazz (the Ron Peck Quartet with vocalist Dave Higgins, which *Globe* critic Patrick Scott termed "a highly percussive ensemble" of vibraphone, piano, bass, and drums)[12] and folk music (Chick Roberts, Jim McCarthy).

On Christmas Day, 1964, Walker locked the doors of the Penny and hosted a staff Christmas party complete with alcohol. At 1:30 a.m., the Toronto Morality Squad raided the premises and Walker was charged with keeping liquor for sale, selling liquor, and permitting drunkenness. The twenty-seven guests, who paid $5 ($49 in 2025) each to attend the party, were charged as found-ins and Walker was ultimately fined $10 ($99 in 2025).[13]

After a crowd of two thousand thronged Yorkville Avenue in April 1965, Walker drew a distinction between the sometimes lawless youths who were crowding the village and the more genteel Penny Farthing clientele. Speaking to the *Globe*, he blamed the influx for reducing his business by 30 percent. "Tonight they scared a lot of the public away . . . The people who listen to our folk music and jazz are not the hoodlums who take part in street riots."[14]

But even as he complained about them, Walker was plotting to capture that young audience with a major change in his live music offerings. As he told the *Globe*, "It's been obvious that a lot of the people who have been coming to Yorkville because they like jazz and folk music have been put off by the teenagers that are here now. So you'll find that most of our audience is younger than we've had in the past. They don't go for the folk bit so much. We decided to give them what they want. So we're after the available market . . . of course, the teenagers we get here, or the ones we allow in, are well-behaved."[15]

Since late 1963 the Penny had been a major venue for folk and jazz musicians, but beginning on May 11, 1965, rhythm and blues and rock and roll music were in order. The name of the music venue within the Penny was changed to the Mersey Club in obvious reference to the Beatles. The club was open every night from 9 p.m. to 1:30 a.m., and the four-piece Sparrows (after Jack London but before John Kay) were the house band. Another major change was that Walker made the Penny, at least technically, a private club with membership cards. Membership was a dollar, with another dollar as admission price. As Walker explained, "This is an experiment as far as I'm concerned."[16]

It turned out to be a short-lived experiment, with the Sparrows the first and seemingly last band to perform under the new format.[17] As they had done with the Half Beat, John and Marilyn McHugh took the business back.

John McHugh: They [Walker] ran it into the ground. I didn't like what they were doing and they didn't make any money. Totally mismanaged it.

John McHugh brought in one of his favourite traditional jazz groups, Jim McHarg's Metro Stompers. McHarg was a Scottish-born jazz veteran, leading his band on double bass with Charlie Gall on cornet, Eric Neilson on clarinet, banjoist Ron Simpson, and drummer Bernie Nathan rounding out the rhythm section. Fronting the group and making his second Yorkville appearance was guitarist-singer Lonnie Johnson.

David Rea, an eighteen-year-old guitarist recently arrived from Akron, Ohio, in the summer of 1964 and already accompanying Gordon Lightfoot, the Allen-Ward Trio and Joni Anderson, was there on opening night. Johnson opened his first set with "I Left My Heart in San Francisco," the Tony Bennett hit that was already synonymous with the previous generation's lounge-lizard crooners. "The assembled blues and jazz cognoscenti were dumbfounded, to say the least . . . As I recall, someone said, 'play "Tomorrow Night"' [Johnson's 1948 R&B hit]. He did, and of course the playing was brilliant. All of a sudden the audience changed, and he realized that people had come to see him and to hear his music. A big smile came over his face: it was a wonderful transformation."[18]

By the end of the first week, Johnson and McHarg's band were packing the room and performing "Blueberry Hill," "St. Louis Blues," and "He's a Jelly Roll Baker." In his *Telegram* review, Sid Adilman enthused: "Lonnie Johnson at 65 years of age outplays, outsings and outdraws the bulk of the hippy moderns."[19]

Johnson soon recorded a studio album with McHarg's group, *Stompin' at the Penny* (Columbia EL 110), released in February 1966. The album is a document of Johnson's supple singing voice and adept guitar playing, backed by the Metro Stompers' spirited accompaniment. By the time he ended his Penny run in February 1966, Johnson had found an apartment on Avenue Road and was beginning to build his venue network around Toronto. He expanded beyond Yorkville to Steele's Tavern and Castle George, a folk venue above George's Spaghetti House at Sherbourne and Dundas.

John Kay: In Yorkville Village one day, I met Lonnie Johnson. He and I got to talking, just sitting outside the Half Beat or the Penny Farthing, having coffee or whatever. I didn't want to be forward and ask questions that may require uncomfortable answers, but I asked him, "Are things more to your liking here?" And he said, "Yes. They treat you with dignity and respect and I feel good here. I want to stay here." That was when I was particularly actually proud of Canada.

The history of 1920s American jazz was alive on the Penny stage in the fall of 1965. Lil Armstrong, a pianist-singer who had been married to Louis Armstrong and appeared on his legendary Hot Five and Hot Seven recordings, performed with the McHarg group from late August to late September, followed by the return of Lonnie Johnson through late October. One night, Louis Armstrong, in town playing the O'Keefe Centre with his All-Stars, stopped by.[20]

The McHughs decided to double the size of the venue in September 1965 by leasing 110 Yorkville, the adjoining house to the east.[21]

John McHugh: When we leased the other side of the semi, then we realized that we could really go. I had several architect friends who helped me with the design of the parabolic arch in between the buildings, which we cut with an electric saw—there was triple brick between the buildings. And then Kid Bastien [Black Eagle Jazz Band banjoist Cliff Bastin] did the brickwork . . . all the Brits really didn't stick together, but they certainly knew each other, you know?

One of the first performers to play the expanded Penny was José Feliciano, a blind singer-guitarist who was then virtually unknown. He appeared September 6 to 17.

Bob Ezrin: He gets up on the stage with his German Shepherd guide dog. The dog brings him up and he sort of slowly sets himself up, and [the staff] come over and help him with the microphone. It's all very awkward and nobody really knew what to expect. Then he started to play and it was like—I refer to these as "holy shit" moments, where you see someone do something that makes you go, *holy shit, I'm in trouble*. Like, that is so good. It makes you go home and try harder and practise and try to get better. That was one of the greatest things about Yorkville: it was wall-to-wall "holy shit" moments. Every club you walked into was another incredibly special performer, from Gordie [Lightfoot] at the Riverboat to seeing José Feliciano play for the first time.

***

By the summer of 1965, the Toronto municipal government was waking up to the popularity of Yorkville, and the problems caused by their having allowed coffeehouses as an exception to the Fishleigh bylaw ten years previous. Following complaints from residents and daytime business owners about the crowds and traffic, the city's welfare, fire, and legislation committee investigated the situation. On May 13, 1965, they recommended that the Metro Licensing Commission put a six-week ban on applications for new coffeehouses in the area bounded by St. George Street, Davenport Road, Bay Street, and Bloor Street, followed by a zoning bylaw change to impose a permanent ban. Alderman Helen Johnston led the charge. "There is a great urgency involved here," she told the *Globe*. "The rowdyism stems from gangs which invade the area primarily on weekends. And it's the coffeehouses and the discotheques which draw this type of person."[22]

On June 4 just before midnight, Mayor Philip Givens arrived in his long black limousine to visit the Penny Farthing, with Pierre Berton as his tour guide. Nicknamed "Go-Go Givens" for his efforts toward the development of entertainment infrastructure in Toronto, the mayor heard the Dirty Shames and later told the *Globe*'s Scott Young, "I enjoyed sitting there—I'd be a hypocrite if I said I didn't. When we left the Penny Farthing after half an hour or so and walked through the crowds to Avenue Road, all I felt was that here young people were living—and so what?"[23]

Three days later, though, Givens sat silently while the Yorkville coffeehouse issue was debated at city council. As he told Young, "Maybe I should have spoken in council. But with the kind of panic atmosphere there was . . . well, I found it difficult in the face of all those massive allegations to do other than sit back and let the alderman, who after all should know her own ward, tell what it was all about. Maybe they knew things that I hadn't seen on my slight visit."[24]

After the debate, council voted in favour of the coffeehouse licence ban for six weeks pending the ratification of a permanent bylaw. Furthermore, a bylaw banning motorcycles from dusk to dawn was drafted and businesses, including coffeehouses, had to close at 1 a.m. at the latest.[25] This was "a clumsy and misdirected law," according to *Globe* columnist Ron Haggart, "rushed through under the guise of an amendment to the zoning bylaw."[26]

It was also toothless. Two days after the vote, the Metro Licensing Commission, defying city council until the ban was ratified by the Ontario Municipal Board, granted licences to three new coffeehouses.

A public hearing was held in council chambers on October 25, 1965. Robert James, whose wife ran one of the boutiques suffering from the influx of teenagers, said, "The proliferation of teenage night clubs is killing the area. It's them or us. Some of the best shops we have are going, some are gone. It's worth taking strong measures to avoid this tragedy."[27]

Mrs. George Fogelberg, described by the *Globe* as "the forceful, white-haired matriarch of the area's ratepayer politics," said, "When the coffeehouses started to get entertainment, they attracted a crowd that was noisy and unruly; we could not sleep until four in the morning for the hooting and the hollering. Our laneways were used like lavatories. We never had that before."[28]

As Haggart concluded, "The sad fact of the Yorkville situation is that those who fought for restriction do not approve of teenagers gathering in large numbers. They attempted to impose their social values and their adult tastes on those with no power and no organization to resist."[29] But in the end, the building committee voted 6–2 to recommend quashing the ban. New coffeehouses continued to open in Yorkville.

* * *

On March 6, 1964, the Night Owl opened at 102 Avenue Road. Like the Village Corner Club and the original Gate of Cleve, the Night Owl was relatively isolated from the centre of the action, being fairly far north on Avenue Road's less-frequented west side. It was a white-painted brick bay-and-gable house, with the door unusually cut into the centre of the bay window and lit by two lanterns on polished wooden pedestals.

The proprietors were Harry Finegold and David Levin, though it is Finegold, or perhaps his partner Dolores, who is remembered as running the club.[30]

Danny Marks (Edward Bear guitarist): Harry Finegold and his common law wife, Dolores: black braids, she was really cute, and Harry was this English guy. They had a dog whose name was Twiggy. I always remember [Harry] saying, "You tell 'em to go piss up a rope!" We thought that was the funniest thing we'd ever heard.

Bernie Finkelstein: Finegold was like Brian Epstein or something, real life. He wore suits and things.

When it opened, the Night Owl had a strict jazz policy, a rarity by 1964. Only the Cellar, not far up Avenue. was direct competition in the neighbourhood. The ubiquitous guitarist Sonny Greenwich appeared there, along with the less-remembered Bruce Stiles's New Jazz Quintet, the Jazz Couriers, and Al Stanwyck's Quartet.

After a year of modern jazz, Harry Finegold changed the music policy of the Night Owl to rock and R&B on June 1, 1965, thus creating one of the most beloved of the Yorkville live music spots. Admission was a low fifty cents ($4.87 in 2025) at first, then a dollar ($9.73 in 2025). Officially, the club stayed open until 1 a.m. on weekdays and 2 a.m. on weekends, but it is remembered as being open until 3 a.m. six nights a week, and then sometimes even later.[31]

Danny Marks: [The Night Owl] was one of the first places we saw late-hour jamming.

The house band at the club was Dee and the Yeomen, who also happened to be managed by Finegold. Dee and the Yeomen were a trio of keyboards, guitar, and drums led by a British émigré named Graham Dunnet, or "Dee" (1941–). Dee had been a member of Johnny Neal and the Starliners, touring the UK in 1962 and sharing a bill with the Beatles at Hamburg's Star-Club.

Shortly after moving to Canada, he formed Dee and the Yeomen in the fall of 1964. Len Lytwyn (1942–2018) played drums, and the classically trained Terry Watkinson (1940–2026), late of Yonge Street bar band Sonny and the Sequins, played Hammond L-100 organ and bass pedals. All three sang. The trio rehearsed a mix of covers and Merseybeat-sounding originals through the winter of 1965, and were soon in the recording studio with Stan Klees for their first single on Quality Records, "Say Baby."[32]

Graham Dunnet: Out of the blue we got a phone call from Harry Finegold, who had sold his stake in the Biltmore Movie Theatre and wanted to manage us. In turn he proposed giving us a stake in the Night Owl coffeehouse.[33]

Harry Finegold's management style was hands-on. He paid the Yeomen an astounding $150 a week each ($1,460 in 2025), plus expenses, and as he told the *Globe*'s Bruce Lawson, "I would have complete say on every item concerning the band. We would discuss things, but my word was to be the last word." He went on to claim that "Dee and the Yeomen are going to be the next Beatles," and that if the man who owned the Cavern—the Liverpool club where the Beatles got their start—had shared Finegold's foresight in managing his club's most popular band, "well, he'd now be the owner of the Beatles, instead of the owner of a club that's gone broke."[34]

Terry Watkinson: We just played there all the time. Great experience. We had close to a hundred songs in our repertoire. It was actually the envy of all the musicians, because we had a home base where we could rehearse every night, and there was always food there of some kind. Coffee. Tons of coffee.

According to Finegold, in the first week, twenty-eight people paid to get in. The next week the number doubled to 56, and to 164 the next week. After hours, Finegold kept the band in the club to rehearse, following Ronnie Hawkins's practice regimen for the Hawks. He told Lawson, "It was then that we made up our policy—what we were going to give the kids. It was going to be a good sound, mostly our own writings, and we were going to have a clean appearance. We do not go for the long hair and wildness."[35]

Terry Watkinson: Harry was good. He was very ambitious, with lots of ideas. Not enough money to carry them out, but I guess we made enough to justify our existence.

Alan Palmquist: Our band, Magic Circus, played the Night Owl a lot. Harry would always say of his band, Dee and the Yeomen, "They're not the fucking Beatles, but we do pretty good."

* * *

Monique Lips (1944–) and her boyfriend, Eric Stettler, were an attractive couple from Switzerland. Monique had worked as a housecleaner in Zurich, and she emigrated to Toronto in 1960. When she met Stettler, he had money to invest in a coffeehouse, so they applied for a licence, which was granted in early June 1965.[36]

Monique Lips: There were many people around, so we took the chance to open. I loved rhythm and blues.

Lips and Stettler remodelled a house at 88 Yorkville and opened Chez Monique with a two-year lease at $350 per month ($3,407 in 2025) just in time to catch the summer rush.[37] In a 1966 guide to nightclubs in the *Toronto Star*, it was described as "an old tumble-down house with a rickety porch fine for leaning against. Twangy music and urgent 17-year-olds come here six nights a week and pay $1.50 to dance 'til 2 a.m."[38]

Bob Ezrin: I used to spend a lot of time at Chez Monique. The stable hands for the racetrack would come after the race, and they were an interesting crowd. They were a little like carnies, many of them petty thieves and small-time criminals. Late at night, after they were finished, they would come to Chez Monique to dance, smoke, and get drugs. There was always somebody selling something in here.

Linda Shilling: I ran the espresso machine in the back room, until being a regular on the dance floor became more interesting. I tended to move between the Devil's Den and Monique's because I was an R&B fan. Monique's crowd was made up of young people between the ages of fifteen and maybe twenty-five, although not too many at the upper end of the range. The girls were white, and while some were living in the Village area, most came from outlying areas.

The guys were a mix of Black and white, except for one very popular Chinese/white guy who I had a terrible crush on for a while. While some of those young men came from suburban areas, most were from inner city and downtown. All of them could dance. All of them got their hair done on Friday. The Black guys got their heads conked [had their afros straightened]. The white guys got trimmed and sprayed. Most of the guys favoured stovepipe pants, Capezio [dancing] shoes, and most carried an umbrella as though it were a walking cane. The umbrellas were fashion statements, and also handy if a weapon were required, because it could take a minute to reach down into your sock and pull out your straight razor.

There was a core group of regulars made up of factions: Black guys who were aiming for the entertainment industry, some who worked regular nine-to-five hours, usually in clothing shops, and a handful who were aiming for pink Cadillacs and sharkskin suits. Most of that ilk hung out at the Devil's Den, but there was a handful at Chez Monique. The white guys fell into two categories: the ones who wanted to be cool, have a good time, and get laid, and the rest who were intern rounders [i.e., aspiring small-time criminals] and thugs in fancy dress.

The girls were almost exclusively white. In fact, I can only remember one Black girl. She was with one of the white gangster guys and was pregnant at the time. Past that, the white girl mix was well-dressed, lots of perfume, plenty of hairspray, and leaning into whichever particular guy group they were interested in or felt safe with.

* * *

Seven months after the Inn on the Parking Lot closed, a new teen rock club opened in its place at 158 Cumberland Street: Charlie Brown's. Bob Johnston owned the club, though the licence was technically granted to Mrs. Barbara Johnston in June 1965.[39]

Dave Bingham: Everybody called [Bob] "Charlie." It was a nickname from his Navy days. "Charlie" was about five foot eight, quite skinny although elegant and sported a greyish blond goatee and slightly long golden locks.[40]

The Ugly Ducklings were a high school band, entranced by the sound of the Rolling Stones and their influences. Lead singer Dave Bingham was born in the eastern suburb of Scarborough.

Dave Bingham: The first 45 I bought was Chuck Berry, "Sweet Little Sixteen." I met Roger Mayne at school [Cedarbrae Collegiate Institute] and he asked me if I'd like to join the folk club. That was when *Hootenanny* and all those shows were on TV. We thought, we'll join the folk club and see if we meet any other people that are into what we're really into, which was like Bo Diddley and Chuck Berry and stuff. We did meet some people, but it didn't turn out that they were anybody who was going to be in the band.

Cedarbrae was a pretty liberal high school, and they had this one room downstairs next to the furnace room. They made that a room that we could go to at lunch hour. It had a jukebox in it, and anybody could put whatever song they wanted on it.

For their first performance at Cedarbrae, the band called themselves the Strolling Bones, in obvious ironic homage to their heroes, the Rolling Stones.

Dave Bingham: Kids that went down [to Yorkville] would tell us how great it was, and "you got to play there, guys, you got to go." So I went down and we drove around and we were just like, *whoa*. And every time we looked up and we saw red lights upstairs, you know, "what's going on?" We were just totally naive. We had no idea. But then of course, once we got down there and we moved in and were living there, you find out people just had a red light or a purple light. There's nothing going on. There's no illegal gambling; there's no prostitution.

Bill Huard: The Ugly Ducklings had a manager named Bill Crabtree. He was the manager because he had a van. I said, "If I can get you some gigs, I'd like to be the manager." I was on the phone at home, my dad's toes curling on the couch, but I was calling all and sundry, trying to get some gigs. I managed to get some gigs, and I got the job.

Dave Bingham: The first three gigs we played there, it was for the owner, Bob Johnston, and after that he said, "You know, you guys could probably make more money, just charge at the door and you manage it. I'll just charge you a straight fee for whenever you're playing. Which was like 35 bucks [$340 in 2025] for the night."

Bill Huard: We tended to attract a crowd.

Keith McKie: I remember thinking they were like a pale Luke and the Apostles, but they actually had a lot of great material.

The *Star* described Charlie Brown's as "wholesome, loud, crowded . . . tube-like room with open back door looks out into a ramshackle garden."[41]

Dave Bingham: When we first started, we were stupid because we would get everybody in there and have the whole place packed and it would get so hot in there. So then we thought, *oh well, let's fix it up*. We opened the back door and we got some gravel put in the back so that people could go out there to smoke. Then they'd wander off, because it would be nice and cool and they could get their clothes dry. Then we'd get a second crowd coming. Second set. We were pulling in 150 bucks [$1,460 in 2025] a night, just charging $1.50 [$14 in 2025] at the door.

Bill Huard: [Bob Johnston] gave us full latitude. They had the coffee machines in there, and Cokes in coolers and all the rest of it. We charged a nominal cover at the door, and the band took the gate.

Dave Bingham: Bill Huard ran the whole thing at Charlie Brown's. He even booked the bands to come in when we weren't there—when we were doing a high school gig or something. There was no alcohol for sale, but that doesn't mean there was no alcohol there. The girls had their purses and the guys were starting to carry their manbags, and they'd just bring their mickey. We didn't search the bags or ask questions, you know.

I think that Bob Johnston sold it. It was called the Booby Hatch, but that only lasted for about a month. We didn't get along with the new owners. They wanted more money and wanted to get in on the door. We ended up going to El Patio and all the other places.

* * *

After soft-launching electrified bands in Yorkville with Mike's Trio in the summer of 1964, Mike Burak at the El Patio booked a succession of promising acts like David Clayton-Thomas and the Shays, who earned $35 ($340 in 2025) a night there in March 1965.[42] This was paltry pay indeed for a five-piece band, and the El Patio predictably refrained from listing these engagements in the Toronto newspapers for fear of invoking the wrath of the Toronto Musicians' Association.

David Clayton-Thomas: I had played the bars down on Yonge Street. We played R&B top 40. That's what they wanted. That's what you were hired for, and they weren't much interested in new original music that was going on in Yorkville. You know, with Gord Lightfoot and all the artists they would bring in from New York to the Riverboat and whatnot. It started a whole scene. We played the little clubs around there, but there was no money. I still paid the rent by working my gig down on Yonge Street. I had a little band that we actually took into El Patio and we played in there. Then a manager told us we were too loud. We told him to fuck off, and we never played there again.

Clayton-Thomas started to spend more time around Yorkville, absorbing the folk scene and the singer-songwriters. Late at night, he would sometimes busk on the steps of St. Paul's-Avenue Road United Church with his acoustic guitar.

David Clayton-Thomas: You had to be tough on Yonge Street. You had to be able to dodge beer bottles in most places, but Yorkville was a totally different vibe. I liked that a whole lot better. I always wanted to be a songwriter, and that's where it was going on. So you absorbed all sorts of stuff. All these great artists came up there from the States and established a connection between Yorkville Village and Greenwich Village.

Chapter Nine: "We want to be the next Beatles."

IN THE MID-'60S, the Yorkville music scene was on a roll. A sentiment was beginning to prevail among some observers that Yorkville could be the next big music scene, like Liverpool or San Francisco. But who would be the breakout act to put the old village on the musical map? For a while, it seemed that it would be the Paupers, a promising original rock act led by drummer and songwriter Skip Prokop.

Ronald "Skip" Prokop was born in Hamilton in 1943. He learned to play snare drum as a teenage Sea Cadet and worked his way up to drumline instructor. After high school he moved to Toronto and worked for the Metro Police in the identification bureau. By 1963, as the urban folk revival was peaking, Skip had started to sing and play the acoustic guitar. He played small gigs around Hamilton with a trio called the Riverside Three that included another guitarist/singer, Bill Misener.

The Beatles' first film, *A Hard Day's Night*, was released in Canada on August 12, 1964, with George Harrison's new Rickenbacker electric twelve-string guitar up front during the band's musical numbers. The unusual twelve-string guitar, though played the same way as a standard six-string, had a jangly, harplike sound that would soon be exploited by the Byrds' Roger McGuinn and a host of imitators. Prokop, who already played acoustic twelve-string guitar, was inspired to create a rock band that had two electric twelve-strings.

Skip Prokop: When I first heard the Beatles, I thought, "I can write this kind of stuff." In my head, I wasn't thinking I could write Beatle songs, but the formula seemed easy. I got together with Bill [Misener] and we just started writing songs . . . I put an ad up at the Larry Sykes Music Store in Scarborough, looking for a guitarist and bass player. I got a response from guitarist Chuck Beal, who was already in the Musicians' Union and worked at Sykes'.[1]

With the addition of talented bassist Denny Gerrard, the group had a Beatles-like four-piece lineup of two guitars, bass, and drums.

Skip Prokop: We had fifty cents among us. Bill said, "Why don't we call ourselves the Paupers?"[2]

Duff Roman was a popular CKEY disc jockey, born David Mostoway in 1938 in Swift Current, Saskatchewan. After running dances around the city and in cottage country, he opened his own coffeehouse, Brave New World, at 230 Davenport Road around 1964. He was also David Clayton-Thomas's manager and financed the release of several singles on his own Roman Records label.

Duff Roman: All this stuff is going on at the club, and Skip Prokop shows up with Bill Marion [Bill Misener's new stage name] and Denny Gerrard and Chuck Beal. "We want to be the next Beatles." They were confident little buggers.

The Paupers signed on with Roman's artist management company, David Mostoway Productions, a firm that also included Duff's brother Dan Roman (born Roman Mostaway). Duff used his real name to deflect accusations of conflict of interest; as an on-air DJ he could promote his own artists and their records. Duff also signed the Paupers to Red Leaf, a short-lived, all-Canadian record label combining the signings of producers Stan Klees, Art Snider, and Duff.

On March 1, 1965, Red Leaf released the Paupers' first single, "Never Send You Flowers." This Prokop–Marion co-write was tight, loping folk-rock with three-part vocal harmony. A twelve-string guitar solo predictably enough capped the arrangement. "Never Send You Flowers" went to #1 on CKEY, and on April 25, 1965, the Paupers opened for the Rolling Stones at Maple Leaf Gardens. It was only their third gig.

The Paupers were suddenly the hottest band in town. When they first played Yorkville with a week at the El Patio (August 9 to 15, 1965), the club was packed every night. But as well as the Paupers were doing, Duff Roman's other client, David Clayton-Thomas, was faring even better, with an appearance on the ABC-TV national musical performance show *Hullabaloo*.

Duff Roman: When David and the Shays hit on *Hullabaloo* it was all hands on deck. This is the break we've been looking for. I said, "Look, there's just my brother and I [in the company]. Dan will work the Paupers. I'm going to work with David." For Skip that wasn't enough.

Born in 1944, Bernie Finkelstein was an air force brat, his family moving frequently around England and Canada before they settled in Downsview, a suburb north of Toronto. His first memory of Yorkville is of poets standing on street corners and flamenco guitarists.

Bernie Finkelstein: Once I got down there [in 1962], I got hooked. High school kind of lost out. For me, everything was new and slightly romantic, because I was really into Jack Kerouac and William Burroughs and the idea of playing chess—and espresso coffee. Then I smoked my first joint, and that was wonderful. That was more of the world I was looking for. I [started] listening to Bob Dylan and it was like the voice of God to me.

Finkelstein was a born entrepreneur with a prodigious gift of gab. "I had answers for everything," he wrote in his 2017 autobiography *True North*, "and I wasn't just fooling around; I really thought I did know all the answers."[3] With a friend, he started a booking agency, the Specter Agency.[4] Their first contract was a February 1964 booking at the Village Corner Club for the Voyageurs, a folk trio led by his Downsview neighbour Jay Telfer. Finkelstein moved into a rooming house on Avenue Road near Yorkville and immediately got a job at El Patio.

Working under Tony Fernandez, Finkelstein was a dogsbody at El Patio. He washed dishes, set up the room for live music, pulled espressos, and occasionally served as a bouncer.

For a while, Bernie managed the Dimensions, Telfer's group that would morph into A Passing Fancy, but when he heard the Paupers at the El Patio, he took notice. Here was a band that maybe *could* be the next Beatles, with strong songwriting, harmony vocals, and powerful musical skills.

Skip Prokop: We'd be rehearsing there in the daytime, and we'd stumble over something and Bernie would say, "Why don't you try this?" and we'd say, "Hey, Bernie. Shut up. Go back and do the dishes or something." He'd say, "I'm telling you, man, you should try it." We'd

Joseph Bloor, founder of Yorkville; he was the Village's first real estate speculator. Circa 1850.

Toronto Public Library

Toronto's first full-time folk singer, Greg Curtis in 1957. He pioneered folk music in Yorkville, but his formal style fell out of fashion and he left music behind around 1965.

Courtesy of Vivienne Muhling

Klaas VanGraft at the Concerto Café, 1958. He wandered from table to table, singing traditional songs.

Courtesy of Shirley VanGraft

Dick Smith, Klaas VanGraft, and Charles Roach playing calypso music upstairs at the Concerto, 1959. Later that year the café was gutted by fire and closed.

Courtesy of Shirley VanGraft

Ian Tyson at the Village Corner Club, early 1960s.

Courtesy of Andrew Henwood

"Mary," Moya McNulty, Max Wickens, and Doug Bush at the side porch of the Village Corner, 1961 or '62.

Photographed by Andrew Henwood

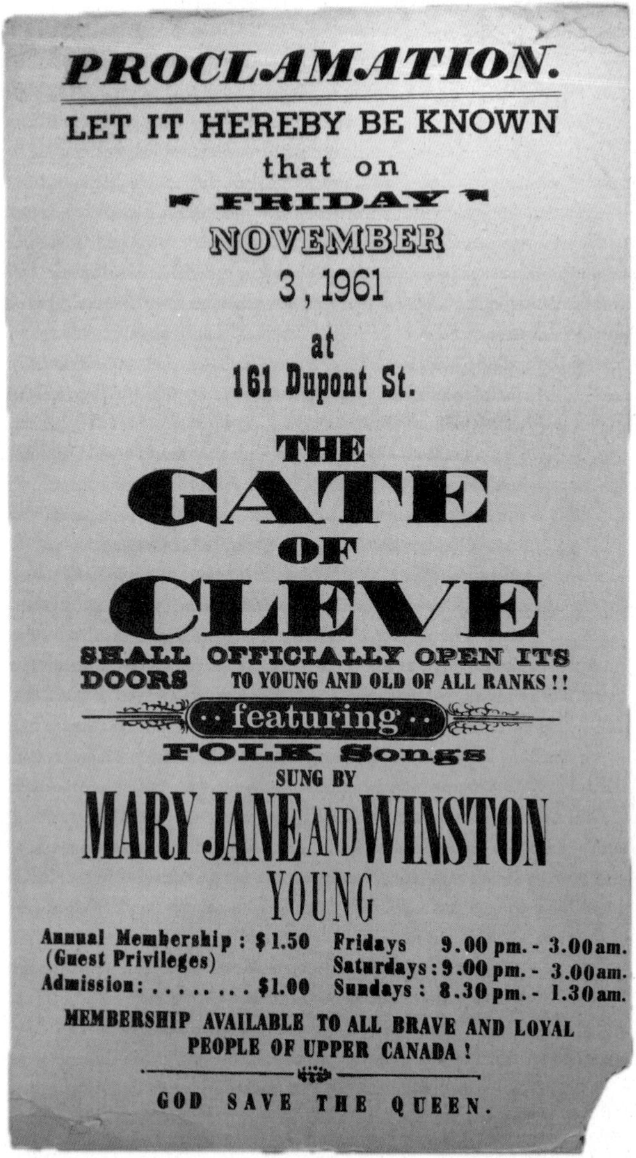

Opening night poster for the Gate of Cleve, featuring Winston Young and his wife Mary Jane, who was, in Don Cullen's words, "incapable of artifice."

Toronto Public Library, Allen and Thomas Suddon Collection

John and Marilyn McHugh on a rare night off from running their two successful Yorkville coffeehouses, the Half Beat, and the Penny Farthing.

Courtesy of Katrina McHugh

The Cumberland Street location of the Half Beat, probably 1961. It was Yorkville's first sidewalk café.

Courtesy of Katrina McHugh

“Conchita,” a waitress at 71 Coffee House, flamenco dances to the accompaniment of Joso Špralja. Werner Graeber sits at the right of the photo. Around 1962.

Courtesy of Leo and Shirley Špralja

A typical night at Werner Graeber’s 71 Coffee House, early sixties.

Courtesy of Leo and Shirley Špralja

Forged in the 71,
Malka and Joso, 1963.

Courtesy of Leo and Shirley Špralja

A poster advertising the Cave, the short-lived jazz cellar on Scollard run by Imre and Hedy Bohm, Holocaust survivors and Toronto shoe-store proprietors.

Toronto Public Library, Allen and Thomas Suddon Collection

The second location of the Half Beat on Avenue Road, where Joni Anderson sang traditional songs and John Kay met the Sparrows.

Courtesy of Katrina McHugh

A stylish Half Beat poster for the new location.

Toronto Public Library, Allen and Thomas Suddon Collection

The Sinners at the Purple Onion, 1960 or '61. Chick Roberts, Harvey Kotler, and Eddie Sokoloff.

Courtesy of Eddie Sokoloff

Judy Collins at the Purple Onion, early March 1962.

Courtesy of Cliff Martin

Cliff Bastin of the Black Eagle Jazz Band in front of the Cellar, Steve Ciotlos's arty jazz venue.

Photographed by Joe Van Rossem

Patti Tancock, centre, and Burnie Fiedler, right, at the Mousehole, circa 1964. Note the fraudulently acquired barnboard interior.

Courtesy of B. C. Fiedler

The Mousehole sign.

Courtesy of Sola Fiedler

John McHugh riding his penny farthing past the Penny Farthing, his long-awaited jazz venue with folk music to pay the bills.

Courtesy of Katrina McHugh

Yorkville's resident trad jazz band, the Black Eagle Jazz Band. Left to right: Geoff Holmes, Jim Falconbridge, Cliff Bastin, Ron Sullivan, Bill Weller, and Joe Van Rossem.

Courtesy of Joe Van Rossem

The Penny Farthing at 112 Yorkville before it expanded into the house to the west.

Courtesy of Katrina McHugh

Jack London and the Sparrows at Massey Hall, March 19, 1965. Left to right: Dennis Edmonton, Jerry Edmonton, Jack London, Art Ayre, and Nick St. Nicholas.

Photographed by Cathie Jacobs

Jerry Edmonton at the Devil's Den.

Photographed by Cathie Jacobs

A poster for Colin Kerr's Mynah Bird coffeehouse, a monument to his talking bird and to bad taste.

Toronto Public Library, Allen and Thomas Suddon Collection

The Mynah Birds at Chez Monique, late 1965. Left to right: Rickman Mason, Ricky James Matthews (later Rick James), Bruce Palmer, Tom Morgan, and John Yachimac.

Photographed by Peter Bieri, courtesy of Yedi Zak

A Riverboat handbill from 1965. Lightfoot's star was on the rise.

Toronto Public Library, Allen and Thomas Suddon Collection

Neil Young at the Riverboat hootenanny, late 1965 or early 1966.

Courtesy of B. C. Fiedler

Michael Sanderson disc jockeying at the Bod Pod, circa 1969.

Courtesy of Linda Buttrey and Yedi Zak

DANGER! DANGER DANGER

HEPATITIS

INFECTIOUS HEPATITIS IS AN EXTREMELY DANGEROUS DISEASE. WHEN THERE IS NO TREATMENT FOR IT 50% OF THOSE CONTRACTING IT WILL DIE. 20% OF TREATED FOR IT DIE, MAINLY BECAUSE TREATMENT IS BEGUN TOO LATE. IF TREATMENT IS BEGUN IMMEDIATELY, AN ALMOST TOTAL RECOVERY RATE COULD BE OBTAINED. THE EASIEST WAY OF FINDING OUT WHETHER YOU HAVE HEPATITIS IS BY TAKING A BLOOD TEST. THE TEST IS FREE, PAINLESS AND FAST.

DOCTORS WILL BE TESTING IN THE TRAILER AND IN FRONT OF THE GRAB BAG TONIGHT :(AUGUST THE 5TH) FROM 9 P.M. TILL 2 P.M.

HELP STOP AN EPIDEMIC.

_____THE TRAILER

A handbill that was distributed around Yorkville in the summer of 1968.

Toronto Public Library, Allen and Thomas Suddon Collection

A reunited Kensington Market performing in Toronto in 2026. Left to right: Tim Timleck, Keith McKie, Gerry Mosby, Luke Gibson, and Gene Martynec. Dave Gray hidden behind Luke.

pass on that, and we'd continue to stumble and fart around and try to overcome the problem. Then we'd be like, "Hey, Bernie . . . what was that you said?" . . . We'd do it, and it would work . . . After a while, we started realizing this guy was very smart, and he started talking to us about other things, like image stuff.[5]

The Paupers asked Finkelstein to manage the band. There was just one problem: they were already contracted with Duff Roman. Duff felt wronged by what transpired.

Duff Roman: Bernie and the Musicians' Union ganged up and basically allowed them to break our contract. We just let it go.

Bernie Finkelstein: I didn't know what a manager really did, exactly. By the time I hooked up with the Paupers, they were not doing well. They really didn't have any money. They weren't all that happy. I didn't steal them from Duff.

Bill Marion soon left the band and decades later told the Garage Hangover website that he quit after refusing to sign a recording contract with Bill Gilliland at Arc Records.[6] Arc was an independent record company founded in 1959 in the East York borough of Toronto. This scrappy and ambitious label issued hundreds of albums and singles in the 1960s, from Maritime fiddlers to Beatles and Monkees sound-alike albums to the first single by a Toronto band to reach #1 on the CHUM radio chart, "Charlena" by Richie Knight and the Mid-Knights.

Bill Gilliland, Arc's vice-president, was known among musicians as an irascible and slippery character. Bill Marion had no interest in being contractually bound to Gilliland, so he left. In the end, the Paupers didn't sign with Arc, but they now had to audition a new lead singer and guitarist. They found him at the Mousehole: the Scottish-born folk singer and erstwhile Folk Guild president Adam Mitchell.

Adam Mitchell: My sister, who used to go to the Village, knew about the Paupers. She told me they were looking for a new lead singer. I actually tried out for the band, but I didn't get the gig because I didn't know the chords to enough Beatles songs. Bernie [Finkelstein] just said to the Paupers, "Listen, Adam Mitchell is a great writer. He's in the band." He had sufficient credibility, I guess, to do it. There was no audition. I joined the band in August of '66. They had a gig coming up, I think like in a week, and I had to learn twenty-two songs, mostly covers. They had a couple of originals that Skip had written.

We suddenly had that really rare thing: chemistry. And we worked harder than any other band; we just did. When we had a new song, we'd go to a rehearsal space, which usually was the Hawk's Nest [Ronnie Hawkins's second-floor teen club at 333 Yonge above Le Coq D'Or Tavern]. We'd start rehearsing at eight o'clock at night, and we would not leave there until we had worked out that song. I remember once we rehearsed twenty-two hours straight. We were so disciplined, we used to get fined if we made mistakes.

Danny Marks: The best thing I ever, ever saw at the El Patio was the Paupers. Chuck Beal was some kind of crazy guitar player, and he had the tape echo going. He made all these like elephant-like shrieking noises on the guitar. Denny and Adam and Skip would all play drums and Skip would turn a bass drum up on its side. So that'd be boom, boom, boom, boom. Skip was—wow, man, crisp technique, like you wouldn't believe. Skip wasn't a sophisticated guy, but when it came to drumming, he was like Buddy Rich. And they were straight [drug-free]. These guys were straight dudes, but they were psychedelic.

Adam Mitchell: [In Toronto] we were starting at the far edge of the solar system. The centres of power were New York and Los Angeles, musically speaking. It was difficult to even get into the United States, especially for young musicians.

To his own surprise, Bernie Finkelstein signed the Paupers with an American label on his first try, selling the band to Jerry Schoenbaum at Verve Forecast, a sublabel of MGM Records.

Bernie Finkelstein: I walked out of there with the deal, not the contract itself, but with the deal, and it was during a period where handshakes were good enough. I didn't know enough about record deals to be worried about what was going to be in the [contract], because it was the first one I ever got.

I went down to the Café Au Go Go [in Greenwich Village] to book the Paupers for a live performance, which Jerry wanted me to do. I wasn't really given a choice [by Harry Solomon, the booker]. I was told, "You play with Ian and Sylvia. They're Canadians. You guys know each other." I could read his booking sheet. He had a big calendar in front of him, quite large, not like the smaller books we use today. I could see "Jefferson Airplane" and I was tuned in enough. They didn't have a hit yet. I'd never even heard them, but I'd heard so much about them and the San Francisco sound and stuff. I said, "What about the Jefferson Airplane show?" He said, "Oh, that's going to be a great show. I'll get it for you." And he did.

Chuck Beal: Not so fast. There were a couple of hitches. The gig was for free, and we had to pay all our expenses including travel costs. We still wanted to take the gamble. So Bernie put us on a strict budget, and we started counting the pennies and days until we would learn whether or not we were going to sink or swim. Finally, the big day came. We had no visas, so the truckload of equipment had to be smuggled across the border. The band would fly as tourists and the eight of us would meet up later that night.[7]

Adam Mitchell: We opened up for the Jefferson Airplane [February 21 to March 5]. It was their first East Coast gig. They had this big reputation, so the Café Au Go Go was full of people. The Beatles' manager [Brian Epstein] was there, [and] Albert Grossman, all to see the Jefferson Airplane.

Chuck Beal: The place itself was in the basement, held about two hundred people and was non-licensed. We were all extremely nervous. When we went on stage to perform our first set, my knees were shaking. I remember praying, "Please God, let somebody clap." We were told later that you could feel the tension in the air . . . All of a sudden, Skip gave the count and away we went, too late to turn back. The first song ended, there was a brief silence, then the place exploded with yells and applause. I don't know what we did that was so different, perhaps they had never heard a band so well-rehearsed . . . The same reaction was repeated every night for two weeks.[8]

Albert Grossman came backstage to meet the band and soon negotiated a co-management deal with Finkelstein. Not long after, with the first Paupers album recorded but not yet released, Grossman bought Finkelstein out of the contract for $20,000 ($180,710 in 2025).

* * *

Colin Kerr (born Christopher Colin Kerr, 1936–2011) was a slight, wiry man, with wavy light brown hair. According to family lore, he had roots in the English aristocracy and by his twenties was a golf pro competing around the globe. Back in Toronto, he owned and ran a nursing home; his wife Jessamyn was a registered nurse, and they had two children, Christopher and Karen.[9]

Kerr had a love for exotic animals and later claimed that he purchased his mynah bird, Rajah, from a local boy in Bombay during a 1956 golf tournament. Kerr came to see Rajah as his ticket to fame and fortune, and trained the bird to talk and whistle, and to say, "Hello, Ed Sullivan," just in case. He later claimed that over six years he earned a quarter of a million dollars with Rajah and appeared on the Merv Griffin, Mike Douglas, Johnny Carson, and David Frost television shows.[10]

Gimmicky, exploitative, and notorious, the club called the Mynah Bird was located in a three-storey house with a narrow eighteen-foot frontage at 114 Yorkville Avenue, on the northeast corner of Hazelton Avenue. The club opened in late 1964 or early 1965, on Fridays and Saturdays only. The front was festooned with ever-changing signage, touting Rajah and the musical talent to be heard within.[11]

Kerr's mother-in-law minded the gate; she was the "old crone at the desk—demanding the exorbitant ($5, $48 in 2025) cover charge" in John A. Reeves's radio script "The Mynah Bird."[12] Rajah was on duty as well, in a cage near the door. "People come from all over the world just to touch his cage," Kerr touted, "hoping that some of the bird's luck will rub off on them."[13]

Facing Rajah was a huge aquarium, stocked with piranhas. After paying the cover charge, patrons parted a curtain and had a choice of the Stage Room, which held folk music performances, and the Jungle Room, a twelve-by-seventeen-foot room with long grass hanging from the ceiling, where rock bands performed.

Christine Young (Mynah Bird go-go dancer): He got away with a lot. No alcohol. When these customers came from the States, the only thing on the menu, it said, "Mynah Bird Cocktail." So of course they all ordered it, because they thought there was booze in it. All it was was a fruit drink with smoking ice. And that was $5. He had chocolate-covered ants and caviar [for $17.95 a plate, $174 in 2025]. He made good money and it was always full. The lineup would go from the front door all the way around to the side of the building.

* * *

Bobbi Lee and the Scepters were a hard-driving R&B group, and the first house band at the Mynah Bird. Lead singer Dan Roach (stage name Bobbi Lee Justice) later told disc jockey John Donabie that they played there about a year and a half, until Kerr wanted them to record a song written by his brother Ben called "The Mynah Bird Song," and they refused.

Dan Roach: We turned it down because we didn't want to change our image, and we didn't want to sing with a mynah bird to begin with. So he let us go from the club.[14]

With Bobbi Lee and the Scepters out of the picture, Colin Kerr needed to find a new band to record his song and advance Rajah's fame. He found it, at least for a time, in a volatile, talented group called the Sailor Boys, soon to be renamed the Mynah Birds.

* * *

Rick James was born James Ambrose Johnson Jr. in 1948 in Buffalo, New York. He played and sang in neighbourhood bands before joining the Naval Reserve to avoid being drafted. He was called to active duty anyway in August 1964—and deserted, crossing the border and landing in Toronto. He ended up on Yonge Street, still wearing his sailor's uniform. He was sixteen years old.

As he recounted in his sometimes fanciful 2015 autobiography, Johnson immediately got into an altercation with some drunk white Buffalonians who were taunting the young African-American man with racist slurs. Levon Helm and Garth Hudson, then playing with Levon and the Hawks, intervened along with their friend Pat McGraw, who took Johnson to El Patio.

Rick James: In the back room we smoked. It felt great, like a weight lifted off my shoulders. "Band's coming on," said Pat. "Let's stay and listen." I was ready. I was glad the band played R&B. The musicians weren't bad, but the singer really couldn't hack it. Pat saw the look on my face and asked, "Think you can do better?" "Know I can," I said. "Well, get your ass up there and try." Nick St. Nicholas, the bandleader, was willing. "You know 'Stand By Me'?" I asked. "What key?" "E." "Hit it!" I hit it hard, and four minutes later everyone was up and screaming for me.[15]

Nick St. Nicholas remembers a different version of the Mynah Birds origin story.

Nick St. Nicholas: I decided to move close to Yorkville Village. I wanted to start a band. We formed this little group called the Swingin' Doors. The Swingin' Doors came to a screeching halt, and I decided to just get some jobs with [a new trio]. I had Ian Gobel on guitar and Rick

Cameron on drums. We were in the basement of the El Patio. You got free lemonade and the band got $20 [$199 in 2025] or something. I think it may have been less.

On a practice night when the club was closed, a Black dude walked in. He came down a winding staircase and stood there at the bottom step, just leaning, looking over. I noticed that he had on a United States sailor outfit. All the Black people that I'd seen were on TV and they all sang. So I didn't ask him if he sang or not, I asked him what songs he knew. He knew Otis Redding, Sam, and Dave, "Hold On, I'm Comin'." He knew all the Motown stuff. I said, "Do you know any Rolling Stones, Beatles?" He's like, "Yeah, I do that." I said, "Grab the microphone," and we tested all these songs and every one of them sounded better than the last one. I said, "Are you going to be sticking around?" He said, "Yeah, I'm here for good." I said, "Okay, you're in." We called ourselves the Sailor Boys.

Pat McGraw's girlfriend was Shirley Matthews, a singer who had scored a big Canadian hit in 1963 with "Big Town Boy." She suggested to James Johnson that he change his name to Ricky James Matthews, after her deceased cousin, to escape detection. The Sailor Boys dressed in Ricky's uniforms—all the clothes he had with him.

Rick James: We switched them up and made 'em funky, but the look was unmistakably Navy. Our sound was unmistakably R&B. We covered everyone from the Isleys to Smokey and his Miracles . . . Some fans of the Sailor Boys would show up wearing bell-bottoms and sailor caps—we started a fad!—to hear us sing harmony tight as the Beach Boys.[16]

Nick St. Nicholas: We had a really good number of songs that people were familiar with. And so we used to pack 'em in, and the price of the band went up. I thought, "This is a really good idea." I met with Colin Kerr. His brother wrote a song called "Old Mynah Bird" ["The Mynah Bird Song"] and "Mynah Bird Hop," and he needed a band to play it and perform it.

The first order of business was a new name for the Sailor Boys. They were now the Mynah Birds.

Nick St. Nicholas: He bought us black leather jackets and gold, long-sleeved turtlenecks. We wore jeans and Beatle boots, but we painted them yellow to look like [bird] feet. We all dyed our hair black but we used some bleach and made the front of our head look like a bird beak. It was too much.

Neil Merryweather: I remember seeing them and they had the yellow boots and they were teaching their manager how to swear.

In what would turn out to be his last act as the Mynah Birds' manager, Colin Kerr booked the band along with Rajah on the after-school television show on CHCH-TV in Hamilton, Ontario, hosted by fast-talking DJ Dave Mickie, a.k.a. Dave Marsden.

Nick St. Nicholas: [Kerr] had sixty mynah birds in his garage on an endless tape loop trying to say "Hello, Ed Sullivan." Only one bird would remember and say it straight, the blind mynah bird.

Rick James: As a gimmick I was supposed to sing to a blind mynah bird. I went along with the program. I let them put the bird in my hand as I sang this dumb-ass song. The girls loved it, but I didn't, especially when the bird started shitting in my hand. When I tried to push him off, he dug his claws into my skin.[17]

Nick St. Nicholas: Kids were sitting out in the bleachers. We were special guest artists for that day. So we're standing and Rick James was gonna sing. [Colin] said, "Oh, by the way, would you give me your hand? You hold the mynah bird." Okay, count down. Nine, eight, before the first note comes up, Rick is saying, "Hey!" He's screaming out loud, "The bird's pecking my hand!" So he flicked it and he flung it on the floor. And the bird's on the floor saying, "Hello, Ed Sullivan. Hello, Ed Sullivan." [Kerr] is out of control. He's madder than a hen. He's screaming at us: "You screwed this up!" We got back in the car and went back to Toronto and we all took our [Mynah Birds uniforms] and burned them.

In their absence, Colin Kerr booked a series of relatively unknown folk singers and obscure non-union bands. Bobbi Lee and the Scepters even returned to the fold for New Year's Eve 1965. The Mynah Birds, now estranged from Kerr, improbably kept their name and soldiered on.

Rick James: Nick [St. Nicholas] was something of a slippery cat. He started gigging behind our back with a group called Jack London and the Sparrows . . . When Nick left us for greener pastures, we recruited a superbad bass player named Bruce Palmer. Bruce brought the funk.[18]

After a dizzying series of membership changes, Rick and Bruce heard a Brantford band called the Bunkies playing in Toronto and poached three members, including drummer Rickman Mason. The post-Kerr Mynah Birds soon found a new investor and manager as well.

John Craig Eaton, a scion of the Eaton's department store empire, became the band's benefactor, putting his friend Morley Shelman in charge of managing the group. Eaton bought the band new equipment, gave them rehearsal space, and booked them at private parties for his well-heeled friends.

Rickman Mason: John Eaton lived on the Bridle Path [a midtown street well-known for its wealthy inhabitants] in a pretty big place. Morley Shelman had a castle-looking place up a couple of blocks. I guess they all knew each other, and we went there one night to meet him. John said, "I want [Morley]," because John didn't want his name out as doing anything for us. [Hollywood actor] Sal Mineo was there and they were all, I don't know what they were into, who knows? But nobody was normal. What I remember was they were dropping their wallets with all their credit cards and "who's got the most credit cards" and all that. I didn't like [Shelman] from the beginning, but he became our middleman. John would give him the money and he'd give us a little bit, and he was stealing the rest. You know, typical.

Morley Shelman's connection to the famous actor Sal Mineo got him an audition for the Mynah Birds with Motown Records, which was branching out from R&B into rock bands. A white rock band fronted by a Black singer was an interesting new wrinkle for the label in the mid-'60s, and Ricky James Matthews was an obvious talent as a singer, songwriter, and frontman.

In January 1966, the Mynah Birds drove to Detroit to audition personally for Motown president Berry Gordy and Miracles lead singer Smokey Robinson. The band was offered a contract, but lead guitarist Tom Morgan refused to sign and abruptly quit the band.

Tom Morgan: I could see what was coming down the road. Soon as [Motown] got [Ricky] back over there, you knew where he'd end up and where everybody else would end up. Nowhere. Just by the way Motown treated people. They were only ever interested in Ricky.[19]

The Mynah Birds now had the offer of a record contract with one of the most successful American record companies in history, and they had just lost their lead guitar player. A replacement had to be found, and fast. The Mynah Birds' salvation was about to arrive in the form of a struggling singer-songwriter and guitarist, Neil Young.

Chapter Ten: "It came down to songwriting."

NEIL YOUNG WAS BORN in Toronto in 1945 to Scott Young, a journalist, and Edna "Rassy" Ragland, an occasional host on local television. After his parents divorced, he and Rassy moved to Winnipeg. Neil became obsessed with the guitar in high school and put together a disciplined instrumental band called the Squires. With a burning desire to make it as a musician, he brought the band to Fort William (now part of Thunder Bay) and then to Toronto on a whim in July 1965. At first he lived with his father, and then in a series of crash pads from 88 Isabella Street to Vicky Taylor's flat above the Night Owl.

On a recommendation from the Allen-Ward Trio's Craig Allen, Neil connected with local manager Martin Onrot, who took on the Squires and renamed them Four to Go.

Neil Young: The Yorkville scene. I'd never seen anything like it. Music was everywhere . . . The Riverboat was an upscale thing—people who played there were really making a living. There was the Gate of Cleve . . . that's where I saw Lonnie Johnson.[1]

We didn't succeed in taking Toronto by storm. It was a tough time. We were small fish in a big pond, had no reputation, and really there was nothing special about us in the big city. We were out of our league.[2]

Four to Go broke up without ever getting a local gig. Neil, who was soaking up Yorkville folk music, tried his hand for a while as a solo folk singer and songwriter but met little success. He does not seem to have played even one advertised gig under his own name during his months in Toronto. The only exception he remembers is a last-minute fill-in for a sick performer at the New Gate of Cleve.[3]

The only way Neil was going to play the Riverboat was by auditioning for the Monday night hootenanny. This was no open stage, but a multi-performer night with a small amount of pay and an audition for Estelle Klein to get a slot. Neil auditioned and did appear at least two times. In a photograph from the winter of 1965–66, Neil sings at a Riverboat hoot, his overgrown Beatle haircut poking out from under a leather fisherman's cap. The microphone stand is too short for his lanky frame, and he is leaning over to sing, strumming a borrowed Guild F-50 acoustic guitar.

The Folk Guild hoot was one thing, but an actual gig at the Riverboat would have been preferable. Neil asked Burnie Fiedler for one, but was turned down.

Vicky Taylor: One night they got into an argument and Burnie said that Neil howled like a dog and told him to take his horrible voice and never come in his club again. Neil said, "You know what, Burnie, some day you're going to beg me to play here."[4]

Adam Mitchell: [At the Riverboat] one night I walked in and this guy Neil Young was up on the stage. I remember standing there hearing that voice. He's playing [affects nasal, shaky voice] "Oh to live on Sugar

Mountain." I remember thinking, "Oh dude, don't give up your day job." You know, dreadful.

Not all of the feedback was negative. A few folkies on the scene believed in his talent.

Neil Young: One night after hearing me at a hootenanny, Chick Roberts of the Dirty Shames told me he really liked my song "Sugar Mountain"—that made me feel like I was somebody.[5]

For a while, Neil lived with Vicky Taylor in her apartment above the Night Owl.

Neil Young: I was at the bottom, kinda like the new guy. I wasn't that good, y'know. My songs were pretty dumb . . . they were what they were. Vicky Taylor was just a good friend. She had an apartment above the Night Owl—I lived there a little while. She was a little bit crazy. She would get real sad about things . . . but not for long. She was a real party girl. Had a little bit of money, liked to have a good time. Let me sleep on her floor.[6]

Vicky Taylor: I was the only one with an actual job; I was making $50 [$500 in 2025] a week. So I rented this apartment over the Night Owl club on Avenue Road. And it was just one huge room. It had a bathroom, but no kitchen. And it had a bedroom in that. That was my private space. But when I came out in the morning, I never knew how many bodies would be there or who they would be. The door was never locked. I was the mama. I took care of everybody and I fed everybody with this concoction that my mother taught me called guck, which is sort of like chili without the chili in it. I would just make a huge pot of this stuff. And then when it was gone, I would make more, but there were times when it was Kraft Dinner, and boy, I have never been able to eat Kraft Dinner since. There was a whole bunch of instruments in there and everything, people's belongings, and nothing was ever taken. There was only one chair in the place, a big green chair in the corner and [Neil] would be curled up in there writing his songs. I remember when he wrote "Nowadays Clancy Can't Even Sing," and that song really impressed me. I saw genius in that boy, that's for sure. Not that I had much power to do anything for anybody, but, you know, I tried to do whatever I could.

Salvation came in the form of Bruce Palmer, Mynah Bird bassist, who met Neil precisely at the moment that the band was desperate for a new lead guitarist.

Bruce Palmer: I ran into Neil on Yorkville Avenue. He was carrying an amplifier on his head. You didn't see many people carrying that around back then. He was looking for people to play music with, so I asked him to join my group.[7]

Neil Young: I became acquainted with Bruce Palmer, who I think I met with some folkies at David Rea's flat in the Village. Bruce was there just hanging, and we became friends quickly.[8]

Neil moved into an apartment on Isabella Street with Ricky James Matthews; this flat was later commemorated by Neil along with other Toronto locations, including the Riverboat, in his 1972 song "Ambulance Blues."

Rick James: Neil and I had just started writing together, and while our songs were good, I was sure that in a few more weeks they'd be great. Neil had this machine-gun style on the guitar that inspired melodies and lyrics out of me.[9]

After the breakup of Four to Go, Neil had traded in his electric guitar for an acoustic twelve-string with a pickup mounted in the soundhole, which lent the Mynah Birds a folk-rock patina. Soon John Craig Eaton bought Neil a Rickenbacker electric to use. Neil played only a handful of gigs with the Mynah Birds before they travelled to Detroit to record at Motown. Holed up at the Pontchartrain Hotel, the band spent about a week in the Motown studios in the winter of 1966.

In addition to recording their own album, the Mynah Birds found themselves being used as studio musicians for other acts, in line with the company's assembly-line approach to record production.

Rickman Mason: Twenty-four seven, day and night until we dropped. They would take us into the studio individually—I bet you I did maybe thirty tracks by myself. I still listen to Motown songs and wonder if that's me playing on them.

Neil Young: It was a very cool time and place. We even went to choreography school to learn how to move, and I'm sure we flunked, but they treated us well. They fitted us for clothes. We were on our way to the big time![10]

A single, "It's My Time"/"Go On and Cry" was prepared for release on Motown's V.I.P. imprint. Co-written by Ricky, Neil, and R. Dean Taylor—another Canadian who had joined the staff of Motown in the early '60s—"It's My Time," offers a glimpse of what might have been. Ricky sings the tightly written, dramatic soul-rock song with a confident swagger and a compelling, gravelly voice. Neil plays a memorable twelve-string acoustic guitar line that floats ethereally on top of the mix.

With the album in the can, the rest of the band went back to Toronto. Ricky was waiting for his share of the $25,000 ($233,632 in 2025) royalty advance from Motown. When the band's handler Morley Shelman couldn't produce it, the two got into a physical altercation. As revenge, Shelman told Motown that Ricky was a Navy deserter. Motown brass, uneasy about this situation, convinced Ricky to give himself up to the authorities. Reportedly the very day that the "It's My Time" single was to be issued, Motown cancelled the release.

Back in Toronto, Ricky broke the news to Neil Young and Bruce Palmer before returning to Buffalo, where he gave himself up to the FBI. He was sentenced to five months of hard labour, escaped, then turned himself in and spent more time in prison.

With their frontman in the Navy brig, Neil and Bruce quit the Mynah Birds. The rest of the group soldiered on with replacements, still backed by John Craig Eaton, and closed up shop in the early summer of 1967. At loose ends, Neil and Bruce hung out at the Cellar at 169 Avenue Road. The club was still open but its founders, Steve Ciotlos and Sam Shirose, were no longer at the helm.

Sam Shirose: We became very busy. We were only open three nights a week, originally Friday, Saturday, Sunday. Then we were getting lineups to get in. Steve wanted to make it bigger. We couldn't make it bigger in that building. I was against it, because I wanted something intimate, small, and homey. Steve found a place on Dupont, and I didn't want to go. That's how I cut away from him and away from the club.

In September 1965, Ciotlos rented the Cellar to Scotty Mair, a former *Toronto Telegram* reporter, and two Yorkville waitresses, Jeanine Hollingshead and Bev Davies.

Jeanine Hollingshead: We had taken over the Cellar and we were keeping it open as an all-night café. Neil played in there and Daisy DeBolt played in there. The jug bands played in there. This was in the days when the *Telegram* was out on strike. Scotty was one of those reporters that got displaced during the strike, and he was very active around Yorkville. He said, "Look, let's just do this. Let's just have an after-hours club." I think we were practically living in it.

Around the corner at 182 Dupont (still standing in 2025), Ciotlos opened a second Cellar, which he called the Cellar Jazz Club (as opposed to just "the Cellar") on New Year's Eve 1965. This was a much bigger space than the tiny Avenue Road location—250 seats—and Ciotlos was thinking bigger with his bookings as well.[11] Now on his own, Ciotlos booked a series of high-profile and expensive concerts by American modern jazz legends—Lennie Tristano, Art Farmer, and Charles Lloyd. The biggest problem was getting the word out. Now there were two Cellars around the corner from each other. The public was confused, and no doubt a few jazz fans showed up at the old Avenue Road location to find a skinny longhair named Neil strumming an acoustic guitar in a corner.

Neil Young: I was in Toronto, in the middle of the night, sitting in a funky after-hours dive called the Cellar. I was with Bruce Palmer . . . The group had just broken up, Bruce and I were just sitting there, probably pretty stoned, and I asked Bruce if he wanted to go down to L.A. . . . He said yes, so we sold all the band's equipment [even though it had been purchased for the Mynah Birds by the group's backer, John Craig Eaton] to buy a '53 Pontiac hearse. We loaded it up with three girls and another guy, all from Yorkville Village.[12]

On Tuesday, March 22, Neil and Bruce headed to Los Angeles with Jeanine, folksinger Tannis Neiman, Judy Mack, and Mike Gallagher. Somewhere along the way, Jeanine, Mike, and Tannis peeled off from the group, which arrived in Los Angeles on April 1. What follows is the stuff of rock legend, as Neil and Bruce found themselves stuck in L.A. traffic when they were spotted by Stephen Stills, an acquaintance of Neil's. This led to the formation of Buffalo Springfield, the innovative group that launched Neil, Bruce, and Stephen into the big time.[13]

Back in Toronto, the Avenue Road location of the Cellar was closed, abandoned by its young proprietors. Around the corner at the Dupont location, Steve Ciotlos was losing money on his new high-profile jazz bookings. He vented to jazz promoter and journalist Dave Caplan about the reception of his ambitious new club. "Where are all those so-called jazz fans who are endlessly screaming for more jazz around town? When I give it to them they don't show up."[14] Just over six months after opening, the Cellar Jazz Club on Dupont was shuttered.

After the club's closure Ciotlos ran Rosedale Art Gallery on Yonge Street near Summerhill and played bebop saxophone a couple of evenings a week at the Hungarian Castle restaurant on Bloor. While splitting his time between Toronto and Romania, he died in his home country at the age of eighty-five. Sam Shirose continued to run illegal poker games for the Volpe crime family up until Paul Volpe's murder in 1983, and afterward for other concerns through the 2000s. In 2025, Shirose is living in the Beaches neighbourhood of Toronto.

* * *

By April 1966, Colin Kerr was claiming attendance of 1,600 people every weekend at the Mynah Bird, his coffeehouse at the corner of Yorkville and Hazelton.[15] By any standards the club was an exploitative ripoff, with Kerr targeting credulous tourists; he was always coming up with ideas to get publicity and draw in the rubes. On July 30, he announced that the Mynah Bird was offering a computerized matchmaking service for $3, "Operation Match Canada."[16] But Kerr's greatest innovation was the introduction of topless dancing to Toronto. While go-go dancers were a popular attraction in Yonge Street Taverns like Le Coq D'Or and the Friar's Tavern, they were always clothed, if scantily so; Ontario's strict obscenity laws saw to that. But in the second half of the '60s the obscenity laws were loosening.

Christine Young: When I was sixteen, I was working at Canada Life Insurance and I wasn't making very much money. So when I got asked to [dance in] the window at the Mynah Bird, that was thirty-six hours a week at a dollar an hour. That was big money ($352 a week in 2025). I was dressed in a white fringe bikini. But anytime I saw anyone that I recognized, I jumped out. I was there for five years, from 1965 when I was sixteen. We were not of age. Carol, who called herself Wyche, was the youngest. She was fifteen.

I had to sign a contract. It stated that if none of the [other] dancers showed up, I would dance topless because I was only upstairs in the window. And I thought, *well, that'll never happen*. There's Kathy, there's Wyche, there's Andrea—no way. And one night, none of them showed up. I was with the owner's wife in the kitchen, putting makeup on these pasties that they made for us. They just cut out circles for Band-Aids and we put makeup on them to make them skin-coloured. [Colin's] wife was like our mom. She was this sweet lady who took care of these young girls. We trusted her. They were very good at business. They knew not to bother the women.

We danced in a room in a corner. He had put up this wrought iron, and it went in twirls and swirls. We'd dance in this corner with this screen in front of us, and then psychedelic lights on us, so you really couldn't see anything. Then he decided to take the seats from chairs and put a motor on it and it became a pedestal. We had to stand on the pedestal topless with a torch in our hand. You weren't allowed to move, with this seat taking us around.

I continued to dance in Toronto until I was thirty-four. Then I went off and part-time still danced. I wanted to get down before they said, "Oh, it's that old broad."

***

On February 26, 1966, the Bloor-Danforth subway line opened. From its launch in March 1954, the Toronto subway system had been a single north-south loop; this east-west line nearly doubled the reach of the underground train and made Yorkville more accessible, more visible, and its properties more valuable. Overnight, the stakes for commercial development in the old Village changed.

Soon enough, the embattled coffeehouse ban, enacted and then quashed in 1965, was back in contention. Over April 26 and 27, 1966, the merits of the coffeehouse ban were again argued at a hearing before the Ontario Municipal Board. After an adjournment to July 3, the OMB hearing resumed, with a new proposal to impose a two-year moratorium on new coffeehouses in Yorkville. Four days later the board ruled against the proposed bylaw. The coffeehouse ban was dead, again.

The city, however, was not done with its war on Yorkville. On July 12, the buildings and development committee authorized surprise inspections of rooming houses in Yorkville, to look for overcrowding. On July 21, a judge vowed to quadruple the usual $25 ($233 in 2025) fine for noise disturbances to $100 ($934 in 2025), or thirty days in jail. Finally on August 10, the city announced a 10 percent tax to be levied on Yorkville establishments offering live entertainment and/or dancing. The tax had been in place for liquor-licensed establishments for some time, and the government realized that they could be charging it to unlicensed establishments as well, with the revenue going to hospitals.[17]

Finally, after a decade of tolerating private clubs in Yorkville despite their prohibition by the still-in-effect Fishleigh bylaw, Toronto City Council passed Bylaw 22972 on September 9, 1966.[18] This bylaw amended the 1959 general zoning bylaw to specifically ban the opening of new private clubs in Yorkville and the Annex, the area immediately to the west. The walls were belatedly closing in on coffeehouse businesses in the old Village.

***

From November 28 to December 2, 1965, and then again on December 11 and 12, the Sparrows played the El Patio at 119 Yorkville. With a raft of new original songs, a tight show and a new, electrifying lead singer in John Kay, they were nonetheless spinning their wheels in Yorkville. They recorded some lacklustre demos for Capitol that included several songs from John Kay's Half Beat repertoire, including the blues standards "Hoochie Coochie Man" and "C. C. Rider" along with Kay's "Square Headed People." Capitol did not call the Sparrows back for more. It was time for the band to try their hand in the US market. Luckily enough, they were approached in the early months of 1966 by Stanton Freeman, a wealthy and connected executive at Clairtone, a pioneering Canadian stereo manufacturer.

Nick St. Nicholas: Stan Freeman was roaming around. He was interested in the band. He really liked John Kay's voice. So we said, "Oh, okay." Stan really thought the band could do something in the United States. He talked to his brother, who was a sports editor at the *New York Times*, and he made a process for us to get H2 [temporary worker] visas for two months and go down to New York.

First, Freeman arranged for an extended gig at Arthur, the New York club owned by Sybil Burton, a Welsh actress recently divorced from actor Richard Burton. Having received a million-dollar settlement from the divorce, she opened Arthur in 1965. While in New York, the Sparrows recorded a three-song demo at Allegro Sound Studios on April 28. All three songs featured John Kay on lead vocal. Barely a year after the split, the Sparrows of April 1966 were already a far cry from the Jack London days, and a far better band. As Nick St. Nicholas says, "We were on fire."

* * *

The Ugly Ducklings continued their residency at Charlie Brown's on Cumberland Street. During the day they would rehearse in the club, attracting fans to hang out outside to listen in. Their sound was all attitude, from Dave Bingham's hectoring vocal style to Roger Mayne's fuzz lead guitar courtesy of his Zonk Machine, a crude early fuzztone guitar pedal, to John Read's busy bass and Rob Boers's rat-a-tat drumming. All of this can be heard on "Nothin'," their first single, which they recorded at Hallmark Studio on June 6, 1966.

Roger Mayne financed the session himself to the tune of $330.50 ($3,088 in 2025) and the record was issued on Yorktown, a short-lived label run by Tommy Graham of local group the Big Town Boys and Fred White, a young music publicist. The record won the Battle of the New Sounds, a call-in contest, on CHUM radio five times in a row.[19] It peaked at #18 on the CHUM chart, #1 in St. John, New Brunswick, and #70 on the national RPM Magazine chart.

* * *

Lonnie Johnson was thriving in his newly adopted home, working more or less steadily at Toronto clubs, making an average of $400 ($3,738 in 2025) a week,[20] had recently appeared on the Metro Stompers' Columbia album, and enjoyed a degree of local fame with a fanbase of young players who saw him as a conduit to a musical golden age.

David Clayton-Thomas: He was the real deal. I followed him around adoringly.

Lonnie decided to open his own club, but he didn't start from scratch. He signed a contract with the owner of the Rive Gauche (Left Bank) coffeehouse at 107 Yorkville, Peter Hill; rent was $50 ($467) a week.[21] The Home of the Blues was launched with a private party on May 4, 1966.

Lonnie could now perform every night from 9 p.m. to 3 a.m. if he so desired, a taxing schedule for a musician half his age. The venue seated about thirty patrons around small rectangular tables, and the $1.50 ($14 in 2025) admission included a cup of coffee. But most nights, he had trouble filling even this tiny club. As popular as Yorkville was becoming, the crowds were looking for rock and R&B, not an elderly solo blues and jazz act.

Bob Ezrin: Talk about playing to an empty house. His place was never really full.

David Rea: It never did very well. I would go down there and he'd be all by himself. We'd sit together, the two of us, and we'd play for a little bit. I had him all to myself.[22]

Peter Hill cancelled their contract in late June. Hill told the *Globe* that Lonnie had appeared at another (unnamed) Yorkville club, and "that night, not one paid admission to the Home of the Blues . . . I didn't think it was fair of him to put himself in competition with the club so I let him go."[23] After the closure of the Home of the Blues, Lonnie found sporadic work at Castle George, the Kibitzeria, and the Italian Villa. In Yorkville, he did a stint at Room at the Top, the second-floor venue in the licensed Gaslight restaurant in January 1968.[24]

On March 12, 1969, Johnson was leaving Webster's restaurant at Webster and Avenue Road when a high-speed collision sent a car hurtling toward the building, pinning him to the wall. Seriously injured and hospitalized for months, he was still recovering when a series of strokes felled him the following year. Lonnie Johnson died in his adopted home of Toronto on June 16, 1970.

* * *

Murray McLauchlan: I had just graduated from art school, seventeen years old, and hit the road, riding freight trains. When I got back, I actually moved into the Village Corner Club. That's where I lived for the first year I was back in Toronto. Nick Garber [brother of Victor Garber] ran this kind of open-mic thing at the Village Corner Club. The concert nights and such devolved into this small collection of people that they knew and loved, rather than trying to find marquee acts anymore. It became, like, literally a club.

1966 was unkind to folk music in Yorkville. The Village Corner Club was one of the first folk clubs to open back in what must have seemed like the more innocent days of 1960, but by the summer of 1966 it was barely hanging on. On June 21, a bailiff locked the doors for non-payment of $775 ($7,242 in 2025) in back rent. By this point another member of the board, Charles Peterson, took over from owner Jack Devoretsky. Peterson was confident that they could reopen the club. "It's a corpse that won't stop kicking," he told the *Star*.[25] Three days later the Corner was back open, but it would not see another Yorkville summer. It closed for good on March 5, 1967.[26]

* * *

The New Gate of Cleve was likewise on its last legs. Talent booker Joe Lewis had worked long months without pay to keep the club going, but the writing was on the wall.

Joe Lewis: The idea was that we'd split whatever profits there were at the end. But there weren't really any profits. In the end I don't think I actually ever collected anything. I couldn't really charge a fee, because the lady [Alyce Haller] was using up her lifetime savings to buy the club, basically to have a place for her son and his buddies to sing in.

At some point before October 1965, Alyce Haller sold the club to one Sergio Rossi. His tenure at the helm of the struggling Gate was short and rocky. The venue was suffering a series of misfortunes in this period, beginning with a break-in in October that resulted in a loss of $700 ($6,814 in 2025) in cash. Later in the month, featured performer Bob Gibson was arrested for heroin and cannabis possession in his Toronto hotel room by the RCMP, resulting in a cancellation of his scheduled appearance. Returning for another Gate engagement in February, he was turned away at the border, leading to a revenue loss for the club of around $2,500 ($24,336 in 2025).[27] The health department shut down the club temporarily in December, demanding that the washrooms be enlarged.

With the venue reopened in January, appearances by the Allen-Ward Trio, David Blue, and the Travellers failed to draw a significant audience. Rossi was late with his rent, leading to a bailiff's notice being posted on the door. Phil Ochs, another popular attraction, was delayed until the last night of his appearance by a fogbound flight in early March 1966. "I think someone's got a doll of me and is sticking pins in it," Rossi complained to Morris Duff of the *Star*.[28] By May 1966, the New Gate of Cleve was no more. Rossi, said the *Globe*, "regrets nothing, would do the same again, but next time . . . would start with more capital."[29]

* * *

Bernie Cugelman had just finished his third year of law school and, with three months off, travelled with a friend to Lima, Peru. After visiting a psychedelic nightclub there with fluorescent paint and black lights, Bernie got the idea to start a similar place in Toronto, and following the demise of the New Gate of Cleve, 45a Avenue Road was available. "I was too stupid to think that I needed experience," he says.

Partnering with a young man from England named Ryan Cove, Bernie opened Boris' "on a shoestring," as he recalls. The name of the club was a reference to monster-movie star Boris Karloff, and a July 1966 *Star* feature described the interior: "A ghoulish white light and coloured wall panels make this downstairs place look very Munster."[30] To *Varsity* writer Volkmar Richter, it was "a fluorescent-monster-decor dance hall."[31]

At least part of the time, Boris' was a discotheque, with a disc jockey and go-go dancers in the front window.

Phyllis Taylor: I was probably fifteen or sixteen. I had a boyfriend who was a DJ, and he looked at me one day and said, "You know, I think you and your girlfriend, we should sew you up some costumes." So we did; we put together some turquoise blue costumes and all that fringe and the white go-go boots, and I started go-go dancing at his dances. I decided to take it to the next level—I was going to start my career by going down to Yorkville and having an interview. And I suppose I got the job because I ended up go-go dancing there, but in order to do that actual go-go dancing, I had to wait for my parents to go to sleep and then I had to crawl out of the bedroom window and hitchhike down from Bathurst and Lawrence [7.5 kilometres away].

I was hired by Boris', and I would dance in the window. My parents had put braces on my teeth, so throughout my go-go dancing career, I never smiled. I danced at Boris' for a couple of years. It was a lot of fun and I made around $20 [$186 in 2025] a night. We were dancing until the wee hours in the morning, and then I would hitchhike back home, sneak back in the window, and go to sleep for a few hours before getting up to go to school the next day. I eventually got caught. My parents grounded me and my father put barbed wire across the window.

The first live music listings for Boris' appeared in May 1966, with December's Children, the Wee Beasties, and the Hue-Men among the acts. "Most of these bands," says Bernie, "confused being loud with being good."

On a chance visit to the Purple Onion (just a few doors over at 35 Avenue), Bernie found the room packed to see Luke and the Apostles. Speaking to the band on a break, he offered them $100 ($934 in 2025) a week each, a big pay hike from the $75 ($704 in 2025) each they were earning at the Onion.

Mike McKenna: We were getting a little tired of the Onion, because we felt we could move on. We were starting to get antsy.

The band began their Boris' residency on July 21, 1966. Not long after, the Purple Onion closed its doors; in founding co-owner Barry Witkin's memory, it was because the new owner, Doug Rodway, forgot to renew the lease.

***

A few doors north on Avenue Road, Murray Campbell rebranded the Devil's Den as the In Crowd in January 1966 and continued to book R&B and rock bands in the venue for the remainder of the year. Newspaper listings disappear for the club by 1967, though the Avenue Road Club upstairs continued to feature live music for occasional special events until 1974, when the building was razed.

***

Luke and the Apostles by this time had a new bassist, Dennis Pendrith, and a new drummer, Pat Little. Pat Little was born in North Bay, Ontario, in 1947. His mother was an English war bride and the family soon moved back to England and then to Malaya, where Pat's serviceman father was stationed and for a time was a prisoner of war. The family, which included older sister Shirley, came back to Canada when Pat was ten. Pat connected with the voice and style of Ray Charles when his father gave him an album, *Modern Sounds in Country and Western Music*. At fourteen he took up the drums, beginning with a single snare drum.

Pat Little: I really didn't know about Yorkville. I had come from a little town called Lake Wilcox up near Aurora [now part of Richmond Hill]. When I got out of high school . . . in those days, you'd get out and it's *get a job, son*. And my life at home wasn't all that good. So when I was sixteen and a half, "I'm outta here." I lived at Pape and Danforth and worked as a draftsman for John Guray and Associates. As soon as I was making my own money, I started to buy nice clothes. I always dressed really well. I rented a drum set from Larry Sykes Music, a set of Sonors. I loved to play music, but you only thought of it as a pastime in those days. People didn't make it except the big stars.

Pat's first band was the Undertakers, a non-union combo playing school dances and bowling alleys around the city in 1964.

Pat Little: I moved to Yorkville—54 Scollard Street, $8 [$78 in 2025] a week—and the first band I saw was the Sparrows. And all these things happened so quickly, within two or three months.

Seven doors down from Pat's apartment, 40 Scollard Street, had been the Clef Club, the Cave, and Café Parisana before reopening in late 1964 as Le Chat Noir with the Black Eagle Jazz Band playing weekends. By the following year, unnamed "top bands" were listed as performing on Wednesdays with "dancing" (presumably to recorded music) for the rest of the week. Shortly after arriving in Yorkville, Pat joined a band, Lost Generation, and played Le Chat Noir. They performed Rolling Stones, Who, and Them covers.

Pat Little: Nick Delar, the lead singer, liked to pretend he was [Mick] Jagger. He was a good showoff, and that's what you needed in those days. He was all over the place. But I heard that the Apostles were looking for a drummer, and so, bang, I zoomed right there right away. I did the audition and they said, "Yeah, cool." I felt like, well, I could turn it into making a living doing it. I had to join the union.

Bernie Cugelman would become, for a time, Luke and the Apostles' manager. After the Paul Rothschild debacle, the band was released from its Elektra contract. At some point, according to Luke Gibson, Warner Brothers Records was interested and attended Apostles gigs at Boris'—as well as at a rehearsal when the club was closed. Nothing materialized from this, though, and the band trudged on. A rehearsal tape from this period has been preserved, and a fragment containing Sonny Boy Williamson's "Good Morning School Girl" and a band original called "Oh Yeah" was restored and recently uploaded to YouTube by Dave Bingham. Recalling early Led Zeppelin, it's a thrilling glimpse into the state-of-the-art of Village blues-rock and psychedelia in 1966.

In November 1966, bands began to appear in a second-floor space at 45 Avenue, as well in the original basement venue, and by December, the Red Gas Room was officially launched as a second venue within Boris'. One of the first bands to play the Red Gas Room was a group from Sault Ste. Marie called the Vendettas, fronted by Keith McKie.

Keith McKie was born in 1947 in St. Albans, England. His family emigrated to Canada in 1953.

Keith McKie: I don't know if I had that much interest in school. I enjoyed the art classes and things like that, but I wasn't really a good student. I think I had ADHD, which nobody told you about in those days. They just said, "poor concentration" or, you know, "should try harder."

Unlike Keith's previous group, the Shades, the Vendettas were Musicians' Union members, making scale playing at teen dances, hamburger stands, and the Sault boat club. The band members, who were starting to write their own material, admired Buddy Holly, Jimmy Reed, and Ray Charles.

Alfred Johns, the band's bassist, soon left for teachers college. Alex Darou (1940–1970) replaced him.

Keith McKie: We find out that [Alex Darou] is a jazz musician. We wanted a rock guy at the time. Alex was second choice. He only played acoustic bass. But you know, he was there and he wanted to do it. Alex turned out to be our band mother, as he called himself. He was basically the guy who was able to get us so that we could leave the Sault. He knew a lot about what was going on in Toronto. He basically was our manager.

A girl from the Sault brought a tape of ours to the big Hogtown [Toronto], and Ronnie Hawkins saw something that he was interested in at the time. So we came to Toronto to play the Hawk's Nest [in the summer of 1965]. We moved here permanently. The idea was to record for Hawk Records [Hawkins's short-lived label].

We were pretty naive, just like every band in those days. We'd do Animals, we'd do the Beatles, we'd do the Stones. We were writing our own tunes, and I have no idea whether they were great tunes or good tunes or not. Ronnie decided to put us on the road in bars, more adult bars, when we wanted to do teen clubs, because we were teens. The drinking age was still twenty-one, but we did play in bars, seventeen years old playing in the Jolly Roger in Thunder Bay. Trying to grow moustaches to look older, so the club owners wouldn't send you home.

The Vendettas played Boris' on October 7 and November 5, 1966, then moved to the Red Gas Room for sporadic gigs from December through March 1967. By the following month, the band was splintering. The two songs they recorded for Hawk Records were never released. Soon Alex Darou decamped for New York to play with David Clayton-Thomas, and the group limped along with a new bass player for a while before disbanding.

Keith McKie: It came down to songwriting. I had just started to write songs near the end of the band and the guys wanted to play rhythm and blues and rock and roll. But I couldn't write rock and roll. Folk seemed to be more of a thing. In Boris' one time [the Paupers'] Adam Mitchell came in and I'd started to write these little folkie tunes and I played him a couple. He told Bernie Finkelstein about me.

When the band started to fall apart, I auditioned for Patti Fiedler, but I wasn't quite ready for the Mousehole. Then Bernie [Finkelstein] came back from doing the Paupers. He had sold the Paupers to Albert Grossman and he was interested in me as the focus for a new band. I had been living in a station wagon at that point, and Bernie had a big apartment. He gave me a little room in his apartment and I worked on tunes.

* * *

David Clayton-Thomas was living in a one-room flat on Yorkville Avenue when he walked into a jazz club (probably the Cellar) and befriended a local jazz pianist named Tony Collacutt; today Clayton-Thomas calls Collacutt "a young genius,"[32] but he was also a heroin addict and a psychiatric hospital outpatient. Tony Collacutt (1946–2014) grew up in Toronto. Inspired by a movie about a popular pianist when he was eleven, he started practising on his own daily. That fall he entered the Royal Conservatory of Music, where he studied under Myrtle Guerrero.

Myrtle Guerrero: [He had] phenomenal technique, extraordinary facility and a very good brain . . . Tony just didn't feel classical music was creative enough.[33]

At the age of sixteen, Tony earned an ARCT music diploma with honours, but his heart was in modern jazz. He began to play at the Cellar on a regular basis with his trio. That group appeared on CBC television on a Phil McKellar-hosted show called *Commonwealth Jazz Club* in 1965. A Bud Powell and Art Tatum influence is evident in his fleet bebop-soaked improvisations on his own composition, "Meditations."

David Clayton-Thomas: We struck up a conversation and he had some very interesting ideas about music. I loved him as a piano player. He wanted to join my band, but to use an avant-garde jazz musician like Tony Collacutt in a rock context was not done.

Clayton-Thomas and Collacutt decided to start a jazz-rock fusion project. Formed in January 1966, the Bossmen combined twin lead guitars "arranged like a jazz horn section"[34] with a rock rhythm section built around Tony's inventive piano playing. Duff Roman financed a recording, spending $2,000 ($18,690 in 2025) to produce a single showcasing Clayton-Thomas and Collacutt's co-composition, "Brain Washed" b/w "Barbie-Lee" (Roman Records DR-1105). This anti–Vietnam War screed, bathed in fuzztone bass and bookended by a strikingly modern jazz piano break, peaked at #6 on CHUM on July 18 and #11 on the national RPM chart on August 8. But Duff could not get a US company to release the single.

Top Toronto agent Ron Scribner booked a rare national Canadian tour for the Bossmen, with the band driving from Toronto to Vancouver in a former bakery van.[35] It turned out to be, in Clayton-Thomas's words, "a total disaster," exacerbated by Collacutt's drug addiction and mental fragility.[36] They had to escape from a riot at their Sault Ste. Marie gig, and then drove their van into a ditch on the way to Winnipeg.

David Clayton-Thomas: That was the end of the Bossmen. By this time Tony Collacutt was deteriorating rapidly. We had to sign him out of the psychiatric hospital for gigs and bring him back afterwards. His brilliant mind was burning out fast, and the years of drug abuse were taking their toll on his body . . . The group disbanded . . . I went back to playing the coffeehouses in Yorkville.[37]

After the breakup, Tony Collacutt played in a band called Chimo! before being finally sidelined by mental illness. He lived his last years in a nursing home in Newmarket, Ontario, still avidly practising the piano and playing for residents. He died in 2014.

The failure of the Bossmen and the "Brain Washed" single ended the professional relationship of David Clayton-Thomas and Duff Roman. Clayton-Thomas put together a new band, the David Clayton-Thomas Combine, and played the El Patio and Devil's Den.

David Clayton-Thomas: The Combine was basically a name we had because we did a gig at the El Patio and we didn't have a name. Some record company up here [Arc/Yorkville, run by Bill Gilliland] gave me 500 bucks [$4,672 in 2025] to go into the studio and record a song ["Spinning Wheel"]. So I went and recorded that and it was just some of the local guys. The record company was horrified when they heard it, and said, "This sounds like jazz. You can't sell jazz. We want rock and roll."

In 1968, Clayton-Thomas signed on as the lead singer of Blood, Sweat & Tears.

The New York-based band had already released a hit album, *Child Is Father to the Man*, before ousting the lead singer, Al Kooper. Clayton-Thomas brought some of his compositions into the band, including "Spinning Wheel."

David Clayton-Thomas: I walked out of [Bill Gilliland's] office and two years later I played the cassette tape [of "Spinning Wheel"] for Freddie Lipsius [saxophonist and arranger for Blood, Sweat & Tears]. He wrote the chart and we went into the studio two days later and recorded it.

Blood, Sweat & Tears' version of "Spinning Wheel," released in the spring of 1969, reached #2 on the US Billboard pop charts, a massive hit by any measure. The only hitch was that David Clayton-Thomas was still under contract to Arc/Yorkville and Bill Gilliland, who, according to the latter's unpublished memoir, had invested $1,200 ($11,214 in 2025) into rehearsals, musicians, and an arranger for a projected David Clayton-Thomas solo album. Gilliland travelled to New York and confronted Bennett Glotzer, Blood, Sweat & Tears' manager.

Pat Little: [Glotzer] gave Bill a cheque for $25,000 [$217,477 in 2025] and basically told him to go back to Canada.

Duff Roman: The funny thing is, Bill Gilliland came crying to me about the lack of loyalty of David Clayton-Thomas. I said, "You understand that you recorded David while he was still under contract to me!"

The follow-up singles to "Spinning Wheel," "You've Made Me So Very Happy," and "And When I Die" also went to #2. The band played at the Woodstock festival and their second album won Album of the Year at the Grammy Awards, over the Beatles' *Abbey Road* among other nominees. Clayton-Thomas left the group in the '70s, only to return as a hired gun on and off until the early 2000s. After releasing several solo albums, in 2025 he has recently retired from performing and lives in downtown Toronto.

* * *

On September 24, 1966, at Maple Leaf Gardens, CHUM radio and the *Telegram*'s After Four teen-oriented supplement presented the Toronto Sound Show. This was a marathon fourteen-hour concert featuring fourteen Toronto bands: Little Caesar and the Consuls, Luke and the Apostles, the Secrets, the Five Rising Sons, the Ugly Ducklings, the Stitch in Tyme, the Last Words, the Paupers, Bobby Kris and the Imperials, Susan Taylor and the Peytons, the Big Town Boys, R. K. and the Associates, the Tripp and the unfortunately named Spasstiks. CHUM broadcast live from the concert all day, a song each from the bands.

It was a triumphant moment as the Toronto band fraternity, or at least those on the Ron Scribner booking roster, became aware of itself. This appears to be the first formulation of something called "the Toronto Sound," even if it would eventually be Yonge Street bands like Ronnie

Hawkins and the Hawks, Richie Knight and the Mid-Knights, David Clayton-Thomas and the Shays, and the Mandala who were later associated with the term, not this pack of largely Yorkville-based acts. In any case, with 16,000 fans filling the old hockey shed, it was a taste of the big time.

Luke Gibson: It was completely amazing, because that was [where] the Beatles and the Stones were playing. We went to see both bands at Maple Leaf Gardens and this was like, *this is what this has all become now, these arenas full of screaming girls*. It was everybody's chance to actually do that. It was incredible.

Neil Merryweather (bassist, the Tripp): We played the Toronto Sound festival, even though we missed the morning show, because our truck engine blew up. We had played in St. Catharines the night before at a university thing, a frat thing or something. We did get there for the afternoon show. That was my first experience with screaming girls. I mean, they even knew some of our names, right? That was a trip.

Chapter Eleven: "Sell them junk. That's what people want."

BY 1966, THE RIVERBOAT was established as the premier folk club not just in Yorkville, but in all of Canada. Burnie Fiedler's competitors, not only for patrons but for the top folk talent, had been vanquished, with the Purple Onion and the New Gate of Cleve closed, and the Village Corner Club running on fumes. That year, he presented Gordon Lightfoot, Tom Rush, Jesse Colin Young, Eric Andersen, Phil Ochs, Odetta, and Richie Havens, along with a one-off appearance by a breakout vocal duo from New York.

B. C. Fiedler: I had to go to New York and visit Sonny Terry and Brownie McGhee's new agent; they had just changed. The guy said, "You can only have them if you take this band." I said, "Oh, who's that?" He said, "Well, just a minute. They've got a funny name." I said, "That's fine. What do you want me to do?" He says, "You've got to book them for at least two weeks." "How much?" "Four hundred dollars [$3,738 in 2025]." It was Simon and Garfunkel. I signed them in the spring [of 1965] and they were supposed to play my club in the fall. By that time, they had the big hit ["Sound of Silence"]. And here I'm sitting with two weeks, except they never signed [the contract]. I signed mine and they knew, and I said, "I'm going to take you to court. I'm going to sue the shit out of you." We came to an agreement. [I said,] "They're coming to Toronto and playing at York University as a concert for one night. Then let them come the next night and play at the Riverboat for nothing." And they did come [for a single set on March 29, 1966]. Lines around the block.

* * *

On January 17, 1966, Malka and Joso won an RPM Award (the predecessor to the Juno Awards) for Top Folk Group, beating out the Courriers and Ian and Sylvia. They also came in second for Best Produced GMP ("good music production," i.e., non-rock) Album for their second Capitol long-player, *Mostly Love Songs*. Their third album, *Autour de Monde*, followed in March 1966. Soon after, the duo signed with the William Morris Agency, working with agent Sheldon Schultz. Schultz booked them into Carnegie Hall and upscale US clubs, along with four appearances on NBC's *Tonight Show*. But Joso was resisting their career advances.

Malka Marom: He grew up thinking that Americans are the devil, Americans are stealing things . . . capitalists. I showed him the contracts and [he said], "So much money? It could be that he's stealing more." I couldn't convince him that William Morris was a legitimate agency.

In the fall of 1966, Malka and Joso began to appear regularly on CBC Television with their own show, *A World of Music*. CBC had decided to cancel *The Juliette Show*, a popular variety show that followed the Saturday night hockey game. In this time slot, Malka and Joso stood to inherit the largest television audience in Canada. First pitched by director Bob Jarvis in the spring of 1966, *A World of Music* was conceived as a half-hour musical variety show with an emphasis on international folk music. CBC signed on for thirteen episodes to start.

Alex Barris was both a powerful newspaper critic and a prominent Canadian media figure himself on panel shows like the much-watched *Front Page Challenge*. He was hired as head writer of *A World of Music*. He wrote about the experience in his 1969 book, *The Pierce-Arrow Showroom is Leaking: An Insider's View of the CBC*.

Alex Barris: [*A World of Music* was] a towering medley of mistakes from start to finish, a snowball of errors . . . somewhat smaller, shallower and sadder than [it] appeared to be in the dream stage.[1]

Show creator Bob Jarvis was committed to another production, so Mark Warren, the director of *The Juliette Show*, was brought in. A fan of contemporary pop music, Warren had little feeling for the traditional folk music of Malka and Joso's repertoire. But a bigger problem was that the predominantly Anglo-American, post-hockey audience didn't appreciate Malka and Joso's multilingual repertoire and heavy accents. Of course, anti-Semitism played a role. Though most of the letters that came in were complimentary, a handful complained about having to watch these "foreigners," particularly "that Jewess."[2] Once the negative viewer mail started rolling in, the CBC brass began compromising.

Alex Barris: Like all compromise (in the arts, anyway) it leads to failure . . . We did our share of sugarcoating. We hired dancers to fill up our set. We cajoled Malka and Joso into singing more "familiar" songs . . . So help me, we even had go-go dancers once.[3]

CBC ultimately decided not to renew the show when its thirteen-week contract ran out. Not long before receiving the bad news, Malka was driving around Toronto trying to cool down after an argument with Joso.

Malka Marom: CBC had hired us, and the minute they hired us they wanted to turn us into white bread. They couldn't take the exotic and sexy and sensual part of our singing. They wanted to change us and have us sing English songs. We sang English songs horribly. They wanted Joso to wear a toupée. He had a split in his teeth, and they forced him to go to a dentist to close it. Joso was willing to do it and I didn't want to do it. He said, "Are you kidding? This is good money. This is a good job. We are in Toronto. We don't have to travel, it's great."

The argument having ended in an impasse, Malka drove around the darkened streets until she reached Yorkville, which was uncharacteristically deserted. She saw a light on at the Riverboat.

Malka Marom: On the lit-up stage . . . stood a girl who must have picked out her miniskirt at the Salvation Army . . . She turned to face the empty seats and, leaning closer to the mike, she strummed a progression of chords with a surprisingly assertive hand. They were unlike any chords I had heard before. I found myself hanging on every note. And then she started to sing. From verse to verse, her songs were like a kaleidoscope that splintered my perception . . .[4]

It was Joni Mitchell, playing her first engagement at the Riverboat.

Malka Marom: The next day I phoned Paul White [of Capitol Records]. I told him, "Do I have a find for you. By now, you know that I have a thing for talent. Listen. Never in my life have I seen such a thing, except Leonard Cohen and Bob Dylan. This is the league that I'm talking about. You must come and see this girl." He said, "Are you kidding? It's a coffeehouse and I never heard of her." "So this is why you will discover her. Trust me." "Okay." He didn't want to come—I had to come to his house and drive him to the Riverboat at 11 o'clock at night.

The place was empty when [we were] there, maybe three people, four people. She comes on, and you know at that time Joni played guitar in open [tunings], so from song to song she had to change the whole thing. It took a long time in between songs. Joni at that time was also very shy, so she would stand and her hair would cover her face. Paul White said, "She'll never amount to anything. She has no stage presence." He left after two songs.

In Canada's centennial year, Malka and Joso were booked to appear at Expo '67 festivities in Montreal, followed by a week at the swanky St. Regis Hotel in New York. They had, by Malka's recollection, half a million dollars in future contracts. But one day in the spring, while she was waiting for him to arrive at rehearsal, Malka got a phone call from Joso.

Malka Marom: He said, "I'm not coming anymore to rehearsals. We are finished." I was shocked.

She still doesn't know why Joso broke up the duo.

Malka Marom: Fear of success? The higher we went, the more he didn't like it. Elsa Franklin—she was Pierre Berton's [manager]—she talked

Joso into singing [solo]. "What do you need Malka for? You are such a better singer." The other possibility was that his wife thought maybe we had an affair or something. I mean, I loved him, but not like that. I loved his fabulous and miraculous voice.[5]

Malka called Nathan Cohen to make the announcement in the *Star*. In the article, Joso explained his reasons for leaving.

Joso Špralja: I couldn't face it . . . We have gone as far as we can in Canada, and for the next two, three years our work in the United States would call for a lot of travelling . . . When you add up the cost, and what you have to pay an agent, and in guitarist fees, and the expense of travelling, you really aren't left with much.[6]

Joso also needed to have an ulcer operation and felt that he had to stop travelling for his health. As Alex Barris wrote, Joso told him, "You work with Malka, you have ulcer."[7] Returning to 71 Yorkville Avenue, Joso and his wife Angiolina took over the Act One, Scene One coffeehouse in 1968 from Franz Wieltschnigg and changed the name to the Continental Coffeehouse and Gallery, then finally Joso's. Joso himself performed six nights a week (excluding Monday) in the cellar from 10 p.m. to 3 a.m. Like his near-contemporary Steve Ciotlos, Joso combined music with an active visual art practice. On the second floor of the building was Joso's studio, where he painted and sculpted, and taught singing and folk guitar during the day.

In Werner Graeber's old space at 71 Yorkville, Joso and Angiolina were building a Toronto institution. They began to serve calamari, octopus, clams, and mussels prepared in the traditional Zadar style. This was so popular that they started to transition Joso's from a coffeehouse to a fine dining restaurant. Their son Leo was now a teenager and getting involved in the business.

Leo Špralja (Joso's son): We had no clue of how to open up a restaurant; what to do in a restaurant, we had no idea. My mother started this place basically with $20,000 [$180,710 in 2025]. Permits, equipment, everything.

In the 1970s, Joso's restaurant was a beloved connection to the early days of the Yorkville coffeehouse scene, with Joso holding court as a celebrity restaurateur. A young classical guitarist named Liona Boyd, later to be one of Canada's best-known musicians, spent many an evening there with her guitar teacher Eli Kassner and fellow members of the Toronto Guitar Society.

Liona Boyd: After Guitar Society [concerts] we would go upstairs at Joso's, way past my bedtime. Picking up guitars and singing. They were probably into drugs, pot, and so forth, but I was unaware of that. They'd be carousing having drinks; I'd be having my lemonade.

In 1977, the house at 71 Yorkville was slated for demolition, so Joso's family dismantled the old place and moved it to a new location at 202 Davenport Road, just east of Avenue Road and around the corner from the old Village Corner Club.

Leo Špralja: We stripped the rest of the old coffee shop to the bone. We took all the wood from the ceiling. We took everything and we incorporated it all into this [new] restaurant.

They also filled it to the brim with Joso's sculptures, paintings, photographs, and other art. Joso continued to serenade late-night visitors in the upstairs space. Malka, who visited the restaurant often, recalled many a night when Joso would express his regret to her that he had broken up the duo. She says his destiny "was not to have a restaurant. He was a born singer."

Joso's is still open and thriving in 2025, a beloved fine dining restaurant and celebrity hangout, still specializing in fresh-caught seafood prepared the traditional Zadar way. In the 1990s, Joso and Angiolina retired to Zadar and Joso's son Leo took over the business, running it with his wife, Shirley. Joso died on August 8, 2017.

After her divorce from Sydney Himel in 1966, Malka met the accountant Marvin Cohen at Joso's coffeehouse when it was still located at 71 Yorkville. Marv and Malka married in 1970, and Malka henceforth used the Hebrew form of Himel, Marom, as her last name. She launched a solo singing career, appearing at the Riverboat and at the Royal York Hotel's Imperial Room. She soon embarked on a second career as a television and radio documentarian; her radio documentary *The Bite of the Big Apple* won an ACTRA award. In 1999, she published *Sulha*, a fictionalized account of her time living among the Bedouins in Israel. For her second book in 2014, Malka compiled her three interviews with longtime friend Joni Mitchell to create the award-winning *Joni Mitchell: In Her Own Words*. After Marvin Cohen's death, in 2021, Malka moved back to Tel Aviv, where she lives in 2025.

* * *

On Werner Graeber's release from prison in the fall of 1967, Burnie Fiedler hired him to work the door at the Riverboat.

B. C. Fiedler: But he was much too restless. Werner had so many ideas. He said to me, "Burnie, let's build the Gordon Lightfoot [of coffeehouses].

I can't rent because I just came out of jail. But you can rent it from your landlord [Harry Jordan] who owns that building on the corner [of Hazelton and Yorkville]." And we built the Upper Crust because he helped me out at the beginning.

Sola Fiedler's version of the story is somewhat different from Burnie's. In her memory, she and Burnie had already opened the Upper Crust at 116 Yorkville and were running it, albeit unsuccessfully, upon Graeber's release.

Sola (Patti) Fiedler: [116 Yorkville] came up for rent. It had a huge terrace outside. And everybody said I was crazy, because most of the year there was snow on the ground. But I really liked the place, and because we made so much money in Yorkville, incredible amounts of money, I was going to call it the Gold Mine. I panelled it in Florida cypress wood, and I built it like a mine inside. It cost me $15,000 [$135,532 in 2025] to renovate the building. I put up this huge paper sign in the window, "Opening soon, the Gold Mine." Marilyn [McHugh] was furious and actually insisted that I couldn't call it the Gold Mine. So I called it the Upper Crust.

I was very impressed with the CNE [Canadian National Exhibition], and the fact that people wandered around with these Belgian waffles. I opened up the side of the building so you could line up there and get one of these Belgian waffles. Well, it was a total disaster. Nobody wanted these waffles. [Werner] came out of jail just as I had opened the Upper Crust. So we sold it to Werner for $15,000—exactly what it had cost me in actual materials and labour to build the place. When Werner took over, he put in soft ice cream cone makers and he made $150,000 [$1,355,328 in 2025] in the first two months.

B. C. Fiedler: What we had was the soft ice cream. That was our Gordon Lightfoot. I must have taken in between $1,000 [$9,035 in 2025] and $3,000 [$27,106 in 2025] a night.

The Upper Crust was emphatically not a live music venue. The Fiedlers were busy running the Riverboat and the Mousehole, and Graeber, with his experience running the 71 Coffee House, was certainly accustomed to running a low-key club with chess and conversation only. Bernie Finkelstein used the Upper Crust as his informal office; Graeber let him use the telephone.

Bernie Finkelstein: I would talk to Werner about what I was about: music. I talked in highfalutin terms about how *this is really good, this is really original, this guy can really play*; it was always about quality or style. [Werner] said, "Bernie, sell them junk. That's what people want: junk."

* * *

With El Patio thriving, Tony Fernandez and Mike Burak opened the Flick at 88 Yorkville Avenue, next door to Chez Monique, in early December 1966. The club was around 1,400 square feet, relatively large for Yorkville. It had a barely raised stage with a drum riser in the centre, no more than eight feet deep and twenty feet wide. Curtains on the back wall of the stage were joined by a valence that ringed the top.

The Stitch in Tyme was a rock group transplanted from Amherst, Nova Scotia. The band (Bob Murphy, Pinky Dauvin, Don Morris, Grant Fullerton, and John Yorke) cultivated a British look and sound and tended to perform cover songs exclusively. They signed to Arc Records and then were eased into Bill Gilliland's new Yorkville imprint, where they scored a minor Canadian hit with a 1966 cover version of the Beatles' "Got to Get You Into My Life."

Bruce Wheaton (later vocalist in the Stitch in Tyme): Grant and Murph and John Yorke were in this band called the Untouchables, and they had an offer with Bill Gilliland to come to Toronto for a record contract with Arc Records. And the drummer wouldn't go, so they had to figure something out. They approached Donny and Pinky and they went to Toronto. But Bill Gilliland changed their name first to the Golden Earrings, then to the Stitch in Tyme. Then they had a falling out with Donny and John Yorke and they started asking me to join. They said, "Come on down to the El Patio and see what you think of the band." I thought to myself, *wow, yeah, the band is cooking*. They were so on fire. I joined and we were given all the best gigs everywhere. We'd play graduation parties at the Royal York Hotel.

A bunch of backers saw all this going on. We had this big meeting on Bay Street. Here we were, six guys from Nova Scotia in this big office building with these oak tables about fifty feet long. These guys from a mining company said they wanted to invest in the music business. They put up $40,000 [$361,420 in 2025] and we set up our own booking agency and record company [Flick Records] and all these things.

The Flick was available. Tony [Fernandez] ran it and he was getting out of it. We told [the backers] at one of the meetings that it would be a real good idea to have a home base for the Stitch in Tyme, and we could run the record company and all these things because there's an office there. We took over the lease of the Flick. We'd play there and then rehearse till dawn.

Andrew Melzer (Flick Records manager): There was a cover charge at the door. We had an espresso machine put in, and I can't remember where we got the mini sandwiches, but we did and some sweets too. They flew off the shelves. We never had anything left. Half the kids were stoned already by the time they got there.

Andrew and the Flick took a page from the Fiedlers' playbook, increasing room turnover to maximize profits.

Andrew Melzer: We figured out that we could do two shows a night. So there'd be two sets each time, one of them being longer than the other, and that way we cleared everyone out by 11 o'clock and got new people to pay money. We had jazz Saturday and some Sunday nights all the way till four, five in the morning.

* * *

Shortly after the Home of the Blues debacle in mid-1966, the Rive Gauche quietly closed. In its place was the Strawberry Patch, owned by New York–born saxophonist Jim Heineman (1943–2024), along with Tom Franey. Martin Robertson (1943–2010) was the London-born manager of the club. Robertson had been a television producer in Britain and recently moved to Toronto for marriage. He worked for the *Telegram* while running the club.[8]

Jim Heineman led the house band, the Strawberry Blues Band. Playing five nights a week, five hours a night, they took their repertoire from the Rogues, the Domenic Troiano-led R&B group that had recently rebranded as the Mandala, and from the Rolling Stones, including songs like "Paint It, Black." Other remembered covers were "Groovin'" by the Rascals and "Shotgun" by Junior Walker. With four strong singers in the band, they could stack stunning harmonies and ably cover Beach Boys songs. Each member earned ninety dollars ($813) a week.

Like its predecessors in the 107 Yorkville location—the Macabre, Le Rive Gauche, and the Home of the Blues—the Strawberry Patch suffered from its small size; seating barely thirty, it was one of the tinier venues in Yorkville.

Tim Elia (Strawberry Blues Band organist): It was so small that before we went in, Jim had to get some guys to help him to dig the basement and then underpin it, because it was too short. And that's where we're going to play.

By August 1967 the Strawberry Blues Band had changed their name to the Sunshine. They were now playing jazzy covers of "The Same Thing" by Muddy Waters, "Papa's Got a Brand New Bag" by James Brown, and Percy Sledge's "When a Man Loves a Woman."[9] The club was gone by July 1968.

Tim Elia: [Jim Heineman] signed the contract. He lost all his personal money.

* * *

Even as venues were failing, something shifted in the local Toronto scene in 1967. This was felt most acutely in Yorkville, where a critical mass of talent had assembled in a condensed area. It was the ultimate hothouse environment for creativity. With all of the competition and cross-pollination, the bands were getting better. Some seemed to be headed for the big time, also known as the United States.

Even CHUM radio DJ and music director Bob McAdorey, who rarely wasted an opportunity to dump on the alleged low quality of Canadian records, now praised recent homegrown releases. As he wrote in his

February 2, 1967, column in the *Telegram*, in which he praised the Mandala, A Passing Fancy and the Paupers:

> We've never had more really great Canadian records than right now. Just a year ago it was like a scavenger hunt trying to come up with a Canadian-produced record that would sound good on the air . . . Now the quality of our local product is just about equal to that of anywhere in the world, and there are so many of them they're given the same treatment as records from the United States or the United Kingdom.[10]

The Paupers' first album on Verve Forecast was *Magic People*, produced by Rick Shorter. The first single, the ballad "If I Call You By Some Name" was written by Shorter. Described as "hokey" by Chuck Beal, the song was not, according to Skip Prokop, "in any way, shape or form representative of what the Paupers were."[11] It failed to chart in the United States but reached #6 on the CHUM radio chart in Toronto and sold some 35,000 copies. The album peaked at a disappointing #178 on the Billboard album chart.

Adam Mitchell: We did the *Magic People* record in a not-good studio with a not particularly good producer or engineer. It just did not reflect the band at all.

The first defining gig in the Paupers' career was their opening slot for the Jefferson Airplane at the Café Au Go Go in New York. That appearance brought them to the attention of Albert Grossman and the New York rock press. The second one, which should have been their passport to a US breakthrough, was the Monterey Pop Festival on June 16, 1967.

This festival, curated by the Mamas and the Papas' John Phillips and others, is considered to be the first great rock festival; like the Woodstock festival two years later, it was filmed and released as a documentary. Otis Redding and the Jimi Hendrix Experience delivered dynamic appearances, the buzz from which launched their US careers. But for the Paupers, everything that could go wrong did.

Chuck Beal: Prior to the concert, we had spent two weeks of rehearsal time working on a medley of what we considered to be our best tunes, thinking that would be a good thing to do, seeing as we had only twenty minutes to perform.[12]

Skip Prokop: We went out on stage and they introduced us and everything's big applause and all that. We started to play "Magic People," and the first thing we realized is that [our] bassist, Denny Gerrard, was stoned on acid. That was to begin with. Then we were pretty sure he'd tuned his bass sharp. He must have been grooving out on that. So, that was going on. We started playing and on Chuck Beal's Echolette [tape echo unit]—this had to be the first or second song—the tape broke. So instead of the huge big thundering drums going and the Echolette delay making it sound like the sky has just cracked open, it was just going *wonk, wonk, wonk*, you know what I mean? These little short bursts of nothing. No echo, no nothing. It was the whole entire sound of what we had been doing. Then I think Denny's amp blew up. Then Chuck's amp blew up. This is right on stage. So now you have a four-piece band but there's only the drums and Adam Mitchell's guitar and some vocals . . . We faked our way through five more songs . . . It was like a Biblical disaster.[13]

Chuck Beal: We were stunned; this had never happened before and we didn't know what to do. What we should have done was to stop; get things fixed, and then continue. Amidst our panic, we didn't stop; we plowed on through the medley. A tragic mistake on our part. That performance at Monterey, although we didn't realize it at the time, was the beginning of the end.[14]

Adam Mitchell: It turned out to be a bit of a disaster for us. And Albert [Grossman] also discovered Janis Joplin at the Monterey gig, so we were shunned to the side to some degree. Albert was distant. It was part of this manufactured personality; he was very, very excited about us for the first six months or so. But then the bloom was off the rose.

Chuck Beal: Now, a word about Denny. Denny Gerrard was at times tough as nails and other times he was gentle as a lamb. In my opinion, he was the most talented musician in the band. He was really incredible. That was why it was so hard for us to watch him get lost in the world of drugs. Denny's drug of choice was speed. His addiction got worse and worse. He began going days without sleep and wearing the same clothes for ages. I can remember getting up in the morning, about to head out for breakfast, and there would be Denny, sitting in the hotel lobby surrounded by empty coffee cups. We were neither equipped to handle him nor could we offer him the help he needed. It was easier for us to stand by and hope that things got better. Well, things didn't get better. The whole situation was frustrating but still bearable right up until the point that he got violent. The band was really frightened. Reluctantly, we had to let him go. Later, he was diagnosed as schizophrenic. If we only knew at the time.[15]

Richard Fruchtman (A Passing Fancy bassist): Skip called me. They were having problems with Denny, I guess for drugs, whatever, I think it was after they went to New York. He wanted me to come audition for the band. I asked my parents and they said, "No, you're going to university. But I was flattered."

Chuck Beal: Denny's replacement was a nice Toronto guy from the Last Words named Brad Campbell.[16]

The Paupers' second album was *Ellis Island*. Released on July 1, 1968, the album sold poorly. The band brought in a full-time keyboardist, John Ord, for live shows, and by that summer some of the musicians—Skip Prokop, Brad Campbell, and Ord—were beginning to branch out into session work, including some for labelmate Richie Havens' album *Richard P. Havens, 1983*. Janis Joplin, also managed by Albert Grossman, dropped into one of the sessions and offered Skip Prokop a job in her next band, the Kozmic Blues Band. He turned her down.

Skip Prokop left the Paupers on September 1, 1968, and joined forces with Paul Hoffert, a jazz piano virtuoso and former denizen of the Cellar and the Green Door, to form Lighthouse, an unusual rock big band. Lighthouse had a series of Canadian successes highlighted by "One Fine Morning" in 1971, one of the first big hits of the early CanCon (Canadian Content rules) era. After Lighthouse's heyday, Prokop was a radio host on CFNY-FM. He ran an advertising agency and a jingle house and issued a solo album, *All Growed Up*, in 1977. While he was writing his autobiography with local music historian Jaimie Vernon, he died of heart ailments in 2017.

Brad Campbell was the next to leave the Paupers; he accepted Janis Joplin's offer to help to form her last group, the Full Tilt Boogie Band, along with fellow Canadian musicians Richard Bell and John Till. All three appear on her album *Pearl*, posthumously released in 1971.

Denny Gerrard rejoined the Paupers on bass and a new drummer, Roz Parks, was brought in. The Paupers began to play again, including stints at the Night Owl, then Denny Gerrard had to be fired again. He went on to record with Rick James among others. In 2025, he is thought to be living in a mental health facility in Barrie, Ontario, still legendary in the minds of his old fans.

With the second firing of Denny, Adam Mitchell left the band. He had a brief solo career before assuming the role of Linda Ronstadt's musical director in 1970. In the 1970s and '80s Mitchell was a successful songwriter; his song "French Waltz" was a hit for Nicolette Larson and he placed other songs with Olivia Newton-John and Art Garfunkel. One of his most successful collaborations was co-writing four albums with the glam hard rock band Kiss. Now retired, Adam Mitchell lives in Mexico and California.

By the fall of 1969, the Paupers had packed it in. By that point Chuck Beal was the only original member. They are remembered today among local fans as one of the most talented and innovative of the Yorkville bands. Though some of the ex-members went on to great success, it's hard not to see the Paupers' story as a tragic one, from their confident beginnings, the methodical and labour-intensive rehearsals, the local hit records and the triumphant Café Au Go Go gig to the disastrous Monterey Pop festival and the slow death of the band that followed. It's hard to know if the Paupers would have caught fire with a mass audience, even with a successful Monterey performance. They never scored a US hit, a critical metric in the development of a major act. But once Albert Grossman lost interest, their fate was sealed.

* * *

Bernie Finkelstein had met the Vendettas when they played the El Patio, and now in the spring of 1967 he was just coming off of the wild ride of the Paupers. He was also flush with cash from Albert Grossman's buyout of the Paupers' management contract. He floated the idea of building a new band around the Vendettas' Keith McKie and his original songs.

Keith McKie: He was a great manager. I always liked Bernie; he was a character. He wasn't very tidy in those days, let's just put it that way. He had a pair of boots that had big, huge holes in them. We called them aardvark boots. He encouraged our band a lot. Bernie got me together with Gene.

Eugene Martynec: I heard Keith playing a couple of tunes in the back seat of a car one night and really liked what he was playing, so we started from there.

Eugene, or Gene, Martynec (1947–) was born in Coburg, Germany, and briefly picked up the accordion after emigrating with his family to Winnipeg. At a Grade 7 dance he heard a rock and roll band, which led to his interest in the guitar. At Runnymede Collegiate in Toronto's west end, he played in a band with guitarist Dave Konvalinka, which led to the formation of Bobby Kris and the Imperials.[17]

The new band, Kensington Market, launched on June 4, 1967, at the Night Owl. Keith and Gene were joined by Keith's Vendettas bassist Alex Darou and Jimmy Watson (1950–) on drums and sitar. The band was paid a salary of $75 ($677 in 2025) a week each by Finkelstein.

Keith McKie: Everyone loved Gene, all the guitar players. Gene was our arranger in the Market. I think he took the least drugs. I mean, all of us did drugs. I did too many. Alex got too carried away and Jimmy really went overboard with some of the more, I think, dangerous drugs, like speed and shit. Jimmy was very young when he joined the band. I think in a way we failed Jimmy, because we were sort of not bad influences on him, but we just didn't become good influences on him.

***

Boris' owner Bernard Cugelman was now managing Luke and the Apostles. He arranged a return of the band in mid-April 1967 to the Café Au Go Go for another week, this time opening for the Grateful Dead. The club owner asked them to return for a second week in late May, again opening for the Grateful Dead. Recently released from their Elektra contract, the band was being courted by MGM Records, who assigned Rick Shorter, fresh off his work with the Paupers, to produce a series of demos for the group.

Luke Gibson: We didn't like [Rick Shorter]. He wanted us to start doing his songs—that scam.

Bernard Cugelman: The band became a bickering fivesome. Each one decided that they were so good they didn't need the other guys.

Peter Jermyn (keyboardist): Cugelman tried to get money up front mostly for him[self], when all we needed was a chance to work with a major label.[18]

With Luke and the Apostles away in New York, Kensington Market began to appear at the Red Gas Room. When Luke and the boys returned, the two bands often shared the bill, with the Apostles in Boris' and the Kensington Market two floors above in the Red Gas Room. Luke often wandered upstairs to hear the Market and sit in between sets.

The American concert promoter Bill Graham arranged for Luke and the Apostles to open for the Jefferson Airplane and the Grateful Dead at Toronto's Nathan Phillips Square on July 23, 1967, in front of 50,000 people, then had them repeat their support act at the O'Keefe Centre from July 31 to August 5. But by this time the group was planning to split.

Luke Gibson: Rick Shorter flew up and said, "Guys, what are you doing? Don't break up."

Luke and the Apostles did their last gig at the Red Gas Room on August 6. Peter Jermyn returned to Ottawa and formed the Modern Rock Quartet along with drummer Robert Coulthart, lead singer John Martin, and bassist Doug Orr. Mike McKenna formed McKenna Mendelson Mainline, a popular blues-boogie act, with Joe Mendelson. Luke Gibson joined Kensington Market.

Luke Gibson: We were young, stupid, and impatient. My thinking was, "Well, I'm playing blues and stuff for all these years." I'd heard the [Kensington] Market, I liked the original songs, and I went, *this is progress*.

Pat Little: If, after we came back from New York City, we'd gone right to California and played that heavy blues with big amps and the whole deal, we would've blown people away.

Keith McKie: What I remember was that the Apostles were breaking up and Luke was now a free person, to play with whoever he wanted. Because you didn't really steal guys from other bands.

With Luke Gibson newly arrived on third guitar and second lead vocal, Kensington Market composed and recorded eight songs for Don Owen's National Film Board movie *The Ernie Game*, followed by an appearance at the seventh Mariposa Folk Festival, the first one to include electric rock bands. Guitarist David Rea recommended the group to Felix Pappalardi, an independent producer who had recently recorded the as-yet unreleased *Disraeli Gears* album by the British supergroup Cream. Pappalardi flew to Toronto to hear the band and signed them to a two-album deal with Warner Brothers in early 1968.

Arriving in New York in February, Kensington Market played a run at the Bitter End and, over five weeks, recorded their debut album, *Avenue Road*, at Century Studio with Pappalardi in the producer's chair.

Eugene Martynec: It was our first introduction to a major studio. I wish I had brought my amplifier from Toronto, because I couldn't get a reasonable sound out of the amps that we rented. Not enough distortion.

Back in Toronto with their major label album in the can, the band played Boris' and El Patio. Meanwhile, their album debuted in July 1968 at Warner Brothers' annual sales convention in Honolulu.

Leading with a re-recorded "I Would Be the One," with quickened tempo and spiffy, if somewhat out-of-tune horns, *Avenue Road* started strong but was somewhat out of step with rock trends in the summer of 1968, which were moving toward hard rock and away from psychedelic folk-rock. In any case, though the single (the re-recorded "I Would Be the One") and album charted in Canada—#59 and #39, respectively—Kensington Market did not trouble the all-important American charts.

Boris' closed around March 1968. Bernard Cugelman and his partner Ryan Cove tried converting the Red Gas Room into a psychedelic discotheque, Infinity One, with "infinite" mirrors. This venture was short-lived and they closed that venue a short time later. Cugelman went on with his law career. He didn't want for clients; he had been informally advising drug possession defendants and bikers at Boris': "I had a built-in criminal law practice."

John Mills-Cockell was born in 1943 in Toronto. He studied classical piano growing up, and while pursuing a music degree at the University of Toronto he got into electronic music, the avant-garde classical world of early sound synthesizers, and manipulated tape recorders. He was among the first to perform with the new Moog synths that were appearing in the late '60s and when he encountered Kensington Market, he was working with a mixed-media group called Intersystems, which also included architect Dik Zander, sculptor Michael Hayden, and poet Blake Parker.

Keith McKie: John Mills-Cockell came along and all of a sudden we were able to do other things we couldn't do before. We went to one of [Intersystems'] shows, possibly at the University of Waterloo [west and south of Toronto] and they had a guy on a strobe machine going around this big, huge room at the university. They separated the men from the women and got them in a room, all these odd things. And they had all this synthesizer music going on. We were all really impressed with a synthesizer. We'd never seen anything like it.

Eugene Martynec: The bloody thing would never stay in tune, you know? And he played loud. So when he went out of tune, he went out of tune real loud. There was talk of amalgamating with Intersystems, and then the whole Intersystems thing broke up and John joined [our] band.

Kensington Market's second album, *Aardvark* (possibly named in tribute to Bernie Finkelstein's unkempt boots), was recorded at Eastern Sound studio on Yorkville Avenue, again with Felix Pappalardi.

Eugene Martynec: Keith [McKie] set the carpet on fire [at Eastern Sound]. It cost us $3,000 [long laugh]. It wasn't funny at the time.

Luke Gibson: I mean, some of the material, it's just, *what?* Clearly drug influenced. There's some pretty good jams. I like "Dorian." Gene Martynec played some brilliant guitar on that. My favourite part is that end part where it just takes off. Whereas, the other one [*Avenue Road*], it's a little wimpy. Frankly, Felix Pappalardi took all the balls out of the band. The Market live at that time was a lot beefier, a lot tougher. The band was so lyrical and musically classical or whatever. This was his chance to write some nice charts and get all pretty. Because he was already working with Cream, so he didn't need another Cream.

A Market gig at New York's Fillmore East with Chuck Berry and the Steve Miller Blues Band didn't go well.

Keith McKie: We were told not to smoke anything and some of us had some hash. We went on and we all started playing a different song. I don't know how it happened. It wasn't a good gig.

Eugene Martynec: Felix got the guys in the band really ripped on pot. We played the first tune and it's going along fine, and then there's a little kind of instrumental interlude that Keith and Luke would play. So they're going into the section in the end. The first note that Keith hits is a fret [i.e., one semitone] off. And he just stayed there.

Luke Gibson: Felix got the band so stoned. It was our own fault. We didn't have to do that. We used to smoke dope like crazy. I don't know if that pot that Felix had was laced, whatever, but it was too strong. It was probably like that stuff they smoke today. But we were just *phhhhh*—we really had a hell of a time trying to hold it together. Also,our buddy Brazilian George was the MDA [a.k.a. ecstasy] distributor in North America. As the Dead were to acid, the Market was to MDA. So half the Fillmore was stoned on MDA for the very first time. The band was just too weird. The audiences were more into blues-rock and stuff, and they'd never heard anything as weird as the Kensington Market. All anybody wanted to hear out there was, guess what? Blues and blues-rock. And what did I do? I just got rid of one of the arguably best blues-rock bands in North America [Luke and the Apostles]. I was in a terrible state after that. I went, "Man, did I fuck that up."

Keith McKie: We wanted to do all kinds of different things. We didn't want to be just playing R&B or whatever. That was our big failing. Luke and I had both done blues and R&B. And we were so foolish not to take that as a thing, because when we went to the States, in a lot of ways our music was like children's rock. All the songs were about, you know, squirrels. We were sort of immature, and in the States they were in the middle of Vietnam. Even though we had some songs that were heavier, they were still very artsy. We'd have little breaks in the middle, like madrigals or whatever.

Eugene tried to quit the band after the Fillmore debacle, but was convinced to stay on for the Chicago dates. In Chicago he finally walked out.

Eugene Martynec: It was pretty bizarre, that whole thing. I was really happy to get out. It got really stupid and drugged out. Things weren't working. I had no money, but I was going home. I just thought, *I don't care. I don't care how I get back, but I'm gone*.

Keith McKie: There were times toward the end of the Market where I think I'd really lost a lot of my inner core. I was just too scrambled up. Too much acid, too much everything.

Even Bernie Finkelstein, the visionary of Kensington Market, decided to step away. Doug Prager took over the management of the group.

Luke Gibson: That was the beginning of the end. He had no more faith in the band.

Keith McKie: "When [Bernie] left the band . . . that was it. The driving force had gone."[19]

First Jimmy Watson, then John Mills-Cockell dropped out.

Keith McKie: Jimmy quit because we had a to-do with him. He was having a few difficulties at the time.

Jimmy was institutionalized for mental illness at one point, and Keith suggests that he had some permanent damage as a result of the electroshock therapy he was given. In 2025, he appears to be still alive, but is unreachable.

Eventually just Luke Gibson and Keith McKie were performing under the Kensington Market name as an acoustic duo.

Luke Gibson: That didn't last long. We played a couple of places here and there. The Market was done.

With the breakup, Keith McKie carried on living above the Grab Bag convenience store on Yorkville Avenue and played the Riverboat and several Canadian festivals, including the Festival Express whistlestop tour with the Grateful Dead, the Band, Janis Joplin, Ian and Sylvia, and others. He left the music business around 1971, after which he built sailboats and worked as a cable puller for Bell Telephone, but returned to music in the mid-'70s with the Village Band along with guitarist Stan Endersby and bassist Bruce Palmer. In 2025, he lives in the east end of Toronto and still makes occasional appearances at Yorkville reunions and at the Black Swan bar on Danforth Avenue.

Eugene Martynec, the Market's brilliant guitarist and keyboardist, enrolled at the Royal Conservatory of Music and studied electronic music with Sam Dolan. Building on the experience of scoring *The Ernie Game*, he wrote soundtracks while nurturing a busy producing career. His albums with Bruce Cockburn are among that artist's best-loved. He also produced "Last Song" for Edward Bear, a major hit in the United States and Canada. In the 1980s Martynec founded the Toronto Improvisers' Orchestra, which he still leads with a laptop computer.

Alex Darou met a sad end in 1970.

Keith McKie: I knew Alex had bad teeth, because he always had a lot of cavities. He always said he'd get his teeth fixed. When the Market broke up, Alex had all his teeth pulled and he got false teeth, but I don't think he was eating well. He told someone else that he'd been losing his hearing. He was very alienated and he didn't want to talk to anybody. I left him some money because I had a little bit of money. I was doing folk festivals. I should have hired Alex to play with me, but I think I was still mad at him because he'd left.

Alex Darou was found dead in his apartment, having died of malnutrition, in 1970.

Chapter Twelve: "There was ferment and energy in that scene."

PAT LITTLE WAS DRUMMING with a band called Transfusion at the Rock Pile (888 Yonge Street) in December 1968, when David Clayton-Thomas invited him to join him as a guest on Blood, Sweat & Tears' American tour. After the tour, they headed back to New York where Pat stayed at the singer's apartment.

Pat Little: We had a bowl of cocaine on the table. I got into heroin at that time. Nobody thought anything of it.

Pat picked up a studio gig recording an album produced by Paul Stookey from Peter, Paul, and Mary, and stayed at Stookey's house in Mamaroneck, New York, for about a month. He shortly met Van Morrison, whose album *Astral Weeks* had just come out. Morrison was appearing at the Ondine nightclub in New York City, and one night his drummer didn't show up. Pat sat in and was invited to join Van's band for around twenty East Coast dates and to participate in sessions for Morrison's breakthrough album, *Moondance*. Pat remembers that he played on the title track and "Caravan."[1] After being let go from the band, Pat returned to Toronto to join Chimo!, which included erstwhile Bossmen keyboardist Tony Collacutt.

Luke Gibson: I bumped into [Pat] at one of the clubs. He said, "What are you doing?" "I'm not doing anything, really." "Well, why don't we talk to Mike [McKenna] and see if he wants to put the Apostles back together?"

We went, "Who are we going to use for bass?" Denny Gerrard from the Paupers. He was working at a carpet store or something, because at that time he wasn't all that stable in his mind. Pat and I talked him into quitting his job, getting back into what caused him all the mental problems in the first place.

We had Mike, we [also] got Danny McBride, great guitar player. Bernie [Finkelstein] handled it. We rehearsed with that second Luke and the Apostles, and then before we played any gigs, Denny had another kind of breakdown and left the band. Then we got Bruce Palmer from the [Buffalo] Springfield. He was back in town. And that was when he wouldn't face the audience. He did a couple of gigs with us, and that didn't work out.

The band recorded "You Make Me High" (True North TN 4-101) for Bernie Finkelstein's new label, True North Records. It reached an anemic #27 on the RPM chart.

Luke Gibson: Mike quit because he wanted to go back to Mainline [he left the band on May 9, 1970], so we got Walter Rossi, and then the band was becoming not what I had [set] out to do. It was so loud and nuts. It lost the Apostles groove.

The band played the Electric Circus, a new "total environment" nightclub at Queen and Church streets, and the Strawberry Fields festival in Bowmanville in August 1970. They made a brief foray into New York with a gig at Ungano's.

Luke Gibson: It was getting out of control, so I split it up [on October 9, 1970]. I went, "Okay, that's it. I need a break from bands."

Luke's next project was a solo singer-songwriter album for True North, *Another Perfect Day*. But without a tour to promote the record, the album was dead in the water. In 1975, Luke moved to a commune at Killaloe, Ontario, with his first wife. They raised two kids on a farm with no electricity.

Luke Gibson: I had a band up there called Killaloe, a very loosey-goosey band with some ex-jazz musicians.

In 1979, Luke returned to Toronto and the next year reunited with Mike McKenna along with Sonnie Bernardi (formerly of Crowbar) on drums and Dennis Pinhorn on bass for bar gigs including Grossman's, the El Mocambo and the Isabella, and an album, *Graffiti Eyes*. Luke continued to make a full-time career of music until the 1980s, when he began to work as a set painter for films.

Luke Gibson: It saved my life, working. I was completely broke. By that time I had to make a living and I had kids, and this is what happens, you know? The film union (IATSE) is great. It's a great place for misfits. They used to say, "IATSE stands for 'I Already Tried Something Else.'"

During this time, Luke and the Apostles reunited periodically, including a one-off appearance at the 1997 book launch for Nicholas Jennings's *Before the Gold Rush*. Luke and Mike formed the McKenna-Gibson Band in the early 2000s. After twenty-five years in the film business painting sets for major films like *A History of Violence*, Luke retired with his second wife to Oakville just outside Toronto. Luke and the Apostles have reunited once more, featuring Luke, still in good voice, and Mike with all of the facility of his young years, along with Ed and Jeff Ham on drums and bass respectively. In 2025, Luke and the Apostles make occasional appearances at Hugh's Room Live and the Black Swan in Toronto's east end.

After the October 1970 breakup of the reformed Luke and the Apostles, Pat Little rejoined Chimo! and released a single, "In the Sea" (Epic 5-10770), written by Pat. He then joined Rick James in Heaven and Earth for two singles on RCA in July 1971, followed by a stint in Fludd. He was a full-time musician in a series of groups, including the Michael McKenna Band, before leaving the music business for a time as a shipper-receiver and hydraulics mechanic in Midland, Ontario, a small town 160 kilometres from Toronto. Out of touch with his old crowd, he led a quiet life.

Pat Little: And then Cathy tracked me down.

Cathy Little: I met Pat when I was about fifteen. I was attracted to him right away. I guess we knew each other for about a year and a half; we were always doing things together. We started a little romance there, but, you know, I was just too young for what Pat had in mind, if you get my drift. He was so busy with the Apostles and we drifted apart. Then he was off with David Clayton-Thomas to New York City. He was gone for a long time, and so when he did come back, I never knew that he had come back. Then there was a rumour that he had died of an overdose out in California, so I always assumed that he was no longer with us. I mean, it was all over town. Even his mom heard it. But it was just one of those rumours.

My brother had taken some pictures of Pat that he'd never shown me. Forty years later, he shows them to me and I started thinking, *what happened to him*? I couldn't find him. I got in touch with a lot of people and used my own little detective work checking all of North America and United Kingdom, nothing. Nobody had ever heard of him or seen him, but I had one address of a Pat Little in Midland, Ontario. The next weekend, I took that information with me to visit my girlfriend Tish in Bracebridge.

That night, there were a million stars in the sky. It was just so awesome. A big shooting star flew across the sky. When we got up in the morning, this Joni Mitchell song, "For Free," came on, and it seemed to be a sign or something. Tish said, "Well, let's go. Let's drive to Midland and look for him." We went to that house, nothing. We went to the music store in town, nothing. The post office, nothing. And we just got back in the car when I saw these three guys walking across the street, so I ran out and showed them these pictures I had of Pat from when he was really young. They said, "Well, that's Pat. We know him. He said he was a drummer and he was in all these bands and we didn't believe him."

Pat Little: Probably a day after I met her, I asked her to marry me.

In 2025, Pat and Cathy are enjoying retirement and living in east Toronto. Pat is again writing and recording new music, making occasional appearances at the Black Swan.

* * *

The Sparrows, having moved to New York, were ready for a change of scenery.

Nick St. Nicholas (Sparrows bassist): Our [US] visas ran out, so now officially we're there working illegally. I don't know how we were going to do this, but there's got to be a way to be able to stay in the United States. The record company, they were excited, but they weren't overwhelmed. My whole thing was, *where are we gonna play*? Because a working band is a happy band. If you don't have jobs, you fall apart. That's just the way it is. The only alternative is to stay here in New York long enough to get up some cash so we can have enough gas to get to California. Go to Los Angeles, Hollywood, whatever else is out there.

Immediately following their second session for Columbia, the band packed up and drove to Los Angeles.

Nick St. Nicholas: We got in our station wagon and we headed out. I had to drive sixty-two-and-a-half hours. Nobody could drive other than me. We had all our equipment stolen the night before, which is kind of handy. We'd have had to drag it across a bunch of states to get to Hollywood. We booked rooms at the Tropicana Motel on Santa Monica Boulevard.

Arriving at Kay's old haunt, the Troubadour Club, they encountered Neil Young and Bruce Palmer, now performing there with Buffalo Springfield. Neil and the band lent the Sparrows equipment so they could rehearse and do gigs. In that long, hot summer of 1966, the Sunset Strip was boiling over into the riots that Stephen Stills memorialized in Springfield's biggest hit, "For What It's Worth."

The Sparrows were now "the Sparrow," singular, playing blues and psychedelic rock at It's Boss in West Hollywood before settling in a band house in Mill Valley, across the bay from San Francisco. There they headlined at the Matrix, and at the Avalon Ballroom they opened for the Doors, the Youngbloods, and Moby Grape. Columbia notified the band that they were not picking up their contract option, effectively dropping them from the label.

Mars Bonfire (formerly Dennis Edmonton, Sparrows guitarist): We played in San Francisco with Janis Joplin and Big Brother and the Holding Company, we played with the Doors and others, and we saw that they got record deals. All we were doing was playing the gigs but not getting a [new] record deal. So that was starting to weigh on us. And then when you had the built-in dissensions of any group, and the fact that I was starting to realize that my main interest was not being a musician. My main love was just creating songs. I hinted at this with the group when we were still in San Francisco, that I was just going to focus on songwriting and, at an appropriate time, leave the group.

By this time all members of the Sparrow were regularly tripping on acid. As LSD filtered out to the counterculture, the distortions of time brought on by a trip were having an effect on live rock music, with musicians and audiences increasingly receptive to long instrumental jams. A recently released recording of the Sparrow performing at the Matrix in San Francisco on May 14, 1967, finds Kay as the sole lead singer of the group. A highly experimental twenty-minute version of "The Pusher" shows the extent to which the group had moved toward psychedelia.

Following a concert on June 28, 1967, at the Oakland Auditorium, with a bill that included Country Joe and the Fish, the Sons of Champlin, the Grass Roots, and the Young Rascals, Dennis Edmonton left the Sparrow, and the band soon broke up.

Nick St. Nicholas: We had a blowout. Jerry [Edmonton, drummer] had a big fight with the owner of the club where we were playing. We didn't have any more dates and the band sat idle. We just wanted to take a break. We sold the equipment and I let Jerry and John take over on that end of it.

The Sparrow was no more. But Gabriel Mekler, a staff producer at Dunhill Records, a West Coast label recently purchased by the deep-pocketed ABC television network, encouraged John Kay to reform the group.

John Kay: After the demise of the Sparrow, Jutta, who had arrived in L.A. from Toronto, and I moved into a tiny flat above a garage on Fountain Avenue in West Hollywood. Shortly thereafter, Jutta's friend Jody, also from Toronto, by sheer coincidence moved in next door with her new husband, Gabriel Mekler. After Gabriel heard a live performance of the Sparrow via a tape I had, he suggested I form a new band, since both Jerry Edmonton and Goldy McJohn [Sparrow keyboardist] were also without new prospects and available.

Mars Bonfire: They invited Freddie Keeler, the great guitar player from Toronto [late of David Clayton-Thomas's R&B powerhouse the Shays], to come down and take my place. This is just secondhand, but I heard that Freddie came down and Goldy gave him acid, and Freddie had never had acid, and he was so disorientated by it all that he just went back to Toronto. So he didn't take my place.

By July, guitarist Michael Monarch and bassist Rushton Moreve joined Kay, McJohn, and Jerry Edmonton. The new band was renamed Steppenwolf, after the 1927 existential novel by Hermann Hesse. Their first single, "A Girl I Knew"/"The Ostrich" (Dunhill D-4109) did not chart. The A-side, co-written by John Kay and his friend Morgan Cavett, is pure fuzztone psychedelia, with a quasi-Baroque introduction and coda.

"The Ostrich" is another uptempo Kay put-down of straight society, of a piece with "Square Headed People." The second single, Don Covay's "Sookie Sookie" backed with Kay and Mekler's "Take What You Need" (Dunhill D-4123) also failed to register on the national charts, despite strong L.A. radio airplay.

Now determined to make a new way as a songwriter in L.A., Dennis Edmonton changed his name to Mars Bonfire.

Mars Bonfire: I then focused a lot on writing songs. I would go around to the publishers and try to get some interest. Leeds Music signed me as a staff writer. I started to listen to more and more early blues, before blues came into rock and roll, where it was basically just one person and a guitar. It had quite an influence on me. What I really appreciated was the hypnotic effect of a good guitar riff, be it Muddy Waters or whoever. I learned all these early blues guitar riffs and would merge one into another, maybe try to play it backward and so on, and that's how I ended up coming up with the riff to "Born to Be Wild." It's based on variations of a blues riff. As I was writing the song, I felt really good about it because it encapsulated my life at the time. I had just got my first vehicle and I started to drive around greater L.A. I didn't even know there were mountains there; I was just stuck in the Hollywood area. I'd drive up into the mountains and out to the beach and everything. I felt really good about the song accurately capturing my experiences and my mood, but that doesn't mean it's going to be a hit or anybody else is going to like it.

Nick St. Nicholas has a somewhat different recollection of the writing of "Born to Be Wild," placing the beginnings of the song back at the band house in Mill Valley while the Sparrow was still together.

Nick St. Nicholas: This biker asked me to hang on to his wheels till he got back. He'd gone somewhere and he didn't have a place for his bike. He said, "You can ride it if you want." I was able to start the bike, and Dennis and I headed across the Golden Gate Bridge to the Fisherman's Wharf. That's where we ran into this guy from World War II. He called Dennis a bunch of names, with bad language. Dennis had his black belt [in karate]. He gave me his glasses and popped this guy so hard, he went flying backwards into a phone booth and got stuck. Then Dennis pushed the phone booth out in the street. Dennis and I came back into Sausalito and we ended up back of the house and he scratched away on the chord changes to "Born to Be Wild" while I'm on the other side of the wall trying to go to sleep. I had to go and see, "What the hell, Dennis, you've been on this chord change for like two-and-a-half hours. Did you get it or do you need some help?" He's saying, "No, I got it." He's grinning, he had something that he felt worked. Just before that incident, I booked us into a place called the Cable Inn on Lombard Street in San Francisco. That's where Dennis saw the movie *Born Free*. Then he added his experience after he got his first car.

Mars recorded a demo late at night with his unplugged Telecaster. This original demo seems to have been lost, but a later demo that appeared on Mars's first solo album has an uptempo psychedelic rock arrangement, with Mars's soft vocal avoiding some of the octave leaps later exploited by John Kay. Mars suggested the song to his brother Jerry as a Steppenwolf candidate. In John Kay's garage, they worked it up in preparation for their first self-titled Dunhill album, recorded in the fall of 1967. The album was released on January 29, 1968, to little fanfare at first. Only after the failure of the first two singles did Dunhill see fit to release "Born to Be Wild"/"Everybody's Next One" (Dunhill D-1438) as Steppenwolf's third single in May 1968. It was their breakthrough, peaking at #2 on the Billboard pop charts.

As interpreted by Steppenwolf, "Born to Be Wild" is a perfect fusion of blues-based rock and roll with pop songcraft, overlaid with a heavy, distorted approach that presaged the heavy metal music of the early '70s. The main guitar riff, heard off the top, was Mars Bonfire's transformation of a John Hammond, Jr. blues riff, possibly Jimmy Reed's "Big Boss Man" from Hammond's 1965 album *So Many Roads*.

The lyrics are a call to action, to fire up the machine and get on the road. Car and motorcycle culture had been a part of song lyrics for decades, but "Born to Be Wild" stepped beyond that tradition. The song begins by associating vehicular technology with freedom, but with the pre-chorus, the lyrics widen into a more expansive vision of universal love and the destruction of the weapons of war. In the second verse, the narrator switches into first person, describing the pleasures of the open road. Mars was the first to use the term "heavy metal" in a rock song, thus helping to name the genre.

The roots of "Born to Be Wild" can be traced back to the early days of the Sparrows, from Jack London's singular drive to get the band signed to Capitol, through the songcraft of "If You Don't Want My Love," the bluesy shuffle of "Take It Slow," the nature worship of "Sparrows and Daisies," the heady psychedelia of "Tomorrow's Ship" and the high-volume freakout of the 1967 Sparrow performances of "The Pusher." In the summer of 1969, "Born to Be Wild" achieved genuinely iconic status after being added to the soundtrack of *Easy Rider*, Peter Fonda and Dennis Hopper's hippie/biker film that became a huge countercultural hit.

Mars Bonfire: I go see the movie. When the movie is over, I go to the restroom and there's a guy at a urinal. He was in a trance, urinating away, singing

"Born to Be Wild," and he's only heard it maybe that once. That's when I realized, "Wow, the song that I actually like myself and feel good about has connected with other people."

The success of "Born to Be Wild" launched Steppenwolf as a premier rock act, with more hits to follow, including the long-simmering "The Pusher" and "Magic Carpet Ride." After several lineup changes, including the return of Nick St. Nicholas from 1968 to 1970, Steppenwolf broke up in 1972. After reuniting from 1974 to 1976, Nick St. Nicholas led a "New Steppenwolf" band until 1980. From that point, John Kay reformed the band with new members, retiring the name with a final concert on October 14, 2018.

In 2004, John and Jutta launched the charitable Maue Kay Foundation, supporting NGOs that work to protect wildlife, and provide education to underserved areas in Africa and Southeast Asia. After selling their music business assets in 2010 and retiring Steppenwolf, they have devoted themselves full-time to their foundation.

For Mars Bonfire, "Born to Be Wild" represented a musical peak never to be equalled. After retiring as a songwriter, he sought other peaks.

Mars Bonfire: I continued to write as a staff writer, but other than the occasional song on a Steppenwolf album, not much happened. I started to become very interested in hiking and in karate. I still do a lot of hiking. Where I live in Reno, Nevada, I'm right next to the Sierra Nevada mountains. There's a hiking group called the Hundred Peaks Group and they have a list of 275 peaks and they have a little competition to finish the list. I ended up going around their list twenty-five times.

* * *

Dee and the Yeomen, the mainstays of Harry Finegold's Night Owl, were coming apart at the seams by 1967.

Terry Watkinson: The band fired Dee [Graham Dunnet] with Harry's permission. We wanted to be tough guys like the Stones, and Dee was kind of a polite British guy.

The new version of the group was called the Rock Show of the Yeomen. Finegold upped the production values and proposed a new aesthetic for the group, beginning with dyeing their hair an identical platinum blonde.

Terry Watkinson: The blonde hair was a Harry Finegold concept. He wanted everything white. It broke the guitar player's heart, because his favourite Gretsch guitar had to be spray-painted white. It just killed the sound completely.

In a May 24, 1968, performance on CBC-TV's *Let's Go*, the group performed a mix of covers and originals including the Rascals' "Good Lovin'," the Miracles' "Mickey's Monkey," and the Left Banke's "Walk Away Renée." As a conclusion to the set, guitarist John Loven and bassist Laurie Keller created a quasi-psychedelic effect by swinging speaker horns back and forth on their wires to create a Doppler effect.

Terry Watkinson: Swinging the horns was my idea. I was using a couple of those horns for the organ, and while Harry was away for a week we tried it and it was a lot of fun. When he got back, we sat him down and did the thing for him. I still remember the big grin on his face, because he thought we had the key to success with the swinging horns.

After personnel and name changes including the Yeomen and Dee and the Quotum (Dee briefly returned to the fold), the group split in 1969.

Terry Watkinson: Too many replacements of musicians, and squabbles about the direction of the band and this and that.

* * *

Bruce Cockburn was born in 1945 in Ottawa, Ontario. He is one of the most respected and popular Canadian singer-songwriters of the last fifty years, and from the summer of 1967 to the spring of '68, he lived in Yorkville.

Bruce Cockburn: My first visit to Yorkville was in '63 with a couple of friends, just going to some coffeehouses. It was the tail end of the beatnik scene and quite different from what it was [later] in the '60s. Some of the same venues were there, Malka and Joso's coffeehouse [presumably the 71 Coffee House].

He returned in the summer of 1967 to play electric guitar with the Flying Circus, a psychedelic folk-rock band with bassist Neil Merryweather. Merryweather, born Robert Neilsen Lillie (1945–2021), was a veteran of Just Us, a Yorkville-based band featuring Mynah Birds co-lead singer Jimmy Livingston that evolved into the Tripp in 1966. Following the breakup of that band, he joined a post-Mynah Birds group with Rick James (Rick had since dropped the Matthews surname from his pseudonym) after his release from the Navy brig. That group rehearsed in Detroit before a blowout with guitarist Bill Ross (late of David Clayton-Thomas's Bossmen) led to that lineup's dissolution.

Neil Merryweather: Rick and I went back to Toronto. I started looking for musicians for the New Mynah Birds. We're sitting outside in the front courtyard of the Night Owl, and the waitress calls the cops. The cops were looking for Rick, because Rick was involved with some breaking and entering thing on Yorkville at a clothes store. So they grabbed Rick and he's saying, "You got to keep going and keep building the band!" And then they drag him away.

That's when I got Marty Fisher and Gordy McBain from the broken-up Bobby Kris and the Imperials. I was looking for a guitar player and one of the drummers from the Staccatos [an Ottawa band later rechristened Five Man Electrical Band] told me about this guitar player in Ottawa that was in a band called the Children, and that he was free and was coming to Toronto. That was Bruce Cockburn.

Bruce Cockburn: He called up and wondered if I was interested. I was, because I was looking for a way to get out of Ottawa. He had two other guys he'd sort of put together. But it gelled sufficiently, at least that we thought we could make something out of it. We hardly had any gigs. We did a lot of rehearsing.

Neil Merryweather: Somehow I had the balls to go back to John Craig Eaton. Rick had introduced me to him before. I got into his office and I said, "We need help. You know, Rick's been busted, but we want to keep the band together and we need some money."

John Craig Eaton sponsored the band for a time, as he had done with the Mynah Birds.

Bruce Cockburn: We went to his house once, and his wife was—you could see the horrified look on her face, you know, hippie goons came in . . . I felt sorry for her, actually.

Neil Merryweather: He gave us money to keep us alive. We found an abandoned building downtown, and there was some old bass [speaker] cabinets in there. Like some other band had been in there at one time, and they left two fifteen-inch cabinets. I thought this was magical. I managed to plug into that. We found a way to lock the door, and we set up our shit and came back and forth and rehearsed there every day, while we were waiting for Rick to get out of jail. Then Rick and some lawyer friend of his came down to see the rehearsal and he says, "Well, you guys ought to think about going out and playing yourselves." That was the end of that connection, but he gave us the green light, so to speak, to go out and do it. I came up with the Flying Circus name. This is, of course, before Monty Python. We started rehearsing Cockburn songs.

After his release, Rick fronted a series of bands before signing again with Motown as a solo act in 1978. 1981's "Super Freak" is the best-remembered of his string of hit singles, but his later career was marred by crack cocaine addiction. He spent three years in prison for kidnapping and assault in the 1990s and died of heart failure at fifty-six, in 2004.

Among the Flying Circus's few gigs was a stint of high-profile opening slots. The group opened for Wilson Pickett at Massey Hall (what Bruce calls simply "an awful disaster"), for the Jimi Hendrix Experience in Montreal, and Cream in Ottawa. They played the Riverboat in a November 1967 listing under Bruce's name, as listed on B. C. Fiedler's Riverboat website.

Bruce Cockburn: Fiedler was good to us. I mean, he wasn't always totally easy to get along with. But he saw something in us and in me, and I definitely benefited from that. He was very proud of the fact that his PA system had reverb [echo]. I wished it hadn't; nonetheless, it had.

Neil Merryweather: We played the Riverboat and it went okay. But the songs were driving me nuts, you know. I just wasn't into that folkie stuff.

Local blue-eyed soul group Jon and Lee and the Checkmates had recently broken up, and Michael Ferry (formerly "Lee Jackson") was moving into music management. He became the Flying Circus's informal manager.

Neil Merryweather: The band became quite popular. I just didn't like the music.

Bruce Cockburn: In a certain way, there was an unrealistically great sense of how important it all was in the scheme of things. There was that sense that we were breaking some kind of ground culturally and aesthetically, and maybe spiritually. I never felt like I was a hippie, per se. There was a lot about the scene that I didn't identify with. I was the same outsider in that scene as I had been in high school and earlier. But there still was that feeling that something was cooking. There was ferment and energy in that scene, and you had to temper it with the realization that most of the people you were looking at were not really gonna go anywhere. And that there was a lot of pretence and a lot of delusion around all that too. That was pretty obvious. I got out of the Flying Circus and I was hanging around Yorkville a little bit by myself. I was a bit adrift. I knew a couple of people. I would go to Brent Titcomb's house on Scollard many evenings, because I had nothing else to do. I was lonely and I didn't know anybody. I had no money. I couldn't do anything. I'd go knock on his door, and they put up with me hanging out and doing nothing—basically playing some songs and just sitting around a lot and mostly not saying anything. I didn't contribute much of anything to anything.

Renting a room at Queen and Augusta, Cockburn developed his distinctive fingerstyle arrangements and incisive lyrics into a solo set that would comprise his first album, released on Bernie Finkelstein's True North label.

Bruce Cockburn: I was always hanging out at Le Hibou in Ottawa. Kensington Market came through there, and I met them. So I knew them, sort of, when I got to Toronto. We didn't hang out together particularly, but if I went to the club where they were playing, they'd say hi or whatever. I ran into Gene [Martynec] in a café and we started talking about making records. He wanted to make a record. So did I, and he knew that Bernie wanted to start a label.

Eugene Martynec: I met Bruce through some of the guys in [Bobby Kris and] the Imperials, because they had a band with Bruce. They said, "You gotta check this guy out: he's a good songwriter, really good guitarist." I went to see him and we became friends. He wanted to make a recording and he didn't want his stuff to be sweetened. We went to Bernie, because Bernie wanted to put a label together. Eastern Sound gave us some studio time. We did it on a very low budget. Bernie supplied some of the money, and he had a friend, Brazilian George, who was a big-time dope dealer in those days. George must've pumped in a few bucks too.

Bruce Cockburn: I knew Murray [McLauchlan] from him playing at Le Hibou. I didn't connect with him when I was in the Flying Circus so much. But later we got to know each other and became pretty good friends. He introduced me to the people in the Toronto folk scene, like the Mariposa crowd and all that. Murray McLauchlan introduced me to Estelle Klein. Estelle and [her husband] Jack were very nice to me. She seemed to be aware of me. I can only assume it was Estelle that decided that when Neil Young didn't show up to perform his set, that

I would do his set instead of him at the festival. That was my big shot, right? It put me on people's radar outside the folk scene.

Murray McLauchlan: There was a sort of tradition [at the Riverboat] that if you were a starving folksinger and the weather was warm enough, the back door of the club would be open. There was a set of concrete stairs that went from the dressing room to the club, and the artist had to navigate the concrete stairs to get to and from the stage. I listened to a lot of shows for nothing sitting on the stairs at the back of the club before I knew Burnie. That's how I met Tom Rush. He was employing a guy I knew who used to be in a band called Three's a Crowd, a guitar player named Trevor Veitch. Tom was coming up the stairs with Trevor, and Trevor introduced me to Tom. He said, "This is Murray. He's a songwriter." Tom just went, "Well, you got any songs?" I sat there on the steps, I played him "Child's Song," and he put it on his first record for Columbia Records. That was huge.

[Later] Tom Rush said, "Come on down [to New York] and we'll get a publishing deal or something together," because he basically wanted the songs [of mine] that he'd recorded. I had no problem with that, because it worked out fine. It was Bernie Finkelstein who asked me to come back to Toronto from New York. He was just starting True North Records. This is now 1969. He said, "I'm starting up a record label and I've got this guy Bruce Cockburn." I said, "I know him." He asked if I wanted to come up and do something, put something together. I said, "Sure, why not?" Going and spending a little over a year living in New York and being part of a scene there and doing a publishing deal with the Albert Grossman office, suddenly there was a frisson of fairy dust on my head. So that when I did come back to Toronto, it's like, *oh right*. And now I'm going to parties at Gordon Lightfoot's house.

* * *

One of the last groups to break out of the Yorkville scene was Edward Bear.

Danny Marks: I was born December 27, 1950. The first records I ever bought were probably Duane Eddy's "(Dance with the) Guitar Man" and Al Caiola, the *Bonanza* theme. My brother showed me how to play the Jimmy Reed lick on the guitar and Ray Charles, "What'd I Say?" My guitar heroes in Toronto were Mike McKenna and particularly Freddie Keeler with David Clayton-Thomas, who I thought was wonderful. I answered an ad, I believe it was in the After Four section of the *Toronto Telegram*. It said, "Blues guitarist wanted." I got down to the basement at 40 Prince Arthur. There was a bunch of other guitar players there auditioning. I said to them, "You can send all these other guys home. I'm here." There was a four-piece group: bassist Craig Hemming, drummer Dave Brown, Paul Weldon, the organ player who was insanely old, thirty-two years old. And Larry Evoy, who was playing with a Roger Ramjet squirt gun for some reason, and Larry was just the singer and he wasn't [yet] the drummer.

Paul Weldon: I was born in 1936 in Toronto and I grew up here, Bayview and Moore [in midtown Toronto]. I started taking lessons from a classical pianist, but I wasn't really learning anything. My uncle said, "Why don't you check out this guy Gus Hahn." Every [lesson] he gave me a mimeographed sheet with a couple of songs on it. The first song I learned to play was "Now Is the Hour," an old waltz.

While still in high school in the early 1950s, Paul played piano in a pop combo in legion halls and private clubs around Toronto. At the University of Toronto, he studied architecture while continuing to play jazz and pop at frat parties; after graduation, he worked as an architect for the Stanford Group and moonlighted as a musician.

Paul Weldon: I played at the Balmy Beach Club [in Toronto's east-end Beaches neighbourhood], on a little Farfisa organ I had. There was a bandleader there who heard me playing, and took my phone number. Later on he called me and asked if I wanted to come up to a rehearsal. I was just getting into this rock thing. I went up there, and it was an eye-opener for me as far as the volume went, because I never played that loud before, you know? Then we took a break, and Larry [Evoy] was talking with Craig Hemming, who was the bass player, and they were saying, "We don't like this guy [the bandleader] very much. We're going to make our own music." That's when I got involved in the group.

The original moniker of the new group was the Edward Bear Revue. Edward Bear was the formal name of A. A. Milne's Winnie-the-Pooh character.

Danny Marks: We had a teaser campaign. Paul Weldon was a graphic artist, so he designed this "Edward Bear Is Nice" [poster]. We had bumper stickers. We were among the very first. When we first started the band, they very tongue-in-cheek wanted to call it the Edward Bear Revue. And the Edward Bear Revue became Edward Bear, because in those days it wasn't "the Cream," it was Cream. We thought, well, okay, this idea of it being the Edward Bear Revue, people weren't getting the joke. We played at St. Gabe's church basement, at high schools. The repertoire at that point was everything from "Born in Chicago" by Paul Butterfield, "My Little Red Book," songs like that from Bacharach and David. I don't think we were writing many of our own songs yet.

Drummer Dave Brown left the band early on. Pat Little, late of Luke and the Apostles, was selling hashish in Yorkville when he ran into Danny Marks.

Pat Little: He said, "Hey, listen, what are you doing, Pat?" I said, "Nothing in particular." Larry Evoy had a place right on Yorkville [Avenue] and he said, "You can stay here if you want." I played with them for a few months.

Danny Marks: He was just an animal. We thought he would be dead by now.

Soon Edward Bear contracted to a three-piece with Larry Evoy on drums and vocals, Danny Marks on guitar and vocals, and Paul Weldon on organ and keyboard bass.

Danny Marks: There was a guy named Walter Honsberger and his partner Dan [Bartollini]; they had a place called Rendezvous Records. Walter Honsberger was also booking the El Patio. The El Patio was tremendous. And that's where Paul White came in and discovered Edward Bear.

Paul White from Capitol Records Canada had already released records by the Sparrows with and without Jack London, Robbie Lane and the Disciples, the Big Town Boys, and Malka and Joso. Now Edward Bear was in his sights. The group signed with him and went into the recently upgraded Eastern Sound studio on Yorkville Avenue to record their first album, *Bearings*.

Paul Weldon: Christine Young [Mynah Bird go-go dancer] and Larry were an item for a while. She went down to Mexico.

Larry Evoy's "You, Me and Mexico," complete with marimba and mariachi trumpets, was the band's first single, and a major hit by Canadian standards of the time, with a #3 showing on the RPM chart and a respectable #68 on the US Billboard pop charts.

From the beginning, there were two Edward Bears. There was the heavy blues-rock side, led by Danny Marks, and the tuneful pop side; this was Larry Evoy's specialty, with his gift for melodic songs and appealingly reedy voice. The heavy blues side of Edward Bear was certainly popular in their live shows. They opened for Led Zeppelin twice in Toronto, at the Rock Pile and the O'Keefe Centre. For their second album, *Eclipse*, in 1970, there was some back-and-forth about which side of Edward Bear to show for the first single off the album.

Danny Marks: "You, Me and Mexico" really did very well and everybody loved it. Then everyone said, "You guys aren't a bubblegum band, like, what are you doing?" I insisted to Paul White that we put out a heavy, heavy song for our second single. He said, "That's not how the formula works, Danny. You have to follow it with the same sound for at least three records." But we thought, well, look at the Beatles. They're always progressing. We were in a hurry to be progressive, so we put out a song called "You Can't Deny It"—which was denied.

"You Can't Deny It" reached #16 on the RPM chart, but did not make the American charts. Tensions crept into the membership of Edward Bear when Larry Evoy became a Scientologist.

Paul Weldon: Larry was a Scientologist for a while. He didn't press too hard, you know. There was an influence. I mean, at one point he was selling the *Dianetics* book.

Danny Marks: I was too young at first to sign [up with Scientology], and Mother said, "You know what? I'm not going to let you be a Scientologist. That's stupid." Then when I was old enough to decide for myself, I said, *you know, Mother was right*.

After leaving Edward Bear in late 1971 or early 1972, Danny Marks played with a succession of Toronto groups before striking out on his own as a bandleader in the late 1970s. In 2025 he remains regularly active as a musician, regularly releasing albums and singles while holding down the post of longtime host of JAZZ-FM's Saturday night blues radio show.

With replacement guitarist Roger Ellis, Edward Bear released the Eugene Martynec-produced "Last Song," a jaunty earworm that hit #1 in Canada and an impressive #3 on the US Billboard Hot 100. Paul Weldon left the group in 1972 and Danny's replacement Roger Ellis in 1974; Edward Bear performed for one more year after that before breaking up.

Christine Young: Larry Evoy from Edward Bear—we went out and he wrote a number of songs about me. And he made lots of money. "Close Your Eyes," "Masquerade," "Last Song." I got a gold record for being inspiring.

* * *

On July 19, 1966, the Stormy Clovers debuted at the Penny Farthing. This folk-rock group, a full band with electric guitars and drums, was an unusual sight at the Penny. Ever since the McHughs took back control from Brian Walker the previous summer, they had presented solo folk acts and jazz groups with the odd jug band. Fronted by the beguiling Susan Jains, the Stormy Clovers were managed by Mary Martin (1939–2024), who also handled the careers of the Dirty Shames and Leonard Cohen. Cohen, a respected Montreal poet and novelist at the time, had begun to set some of his poems to music, and the Stormy Clovers were performing a handful of his compositions. Around this time Cohen dropped into the Penny Farthing and sang with the band; this was one of his very first public musical performances.

Marilyn McHugh: In the back room of the Penny Farthing, Leonard Cohen used to come and he used to sit, writing. He liked the Stormy Clovers. He used to scribble and write his stuff on the red-and-white-checkered tablecloths. I'd say, "Stop that, I've got to wash them." I used to buy pads of yellow paper for him to write on. When he did write on paper, he'd tear them and throw them all over the place.

In April 1967, John McHugh made the *Star* by staging a week of life-drawing classes with scantily clad models. "Another first in Yorkville," he boasted at the time,[2] but later he would downplay the intentionality of such attractions.

John McHugh: That was only because there were cancellations. You had to fly by the seat of your pants, you know. Some nights the musicians [who] were booked in for two weeks said, "We have to go back." Sometimes I was really glad to get rid of them [because] they weren't making any money anyway.

Another first in Yorkville was a murder in front of the Penny on May 11, 1967, when seventeen-year-old Zigmond Nowoszynski jumped on the stone wall in front of the venue and kicked thirty-seven-year-old William Brigiatis, causing him to fall and sustain a fatal brain injury. Brigiatis had apparently jostled Nowoszynski in passing.[3] The assailant was found guilty of manslaughter and sentenced to four years.[4]

On July 18, 1967, the Penny—along with the Riverboat, the Mousehole, El Patio, the Flick, Boris', Kiki Rouge, Jacque's Place, the Mynah Bird, Chez Monique, the Putzy Futzy Discotheque, and the Strawberry Patch—were all served with summonses by the Metro Licensing Commission for operating public halls without licences. If the charge resulted in convictions, each establishment could be fined $300 ($2,710 in 2025) and would thereafter have to close at 1 a.m. on weekdays and at midnight on Saturdays. The coffeehouses had been operating up to this point with refreshment licences, which stipulated that no charge be made for entertainment.

The owners banded together to retain a lawyer for the whole group.[5] The test case was against the Penny Farthing, or rather, its umbrella company J.M.S. Coffeehouses Ltd. In the end, the charge was dismissed on November 29 by Magistrate Charles Opper.[6]

* * *

Allan Lamport, born in 1903, was first elected to civic politics in Toronto in the late 1930s. He served as mayor from 1952 to 1954. By the 1960s, despite his efforts to ease the effects of the Lord's Day Act to allow sporting events on Sundays, he was viewed as an establishment figure; balding, paunchy, and jowly, "almost a caricature of the older generation," to historian Doug Owram.[7]

David DePoe, born in 1944, was the son of prominent CBC journalist Norman DePoe. He came to Yorkville as a volunteer for a government agency, the Company of Young Canadians, and soon founded the

Yorkville branch of the Diggers, an anarchist humanitarian collective modelled after the Diggers in Greenwich Village and the Haight-Ashbury neighbourhood in San Francisco. He was charismatic and adept at handling the press; *Star Weekly* magazine dubbed DePoe "Super Hippie."

While Lamport called on police to sweep the Yorkville rooming houses looking for unmarried couples, DePoe helped to organize events like the Love-In on Victoria Day 1967, when five thousand people crowded Queen's Park, and a sit-in protest at Toronto City Council chambers. DePoe's group wanted the city to make Yorkville Avenue a pedestrian street.

Globe and Mail columnist Ron Haggart had suggested this two years earlier, in his critique of the proposed coffeehouse ban: "The most obvious solution is to ban cars completely from Yorkville Ave., turning Yorkville into a pedestrian mall, for it is the confusion, the conflict and the friction between cars and crowds which is the source of most of Yorkville's troubles."[8]

David DePoe: We were choking on the exhaust fumes, especially Friday and Saturday night in the summer. There were no catalytic converters. It was the Crawl. People were coming down to gawk at the hippies. We were saying that they should close the street so that some of these people would come out and talk to us like we're human beings. Turn our village into a cleaner place, and a place where we could communicate our values to people. We went up to City Hall and occupied Committee Room Two. They rejected us. So we organized. I went around to every hippie I knew: "At seven o'clock, we're going to walk down to City Hall Square." We walked down Bay Street all the way to City Hall Square, and we assembled. Of course, the cops followed us, because they thought we were up to something. The staff sergeant said to me, "We're going to charge you with trespassing." I said, "This is a public space. This is not private property." We decided to block [Yorkville Avenue]. We all gathered on Friday night, just west of Hazelton. The cops came and they were directing the traffic up Hazelton. We were there quite peacefully for maybe an hour or two, and all of a sudden in came the wagons and the clubs. That afternoon we'd gone to Queen's Park, we had nonviolence training from our peace movement friends—how to go limp and stuff like that. Some of them also suggested we could link arms, which was wrong. It made the cops lots rougher pulling people apart. It was bad.

The police sweeps continued afterward. With frequent arrests and routine police brutality, the Yorkville crowds began to thin. In retrospect, David Clayton-Thomas saw the police crackdown as the beginning of the end of Yorkville's glory days.

David Clayton-Thomas: Finally, the founding fathers or whoever, or the city police of Toronto, decided that Yorkville was a den of iniquity with dope fiends and sex addicts and musicians, and it needed to be cleaned up. They would pull a paddy wagon up to the Avenue Road entrance, and about forty cops would start from Bay Street with the billy clubs and they just cleared the street. You didn't move along, *bang*, you got hit in the head, were arrested, and thrown in a paddy wagon and charged with trespassing. About three nights of that. It was over, an era ended. And they did it. They did it right through all one long weekend.

Chapter Thirteen: "It finally collapsed."

CATHY YOUNG: THE FAMILY broke up when I was twelve, and we went with my father. My father took a job out west, and we hadn't seen my mother for two years, and then we went with my mother, who had been two years away with a guy, whatever. So there was no parenting. Really, we were on our own from a very early age. I followed my sister [Christine] because she went to Yorkville. And she didn't want me to go to Yorkville. I thought it was because, you know, she was my big sister and "don't hang where I hang," but she really didn't want me to go down the path she was going. She was drinking and hanging out at Charlie Brown's and hanging out with Luke and the Apostles. I started hanging out on the weekends, sitting in front of the Grab Bag [convenience store] learning how to play guitar. The little vagabonds sitting out in front—we'd all play music. It was just what you did. I was fifteen.

After dropping out of high school at sixteen, Cathy got a job running the Head Shop at 100 Scollard Street, owned by Larry Cherniak.

Cathy Young: I moved into this room above the Head Shop. It's spring '67 and I would get up and go down to the Mont Blanc restaurant and get a toasted honeybun and a tea. That was breakfast. I'd come back and open the shop. Dope dealers came through, and you'd trade a pair of trip glasses for a piece of hash, things like that. I didn't last too long at the Head Shop. [Larry] says he doesn't remember why he fired me. Well, where do you go after that? I was homeless, but I remember going somewhere and a band member who shall be nameless took me home with him. And I said, "Oh great. I'll stay here tonight." He told me I had to leave because he liked to sleep alone. So here I am at three, four in the morning, out on the street. You couldn't sleep in the street back then, because at 11 o'clock there was something called a vagrancy law, and they were looking for you. If you were walking on the street, they would pull you over. You had no privacy and you'd be in the back of a cop car, [with them] explaining if you didn't have an address, you're going to jail. So it was pretty scary.

Cathy survived by selling the *Harbinger* underground newspaper and dime bags of weed.

Cathy Young: Who cared about food? I always had smoke. I was singing and playing on the street. A guy heard me and he said, "You know, you're really good. Maybe you want to play in the Mynah Bird." I said, "Yeah, I wouldn't mind." I worked there for ten days [probably in late July 1967]. Doug Henning was the house magician. Doug used to have these marked quarters; he would make them disappear. Well, they kept disappearing. Where did they go at the end of the day? He went to pick them up. They're gone. He asked Mrs. Kerr, "Can I get change for a dollar bill?" She opened up the cash register and Doug saw three of his coins. That's [Mynah Bird owner] Colin Kerr, God bless him. Somebody said, "We're going off to Mariposa [Folk Festival], you want to come?"

I thought, "Ten days, yeah, I've been on this gig long enough," and I left. Later I came back and I was there three months.

At the Mynah Bird for an extended run at $60 ($542 in 2025) a week, Cathy wrote and performed many of the songs that would appear on her first album, *A Spoonful of Cathy Young*. She recounted her Mynah Bird experience in the song "Circus."

Bare-breasted women and talking birds are driving me insane
Man-eating fish make quite a dish for the weak, the sick and the lame[1]

Later, Cathy Young was noticed by Shel Safran, an American record producer. This resulted in a deal with Mainstream Records for her debut (Mainstream S-6121). After her second album, *Travel Stained* (GRT 9230-1035), Cathy was nominated for a Best New Artist Juno award, but her career did not take off, and she left the music business. In 2025 she lives in Toronto.

* * *

The Ugly Ducklings' biggest hit was a song that featured only Dave Bingham on vocals, backed by New York studio musicians; written by Carl Spencer, it was called "Gaslight" (Yorkville YV45013).

Dave Bingham: I was lured to New York to do jingle recordings, and once in the studio they showed me the song and I couldn't resist.[2]

The record went to #1 on the CHUM chart on October 2, 1967, displacing The Rolling Stones' two-sided hit, "We Love You" b/w "Dandelion" (London L.905). On the national RPM chart, "Gaslight" peaked at #17. But this was not enough to sustain the group. Being in a full-time touring band demanded full-time commitment; income was unstable and record royalties were nonexistent. John Read, the bass player, left first. He wanted to get married and work full time and was replaced by Howie Smith, who had been the road manager. Kevan Staples, later of the hit Canadian band Rough Trade, became the new road manager. Lead guitarist Roger Mayne was fired by the band in late 1967 and Mike McKenna was brought in as a replacement.

Keith McKie: Pity they lost Roger. He went a bit too early.

Dave Bingham: When we got Mike McKenna in the band, in order to keep him we wanted to get our recording situation going again. We had to get out of a recording contract, so we hired a lawyer and sent off the letter to Yorkville Records [a subsidiary of Arc, run by Bill Gilliland], and they sent us back this thing that was just—it was amazing, like a bill for everything. We paid for the recording of our album, as well as the singles. Yorkville sent us a bill for all that stuff, the studio time and the unpaid management fees, et cetera. They said that we owed them $7,500 [$67,766 in 2025]. All we would have to do is pay that, and they would let us out of the contract. The band was bringing in $4,000 [$36,142 in 2025] a year. And so we couldn't do it. In the spring, Mike left the band because he wanted to keep recording.

After the breakup of the Ugly Ducklings Dave Bingham continued to sing and lead bands, some of them reformed versions of the Ducks. For a late 1979 reunion, Roger Mayne returned to the fold. They released a new album and did a few live gigs but that seemed to be it. Then something unexpected happened. The Ugly Ducklings' first single, "Nothin'," was included on *Nuggets II: Original Artyfacts from the British Empire and Beyond, 1964–1969*, a 2001 four-disc box set from Rhino Records. This was the spark for a second life of the band, as a younger generation of fans sought out '60s "garage rock," the retrospective genre name given to guitar-based bands composed of untrained musicians playing at the nexus between the British Invasion and psychedelic rock. It turned out that "Nothin'"—raw, fuzzy, and full of attitude—fit perfectly into that aesthetic, seeming to presage punk rock.

Since that first reissue, the song has been featured on several 1960s compilation albums. Their Yorktown and Yorkville singles, and their album *Somewhere Outside*, have become valuable collectors' items. The Ugly Ducklings reformed again in 2001 for the album *S.N.A.F.U.*, but Roger Mayne's death in 2004 marked the final end. In 2025, Dave Bingham lives in Mexico and continues to sing and play the harmonica with local blues bands. In November 2015 he released an autobiography called *Noise From the North End.*

* * *

On the evening of February 24, 1968, after playing Toronto's CNE Coliseum with his band the Experience, Jimi Hendrix and his drummer Mitch Mitchell made their way to the Night Owl and jammed with the BTB-4 (formerly the Big Town Boys). Tommy Graham and the Big Town Boys had previously met Hendrix in New York City in the spring of 1966, when they alternated sets at the Eighth Wonder in Greenwich Village. Back then, Jimi called himself Jimmy James, and he was playing in Curtis Knight's band, the Lovers.[3]

Lance Vaughan (BTB-4 drummer): I'll never forget it. All of a sudden in comes Jimi and Mitch. Harry and Dolores, who owned the club, as soon as [they] walked in, they just went over and locked the door and the place was closed. That was it.

Tommy Graham: After he sat down, I went up to him and reminded him about the Big Town Boys' double bandstand with the group he was playing with at [the Eighth Wonder]. That's when he acknowledged this and said, "Let's jam."

Lance Vaughan: So they jammed all night. Jimi played bass and Mitch got up and played my drums. We had a great old time.

An uncirculated tape is said to exist of Hendrix playing bass guitar with Mitch Mitchell on drums, along with BTB-4 members Tommy Graham on guitar and Bill Speer on organ. At some point that night Hendrix also dropped into El Matador (the former Half Beat) and asked waitress Brenda Meecham Armstrong if she knew where he could get heroin; he apparently also asked patron David Cooper about the availability of mescaline.[4]

If Jimi had asked around some more, he probably could have easily found some heroin, or mescaline, or methamphetamine, or LSD. He could have walked across the street and up a couple of blocks to go to the twenty-four-hour Webster's Restaurant, where drug dealing in the less supervised upstairs room was common. Yorkville was a thriving drug market by 1968.

David DePoe: There were some hard drugs coming in. There was also meth coming in, which is, you know, bad shit. Some of the hippies turned to that stuff.

B. C. Fiedler: [Yorkville] was the place for parents not to let their kids go. And they probably shouldn't have. I actually lost some people there. There was a guy, a real sweet guy. He was from Belgium and he jumped off the [Bloor Street] viaduct because of the acid.

In the fall of 1968, a twenty-seven-year-old Indian-Canadian graduate student named Gopala Alampur went undercover in Yorkville, infiltrating the hippie community over a six-month period and collecting an astounding amount of ethnographic data. Alampur's notes were written up as a report for the Addiction Research Foundation. The report, as described by *Making the Scene* author Stuart Henderson, paints a grim picture. It is "a fascinating but gloomy vision of an alien community in crisis, a factionalized, dangerous and foreign ghetto."[5]

Dave Bingham: You know, all the stuff that was written in the *Telegram* and the *Star* about how bad the Village was, it was all a bunch of malarkey. It didn't get bad until near the end, when it finally collapsed. That's when all the drug pushers and everybody moved in. You know, same thing that happens with any place. Once it becomes really successful, then the scum come in and they try to take advantage of the situation.

Blaik Kirby's July 13, 1968, article in the *Globe* revealed a Yorkville music scene in precipitous decline. From a high point of around twenty coffeehouses with live music in the spring of 1965, only five remained: the Riverboat, El Patio, Act One, Scene One, the Night Owl, and the Flick. At least part of the decline could be blamed on discotheques. "Club owners are finding out that you have to pay a band every week," Kirby wrote, "but you pay for a hi-fi set (12 speakers, 300 watts, enough to fill Maple Leaf Gardens) only once."[6]

Kathy Smith (disc jockey): They had huge sound systems, two turntables, and lots of records. The DJs would always be on the lookout for new stuff every week. Every disco had a unique music preference—some were British music venues, and some were R&B dance clubs. The music was usually great, but the dance floors were not too big. That was part of the fun, I guess.

By 1969, the north side of Yorkville Avenue was dotted with discos. In 1967, Jacque Amoch outfitted his long-running discotheque, Jacque's, with an elaborate psychedelic lighting system. Rebranded as the Psychedelic Discotheque, the club operated into 1969. The Golden Gate (118 Yorkville), was opened in June 1968 by Jacob Eliav and Edmondo Ohron as a basement club with a $2 ($17.40 in 2025) cover charge for men, with women getting in free on weeknights.

At 84 Yorkville was Picasso Key Club, a private disco club co-owned by Miguel Maropakis and Carl Schrupp[7] and opened around May 1968 with an annual membership fee of $25 ($217 in 2025), but no cover charge after.[8] There was Le Spot at the Regency Towers Hotel at 89 Avenue Road, and the Putzy Futzy, a basement club opened briefly somewhere on Yorkville Avenue around 1967–68. But the best-remembered Yorkville discotheque from the period was undoubtedly the Bod Pod, run by none other than Patti Fiedler. She had personal reasons to look for a new venture of her own.

Sola (Patti) Fiedler: Burnie and I lived completely separate lives. We only saw each other at around two o'clock in the afternoon. I was in the living room, and he popped his head in the door and he said, "I want to live like Gordon Lightfoot and fuck anybody anytime I want to. So I'm leaving," and he left. That was the end even of pretending we were married.

Ten days earlier on August 23, 1967, Patti had given birth to a daughter by emergency Caesarian section.

B. C. Fiedler: I was always a hound, chasing, you know, and she was the same, trust me, because I wound up with a child which wasn't mine. And she's still my daughter today.

Sola (Patti) Fiedler: The only [folk music] person I liked was Leonard Cohen. I loved his song "Suzanne." I named my daughter after that song. I was in the hospital and Burnie registered it as Susan.[9]

Earlier that summer, Patti closed the Mousehole and spent $42,000 ($365,362 in 2025) transforming it into a psychedelic discotheque. This was the Bod Pod.

Sola (Patti) Fiedler: When the big performers, their entourages or the managers, came up to my house at three o'clock in the morning, they all wanted to go back into the womb. So I decided, to get them out of my house, I would do the womb, which was the whole concept of the Bod Pod.

Star writer Marci McDonald described the Bod Pod as "small, narrow, curving womb-like to a mirror-lined dancing nook . . . its rich, red upholstered benches climb half-way up the walls while projectors ply everchanging light patterns on the white curved ceiling above."[10] In the *Globe*, Blaik Kirby extolled its "deep, soft, entrail-coloured upholstery; curved walls; softly shifting blobs of light; and the recorded howls of Wilson Pickett . . . an entrance carpeted floor-to-ceiling in bright blood red; a 35-foot-long bas relief showing intertwined human forms in stark white plaster and styrofoam, and a circular dance floor, a whole 10 feet in diameter."[11]

Linda Buttrey (patron): You entered from Yorkville Avenue, to see a two-and-a-half-foot-tall wood carving of a hippie girl on the right side, done by Gert Olsen. There were windows facing Yorkville. On the left was an area known as "King Arthur's Court," which had trestle tables and high-backed chairs of purple velvet, very Gothic. To the right of this was the DJ section with stereo equipment, run by Michael Sanderson. Then, to the right side of the club, there were benches, long and built-in, which were in orange tweed and had high backs. Behind the benches, above them, and to the ceiling, was a huge mural. To make this, Gert glued six-inch styrofoam to the wall, and he then took a drill with a wire brush and carved nude ladies into the styrofoam. Finally he covered the styrofoam ladies with white plaster. The dance floor was round, fully mirrored on all sides, and with a light organ on the ceiling above, which was built by Bruce Jones.[12]

Sola (Patti) Fiedler: I was essentially a dancer, and so dance music was my be-all and end-all. I found folk music actually boring when we opened the Mousehole. [The Bod Pod] was known as the "FM discotheque," because most discotheques played 45s [single records, but] we played whole albums. My disc jockey, his name was Jack. He was twenty-six years old and an American draft dodger. He had the most extensive knowledge of rhythm and blues and soul music, jazz, of anybody I've ever known. I got a lot of people across the border thanks to him. They needed a note to say they had a job. We smuggled twenty-six draft dodgers across the border with notes that they were going to be a disc jockey at the Bod Pod. I had another disc jockey and it didn't work out, so I fired him. He came back the next night and slipped a tab of acid into my hot tea. It was a Saturday night and I actually had to leave because the walls were breathing. The Bod Pod was a total acid trip anyway, even if you weren't on drugs.

And there were bikers because of the drugs and because it was their place to relax. Edjo, who was the head of the Vagabonds [motorcycle club], was extremely protective of me and he kept his guys in line when it came to the Mousehole, the Bod Pod, and the Riverboat. It was a cash business, so there was a lot of cash. Everybody knew. Often there would be a police car parked outside and they would insist that I got into the cruiser, and they would drive me to the bank.

Someone waited in my house on a Sunday night and beat me unconscious when they discovered I did not have any cash. I came to about an hour later, and I got in the cab to the hospital. I thought: "I have a little girl to bring up," because Burnie wasn't interested, "and I'm not going to survive if I keep this up." The next day I put the Bod Pod up for sale.

I came back into the coffeehouse the night after I got beaten up wearing a huge pair of sunglasses to cover the black eyes, and my right arm in plaster because my arm had gotten broken. One of the Mafia people came in. They heard it on the grapevine. He said, "What happened?" I said, "I fell off the ladder." I was not willing to send them his way. They just kill people. I wouldn't say who did it, but they found out and they smashed both his kneecaps. I left Toronto in '71 or '72.

* * *

Just as the so-called "hippie hepatitis" was ravaging Yorkville's reputation, a new epicentre for Toronto's hippiedom launched a few blocks east of the village. Rochdale College at 341 Bloor Street West was first incorporated in 1964 as a U of T student residence, to try to alleviate an on-campus housing shortage. When administrators found out that they could save $175,000 ($1,522,341 in 2025) a year in property taxes if Rochdale had an educational component, it was conceived as a radical new approach to higher education: a student-run free university, the largest of three hundred across North America.

Almost free. There was no tuition fee, and rent was far below market value. Professors were replaced with "resource people" who led informal discussion groups. And Rochdale was not some walled-off academic enclave; anyone could live there, not just registered students. The *Globe* estimated that around 20 percent of the student body were draft dodgers from the United States.[13]

Much of the Yorkville counterculture gathered there in the fall of 1968. The bikers came too, and the drug dealers. Rochdale would become notorious as an illegal drug superstore, but it was also an important creative site. Coach House Press, a long-running independent book publisher, came out of its ferment, and Rochdale was home to Dennis Lee, the prominent poet and children's author. Musically, it hosted C. J. Feeny, former Sparrows keyboardist and now a distinctive guitarist, as well as early performances by bluesman Morgan Davis. Downchild Blues Band, soon to break through with their version of "Flip, Flop and Fly," recorded their first album in Rochdale's recording studio, named Sound Horn. Rochdale would finally close in 1975. Its building, now the Senator David A. Croll Apartments, is a community housing property in 2025.

* * *

At a time when Yorkville seemed to be overtaken by bikers, drugs, and clouds of infectious disease, Ian Richard "Dick" Wookey (1928–2014), a stockbroker turned real estate developer, saw potential.

Richard Wookey: In 1966, I had somewhat casually and on instinct bought [for $515,000, $4,812,836 in 2025] an exceptionally fine piece of property in the middle of Toronto. It was an amusing transaction, which proved to be the basis of my company's fortunes and most of my business activity for the next thirty years . . . [It was] a block fronting on the east side of Avenue Road just north of Bloor Street [actually just north of Yorkville Avenue] . . . It was obvious that the land was the valuable part, not the buildings . . . The adjacent corner was a gas station, and I realized that if I could buy the gas station, I would have a property fronting on three streets—Cumberland, Avenue Road and Yorkville.[14]

Wookey eventually developed this site into the Four Seasons Hotel, Yorkville's first luxury hotel. But he was looking at Yorkville as a whole, and he had a vision.

Richard Wookey: In London I had seen how attractive and interesting it could be to live in the middle of a great city if you could have all the amenities close at hand . . . In Toronto, I realized that whether you lived in the suburbs or in a city residential district, you still had to get into your car to do your shopping or go to the office. There wasn't the integrated, community feeling that existed in so many of the London districts . . . With these thoughts in mind, I began buying up smaller Yorkville properties with the idea of redeveloping the whole area. I began to think that this small old part of Toronto could be redeveloped to become an ideal city community . . . I felt that the right approach was to restore the old Victorian buildings as they came available, and to intermix residential apartments and homes, offices, stores, restaurants, art galleries . . . into this small area . . . The area was getting some bad publicity. The price of real estate crashed . . . I began buying these houses for as low as $16,000 [$139,200 in 2025], and I think the maximum I paid was $50,000 [$435,000 in 2025]. We bought about seventy houses.[15]

Around 1968, Wookey bought the properties along Avenue Road north of Yorkville: the houses that had hosted the Purple Onion, the New Gate of Cleve, Boris', the Half Beat, El Matador, the Hamburger Joint, and the Avenue Road Club/Devil's Den. He developed the block as York Square, an innovative scheme using a new modern brick facade to tie the houses together with a courtyard in the back. He installed two restaurants in the complex, which had no tenants when it opened. Soon Vidal Sassoon built a large salon, and York Square seemed to be on its way. Wookey just had one more obstacle, the hippies and bikers who made Yorkville their home base.

Richard Wookey: My main concern was a motorcycle gang called the Vagabonds. These tough-looking guys, with their equally tough-looking girls, were constantly hanging around the coffeehouses or revving up their massive bikes, making a fearful noise as they rode around and around the block . . . People were fascinated but they were also afraid to stop in the area. The result was a constant traffic jam, as the more timid sightseers just drove slowly along the narrow streets, peering out of their car windows. I decided to deal with the problem directly and approached the gang at their favourite coffeehouse.[16]

Meeting with a gang leader named Jesus, Wookey made an offer.

Richard Wookey: I told him, "Look, I'm not trying to push you out of this area but I want to restore some of the buildings. Little old ladies are terrified of you and your gang. I'd like your help in policing my corner. Don't hang around it but also don't let other gangs bother us . . . In return I'll let you have two old houses as headquarters for you and your lieutenants." To my surprise, he accepted the deal, and he and his gang, true to their word, kept away from my property.

The next problem was the thousands of kids who just hung around the square, blocking the entrances, sitting on steps, and littering the place. I spread the word that I wanted a meeting, and standing on a packing crate I addressed about seven or eight hundred young people. "You see this beautiful courtyard?" I told them. "If you do not block the approaches, do not litter, and respect the place so that customers can come and shop here, I will give you the use of the courtyard on Sundays and you can try putting on theatre or mime, or make whatever artistic use of it you wish." The proposal was enthusiastically received.[17]

Wookey went on to build the Hyatt Regency (later Four Seasons) Hotel and Hazelton Lanes, a sprawling indoor mall between Avenue Road and Hazelton Avenue. The ever-renovating upscale mall is still in operation, its new name a tribute to Yorkville's roots: Yorkville Village.

* * *

John and Marilyn McHugh, proprietors of the Penny Farthing, ceased to book live music in the late summer of 1967. John McHugh returned to his entertainment approach from back in 1960 when the Half Beat first opened on Cumberland Street: he would spin jazz albums on his fine hi-fi system. Live music or not, the Penny was largely empty in 1968. The McHughs were looking to get out of the business, and on November 20, 1968, they got their chance.

John McHugh: A friend who [had been] in England phoned and asked if I was interested in the Beatles. He brought [an advance copy of the "White Album"] in and I put it on the turntable at the Penny. By this time, Yorkville was going through a rough [period]—it was crumbling, frankly. I put this record on and everyone was just amazed. CHUM [radio] was then announcing there was a place on Yorkville playing the new record. The place was swamped . . . Somebody saw it was busy and offered to buy the place. I accepted, said, "'Thank you very much,' and that was it."[18]

Wesley Knapp: I owned the Penny Farthing [with two partners, Wayne Tucker and Bruce Newmark] from '68 to '70. We bought the name, the goodwill associated with it, and the leases to their building and the other half next door. John McHugh retained the ownership of his half of the building. We renovated when we bought it, put a new front and entrance on, and did some interior work also—including excavating the basement to install a sauna, shower, and lounge for a private club where we would host the likes of Led Zeppelin, the Hendrix Experience, and the Butterfield Blues Band after their Maple Leaf Gardens gigs. We did continue as a music venue, but not formal, advertised performances. We featured first-time live performing garage bands like Milkwood and the Good Brothers, who were friends of my partner Wayne.

Lindy Tucker (wait staff at the Penny, married at the time to Bruce Newmark): Led Zeppelin came through one night and played for free. And we had the Marshall Tucker Band, and Leon Redbone was a regular guest.

Wesley Knapp: We were shut down for the summer of '69 by [John] McHugh's contractor. Part of our deal was to build a new front. He hired a contractor from the east end, who demolished the existing front, made a huge excavation across the front, then did nothing more for most of that summer's months, which of course meant we had no business, as the public could not access the building. They didn't maintain the lease payments on the east half of the building, either. So when that lease expired, they wouldn't renew it to us and they bricked in the arch between the two halves of the building. Now the main floor was only half the size of what it had been when we bought the place, and we didn't have the use of the upper floors on the other side either! But the partners had money and used the downtime to develop the basement. When we finally won our litigation, his contractor had to finish the front in the fall and we were back in business.

At the same time as we bought the Penny, I met a Buddhist teacher. Eventually—August '70—he sent me to the Yukon to help found a "universal awakening community" there. Apparently my two partners shut down the Penny two months after I left for the Yukon; I was later to find out.

The McHughs had moved on. John enrolled at the University of Toronto studying history.

Marilyn McHugh: I had a different kind of job. I worked on the street; I went into child abuse prevention. We travelled for three years in a [converted] Greyhound bus. We travelled all through Canada, all through the States.

In the 1970s, John and Marilyn moved to the Toronto Islands.

Marilyn McHugh: I've had five houses on the island. John and I lived together on Seneca [Avenue, on Algonquin Island].

In the early '80s, John and Marilyn broke up. John went back into the hospitality business, running the café in the New Yorker theatre on Yonge Street and Chez Cappuccino on Charles Street. When I met him, John and his second wife, Patricia, were winding down a bed-and-breakfast in Jordan, Ontario. Marilyn never remarried and lived on Ward's Island for the rest of her life, a respected member of the community. Marilyn McHugh died in 2022 after a long illness.

* * *

The Flick, owned and run by The Stitch in Tyme, limped along for a few months before closing on January 26, 1969. Ron Owen, the manager, told journalist Ritchie Yorke: "We didn't pick up after the hepatitis thing, and the overheads have gone sky high . . . I predict the Village has one more summer left: it'll be a big blast this summer but by September, you can forget it."[19]

Andrew Melzer: Two things really killed that deal. One was the hepatitis in Yorkville. The investors got really cold feet over that. And the second thing is that I went ahead and recorded two songs with A Stitch in Tyme, and it was fantastic. Bob [Murphy, from the band] and I drove down to New York City to get it mixed and mastered down there. On the way back, we didn't declare the fact that we altered the tapes. [Modifying an audio recording without a customs declaration was, and is, illegal when crossing the US–Canadian border.] So they fined us ten grand [$86,990 in 2025]. The investors, after seeing the Flick closed for two or three months at that point, and getting a bill for ten grand, they said "it's over" and they pulled out.

Bruce Wheaton: Bill Gilliland [from Arc/Yorkville Records] really believed in the band and he made things happen all the time. He got us on TV shows and things like that. But Murph was kind of a headstrong guy, the leader. They didn't get along. So we just left Bill. We didn't end it officially. We hired some people to produce a few recordings, and we released a song, "Stop Wasting Time." As soon as we did, Bill put an injunction on it, because he still had us under contract. Basically that was the end of the band.

* * *

Neil Young finally played the Riverboat in early February 1969, with a week of appearances. Some of his performances were captured live and have been released as part of Neil's *Archives Vol. 1* CD box set. On the Riverboat recording, Neil seems relaxed and almost chatty as he rolls out a series of now-classic early compositions, among them "Sugar Mountain," "I Am a Child," and "Expecting to Fly." He was on the cusp of superstardom, and his club days were numbered.

When Neil returned to Toronto for two triumphant concerts at Massey Hall on January 19, 1971, John Craig Eaton got a court order to place a lien on the performance fee, to recoup his losses when Neil and Bruce Palmer pawned his equipment back in 1966.

John Craig Eaton: It was the end of my dalliance in trying to help people in showbiz.[20]

* * *

In the 1970s, Burnie Fiedler, now modifying the spelling of his first name to "Bernie," expanded into artist management and concert promotion, handling the careers and tours of Dan Hill, Liona Boyd, the Nylons, and in collaboration with Bernie Finkelstein, Bruce Cockburn, and Murray McLauchlan. But some financial setbacks in that decade forced him to sell his beloved Riverboat, the last club standing from Yorkville's musical heyday.

B. C. Fiedler: I got into trouble with the tax department, and Gordon [Lightfoot] took care of me. His manager came in and said, "No, Gordon don't do that." [Gordon's then-manager] Al [Mair] tried to do his job. First of all, I went there to ask for $35,000 [$184,051 in 2025]. [Gordon said to Al] "Okay, go ahead and just write him the cheque." "What terms?" "No terms. Whenever he can pay it back, then he can pay it back." After I paid that, there was the provincial and federal case. By the time it was done, three times I had to go to Gordon—$95,000 [$499,568 in 2025]. That was a lot of money, and I paid it back. And I was fined $18,000 [$94,655 in 2025] or jail time, whichever. And Gordon paid it so I didn't have to go. I sold the Riverboat. They called [the new place] the Ship of Fools, and I had to repossess it because they didn't have the money.

In 2025, B. C. Fiedler is splitting his time between homes in Toronto and near Frankfurt, Germany. The death in May of 2023 of his longtime friend and client Gordon Lightfoot seems to spell the end of his long and successful career as a concert promoter and artist manager. He has two adult sons, Robin and Arthur, in addition to his non-biological daughter Susan. He is, in his words, "mostly retired."

Sola (Patti) Fiedler ran the Soft Rock Café, an all-ages coffeehouse music venue in the Kitsilano neighbourhood of Vancouver, from 1976 to 1983, then moved to Key West, Florida, to open a restaurant, the Sanctuary. The innovative Sanctuary followed the Pritikin Diet, with no salt, sugar, or flour. When I spoke to her in 2020, Sola Fiedler was a full-time art weaver with a studio/shop on Granville Island in Vancouver. Her stunning and detailed pieces, including a series of large scale "city tapestries," use yarn recycled from estate sales and thrift stores. Eighty-two at the time, she was voluble, sharp, and outspoken, but she otherwise values her privacy. Near the end of our two-hour phone conversation, she told me: "I call myself Sola now because I love being alone."

The block of Yorkville Avenue between the former sites of the Riverboat at 134 and the Upper Crust at 116 is occupied in 2023 by the Hazelton Hotel, hailed by its PR department as "Canada's first and only Forbes five-star boutique hotel in Toronto." The Hazelton Hotel has sixty-two rooms and fifteen suites, and was purchased by Hennick and Company in April 2023 for $110 million. Along with amenities like a spa, an indoor saltwater pool, and a video screening room, the Neil Young Room is a private meeting room with red suede-covered walls, a long table and a dozen leather chairs. Black-and-white photos of Neil in performance, all wild black hair and flailing guitar, cover the north wall. The room rents for $1,200 a day.

* * *

In the later years of the Mynah Bird coffeehouse, Colin Kerr leaned into the more prurient side of his entertainment offerings. He put a sign up over the door, a reproduction of the "Restricted" designation on movie posters of the time, limiting entrance to patrons eighteen years old and over. The topless dancing, and then topless and bottomless dancing, continued, with the usual overpriced drinks and relatively high cover charges into the early 1970s. In the spring of 1971, Kerr got press attention for hiring a male nude chef. The bands and folkies continued, including a young Mose Scarlett, who went on to be a folk festival and club staple into the 2000s, especially after partnering with Jackie Washington and Ken Whiteley.

The Mynah Bird changed location in early 1973, to 284 King Street East, where Kerr tried to turn it into a gay club. It closed a short time later, but Kerr's attempts to ride Rajah the Mynah Bird to fame continued.

Having briefly run Rajah as a Toronto mayoral candidate in 1967, Kerr himself launched a novelty bid to lead the federal Progressive Conservatives in 1983.[21] In his later years, Colin Kerr located to Tahiti, where he raised exotic birds and married for a second time, to Gloria Tanala, and had a daughter, Miracle Kerr. Colin Kerr died in 2011, reportedly outlived by Rajah.

* * *

Werner Graeber ran the Upper Crust in partnership with the Fiedlers until around 1969, when he may have opened an ice cream shop two doors to the west.[22] When the hepatitis scare hit Yorkville in the summer of 1968, he closed the ice cream store and opened the Junk Shop, a name that recalls Graeber's admonition to Bernie Finkelstein: "Sell them junk, Bernie!" He enlisted his girlfriend and former Upper Crust waitress Rheta Maroosis to run the shop, which sold rolling papers, posters, and other head-shop items, along with more exotic offerings like waterbeds.

By 1969, the Upper Crust had closed and Graeber was running a new venture, the Witchcraft Boutique at 104 Yorkville. He had given up drinking and was slimmer than he had been in the '60s. Rheta, who was running both stores, sold a combination of imported clothing, occult supplies, and cannabis paraphernalia.[23] By 1973 Graeber had added Toba Metal Designs Ltd. to his businesses. Toba Hausman, the woman who Graeber assaulted before breaking into her house with a handgun, was now working with him. She made jewellery in the shapes of astrological symbols for the Junk Shop and Witchcraft. Toba died of cancer in 1971, at the age of thirty-two.[24]

Yorkville had changed, and Graeber was adapting. He ran two restaurants outside of Yorkville, Griffin's Café and Café New Orleans. In

1977 Graeber partnered with a younger man, Stephane Sefter, to open La Crepe Francaise at 92 Yorkville with $5,000 ($24,336) in startup capital.

Stephane Sefter: [Werner] could open a business in an afternoon. He was very quick and very full of ideas. He was the idea man.

Within eleven days of taking possession of the property, they had built a two-level restaurant of 102 homemade tables[25] and a patio festooned with hanging plants and red Victorian lampposts.[26] That summer, Graeber and Sefter opened a store called Pots and Plants upstairs in the same location and Graeber began making yearly pottery buying trips to Acapulco, Mexico, in a school bus that he had outfitted as a mobile home, complete with bathtub.

On October 30, 1978, at 1:45 a.m., Graeber was driving near Santiago de Querétaro, 160 kilometres north of Mexico City. According to the police report, he was involved in a collision with another vehicle. His lifeless body was found outside the bus, and the official cause of death was head trauma.[27] Interviewed by the *Globe*, Bernie Fiedler immediately called the verdict into question and divulged to the reporter that he had been told unofficially that Werner's money and valuables were missing.[28]

B. C. Fiedler: Werner was always still drinking a lot. When you're at the bar, you don't open your wallet and show how much money you've got. He must have done that, because they killed him. There's no question in my mind that they killed him.

Sola (Patti) Fiedler: The story I heard was that he took $150,000 [$670,258 in 2025] down to Mexico to buy drugs, and his bullet-ridden body was found. When the drug dealers took the money he delivered, they just shot him.

B. C. Fiedler: He was a wonderful man . . . a *Lebenskünstler* [life-artist].

Sola (Patti) Fiedler: He was an absolutely lovely man. He was so kind, and he was so good to us in the beginning and getting us started, but he was like that to everybody.

Jutta Maue Kay: [Werner] was just a good-hearted person.

Stephane Sefter: Not everyone liked Werner. He was a difficult person.

Malka Marom: He was totally crazy. But in the real sense. I think he was violent, also. Joso was terrified of him.

What is not in question is that Werner Graeber did more than anyone to establish Yorkville, and especially Yorkville Avenue itself, as a busy coffeehouse enclave. When he opened the 71 Coffee House in 1961, he created a welcoming meeting place for European immigrants and fostered the formation of the innovative folk music duo Malka and Joso. He ran four coffeehouses: The 71, the Inn on the Parking Lot, the Place, and the Upper Crust. He was likely the first venue owner in Toronto to hire Joni Mitchell as a professional musician, and he was the first to advertise rock and roll in the Village. His assistance in getting the Fiedlers up and running as venue proprietors led to the establishment of the Mousehole and the Riverboat, two important folk music venues. Though Graeber's shocking crimes and personal struggles cannot be ignored, he was without a doubt the visionary of Yorkville.

The row of houses on Yorkville Avenue where the 71 once stood is long gone, replaced by a nondescript brick office and retail building with a hair salon and a tattoo studio. But outside the door of the club—where immigrants gathered to socialize and sing, and where Malka and Joso found their transcendent vocal blend—there is a blue-painted lamppost with a small metal plaque affixed. It reads: "Time's passing must bring regret / If this place ever I forget—Joso Špralja 1978."

* * *

Through all of Yorkville's changes in the '50s, '60s, and '70s, the 1949 Fishleigh bylaw was very much in effect. It was officially repealed in 1982, though the new bylaw that replaced it carried on many of its prohibitions. At the turn of the millennium, the city's planning department could boast that "with the known exception of Joso's Restaurant at 202 Davenport Road, the intent of the Fishleigh bylaw . . . has been held up for over half a century."[29]

Afterword

IN 2025, MUCH HAS changed in Yorkville. Undervalued no more, the neighbourhood now boasts some of the most valuable real estate in North America; detached homes routinely sell for four million dollars, and condominiums cost around $2,000 per square foot. Rooming houses have been replaced with condominium towers and luxury hotels. Much of the old built infrastructure—Victorian and Edwardian houses—has been razed in the past five decades, replaced by sleek, modern structures. Licensed restaurants and bars abound, with Fishleigh's restrictive bylaw a distant memory. The demographic skews older now; Yorkville is no longer a magnet for the young, except in service jobs. And the district is almost devoid of live music.

And yet, much is the same. Yorkville still feels like a place apart from the rest of the city; there are enough of the old houses left standing to impart a quaint, old-timey feel in places. Even some of the '50s and '60s coffeehouse buildings are still standing, albeit with heavily altered interiors: the outer structures of the Concerto, the Inn on the Parking Lot/Charlie Brown's, the Penny Farthing, the El Patio, the Night Owl, and Village Corner still exist in 2025. The area is still full of boutiques, an unbroken tradition since the 1950s. Well-heeled shoppers can find in Yorkville the finest varieties of perfume, jewellery, fashion, shoes, and cannabis. There is even a basement coffeehouse, Goldstruck Coffee, where an Americano costs $5.30, or around 52 cents in 1963 money.

* * *

Did Yorkville's coffeehouse scene change popular music? Judged by the influence of the musicians who emerged from it and the crucial role Yorkville played in their development, the answer is unequivocally yes. But what was it about these modest venues that produced such an unusually dense, creative, and competitive musical ecosystem? And could anything like it happen again?

My research into Yorkville's coffeehouses reveals several distinctive characteristics. The most successful proprietors approached their businesses with extraordinary dedication. They worked long hours, undertook significant financial risks, and sought to book the best musical entertainment they could afford. The intensity of their commitment may have stemmed in part from inexperience: as far as I know, none of the proprietors discussed in this history had previously operated a coffeehouse.

Entry barriers were low. A coffeehouse could be opened with minimal startup capital, allowing even short-lived venues to contribute to the vitality of the scene. This was made possible by Yorkville's unusually low rents at the time. Despite its central location and proximity to the University of Toronto, the neighbourhood was undervalued—an anomaly that would disappear with the opening of the Bloor subway line in 1966 and the late-1960s real estate boom, exemplified by the acquisitions and upgrades undertaken by figures such as Richard Wookey.

Equally important was the regulatory environment. The Fishleigh bylaw restricted the issuance of liquor licences, discouraging the proliferation of taverns, which would have attracted heavy oversight. Coffeehouses, by contrast, operated with relatively little scrutiny from city hall. Functioning largely outside the purview of both municipal regulators and the musicians' union, they existed as semi-underground yet public spaces. Crucially, there were no meaningful limits on how many could operate within a small area, allowing for an extraordinary concentration of venues within easy walking distance. This density was central to the scene's appeal for audiences and its collaborative potential for musicians.

The effects of this proximity were profound. Patrons could easily move from venue to venue, while musicians encountered one another constantly, hearing each other perform and forming connections that often led to collaboration. This dynamic is evident in pairings such as Malka Himel with Joso Špralja in 1963, John Kay joining the Sparrows in 1965, David Clayton-Thomas working with Tony Collacutt in 1966, and Murray McLauchlan connecting with Tom Rush in 1968.

Another unusual feature of Yorkville was the degree to which musicians themselves owned or managed venues. In several cases, performers directly ran the clubs in which they played: the House of Hambourg (co-run by Clem Hambourg), the Cellar (co-run by Steve Ciotlos), Charlie Brown's (run by the Ugly Ducklings), the Flick (run by the Stitch in Tyme), the Home of the Blues (run by Lonnie Johnson), and the Strawberry Patch (run by Strawberry Blues Band leader Jim Heineman).

Could a scene like Yorkville happen again? In theory, if low rents and proximity to a large audience were to coincide, a similarly dense ecosystem of venues might emerge. But it is unclear whether the audience would follow.

The musical landscape has changed dramatically in recent years. In the 1950s and 1960s, music was relatively scarce and costly: radio offered low-fidelity sound, records were expensive, and folk music—cheap and easy to present—enjoyed widespread popularity. Live performance was the primary mode of listening. Today, recorded music is ubiquitous, inexpensive or free, high-quality, and portable. For many people, music has lost not only its exchange value but much of its perceived cultural value. Even if Yorkville's physical infrastructure could be replicated, it would be unlikely to generate comparable economic or cultural momentum.

Yorkville was a perfect storm of accessible entrepreneurship, minimal oversight, the popularity of live music, and profound cultural change—a convergence that cannot easily be recreated. All the more reason to appreciate how remarkable it is that it happened at all; that an obscure former village, in what was then seen as a cultural backwater, became the site of an extraordinary flowering of creativity and collaboration, shaping decades of music-making and placing Toronto—and Canada—firmly on the musical map.

Acknowledgements

To have written this book is to have received many gifts. Thank you to my interviewees, who brought history to life: Bob Abbott, Craig Allen, Rubin Barna, James Barrass, Peter Bartram, Dave Bingham, Terry Blersh, David Bluestein, Hedy Bohm (RIP), Mars Bonfire, Liona Boyd, Bob Brough, John Brower, Paul Burak, Bob Burrows, Terry Bush, Doug Chappell (RIP), Stefan Ciotlos, David Clayton-Thomas, Leigh Cline, Bruce Cockburn, Yvonne Cocomile, Joe Colonna, Joanne Crabtree, John Crone, Bernie Cugelman, Don Cullen (RIP), Pearl Dacks, David DePoe, Bonnie Dobson, Tim Elia, Astrid Elkins, Stanley Endersby, Bob Ezrin, B. C. Fiedler, Sola Fiedler, Bernie Finkelstein, John Finley, Greg Fitzpatrick, Allan Fraser, Richard Fruchtman, Amos Garrett, Luke Gibson, Bill Gilliland (RIP), Greg Godovitz, Linda Goldman, Tom Graham, Jerry Gray, Catherine Haller, Fergus Hambleton, Sharon Hampson, Jane Harbury, Ronnie Hawkins (RIP), Piers Hemmingsen, Paul Hoffert, Jeannine Hollingshead, Peter Houston, Bill Huard, Richard Hubbard, Mel Isen, Jay Jackson (RIP), Mendelson Joe (RIP), Gord Josie (RIP), John Kay, Jutta Maue Kay, Steve Kennedy, Jack King, Stan Klees (RIP), Deborah Lake, Robbie

Lane, Larry LeBlanc, Bernie Letofsky, Joe Lewis, Monique Lips, Anni Lissee, Cathy Little, Pat Little, Alexander Mair (RIP), Cheryl Mandel, Mitch Markowitz, Danny Marks, Dave Marden, Malka Marom, Rheta Maroosis, David Marsden, Eugene Martynec, Rickman Mason, Brian Massey, John McHugh, Marilyn McHugh (RIP), Mike McKenna, Keith McKie, Andrew Melzer, Eric Mercury (RIP), Neil Merryweather (RIP), Marty Morin, Bram Morrison, Vivienne Muhling, George Olliver (RIP), Judith Orban, Shelley Posen, Tony Quarrington, Noni Raitblat, Chick Roberts (RIP), Beverlie Robertson, Duff Roman, Ed Roth, Elena Saldini (RIP), Jean-Marc Saldini, Arlene Sarner, Virgil Scott, Stephane Sefter, Norm Sherratt, Sam Shirose, Dan Sneddon, Eddie Sokoloff, John Soules, Leo and Shirley Špralja, Denyse Sterio, Nick St. Nicholas, Phyllis Taylor, Vicky Taylor (RIP), Brent Titcomb, Gary Topp, Lindy Tucker, Sylvia Tyson, Klaas VanGraft (RIP), Joe Van Rossem, Lance Vaughan, Terry Watkinson (RIP), John Wetherell, Bruce Wheaton, Tom Wilson, Barry Witkin, Cathy Young, Christine Young (RIP), and Mary Jane Young.

Thank you to those who connected me to the interviewees: Jaymz Bee, Brian Blain, Colin Bray, Paul DeLong, Alec Fraser, Susan Freedman, Eliza Rose Gamble, Gaye Gergley, Sandy Kilgour, Doug Lounsbury, Jennifer Marcoux, Catherine Oxenburg, Lynda Rapp, Lynda Roth, Lenny Shirose, Val Stevens, and Chloe Watkinson. For helpful information and materials, thank you Will Cardinal, Gary Cristall, John Harris, Jan Haust, Nate Hendley, Jay Jackson (RIP), Miracle Kerr, Wesley Knapp, Bill Prosser, Ted Roberts, Don Robinson, Linda Shilling, Tom Taylor, Jaimie Vernon. For access to materials and background information, thank you Ralph Robert Coram, Eddy Curtis, Greg Hobbs, Cathie Jacobs, George Blake, David Lennick, Aaron Lusch, Elaine Magder, Bruce Marshman, Cliff Martin, Gord Martineau, Doug McClement, Jane Moore, David Reville, Ben Shulman, Marna Snitman (RIP), Russell Strathdee, Frank and Rita Troiano, Debra Valevicius, Duke Wilson, Yedi Zak, and Alan Zweig.

Thank you to my former thesis supervisor, friend, and mentor, Rob Bowman, for encouragement and needed criticism. Likewise, Mark Miller, who gave early encouragement and advice and shared critical materials with me. For inspiration, encouragement, and oblique Joni access, thank you to Cameron Crowe. For your tireless work collecting, compiling, and contextualizing the newspaper listings of the Yorkville venues, thank you Doug Harper. Doug, I couldn't have written this book without you.

To the members of my Facebook groups *The Toronto Sound 1955-1975* and *Yorkville Music Scene 1954-1968*, thank you for sharing your memories, pictures, clippings, and more. You have been an invaluable community for me over the years of research and writing. Gerry Miskolczi and his Facebook group *Canadian Records & Artists Appreciation Society* likewise were an essential source of connections and information.

The original Yorkville historians: Stuart Henderson, Michael Panontin, Nick Warburton, and Nicholas Jennings, thank you. Nicholas in particular has been helpful in my research, sharing his ongoing discoveries and connecting me with elusive interviewees.

Thank you to Shaughnessy Bishop-Stall and his 2023–24 Zoom writers' groups for encouragement, criticism, and a crash course in writing.

From Sutherland House, thank you to Ken Whyte for believing in my project, to managing editor Shalomi Ranasinghe and editors Michael Barclay and Kimberlene Francis. For connecting me with Sutherland House, thank you to Deirdre Kelly.

Thanks to Daniel Norman and Steven Mackison at Church of the Redeemer for giving me the time off I needed to get this project over the finish line. Thanks also to my daughter Rowen Daley for the spiffy map.

And to Jill: my love, my partner in the journey of discovery that is our life together, my first reader, thank you for sharing this adventure with me.

Notes

CHAPTER ONE

1 Johnson, William, "The Street Where the Action Isn't," *Globe and Mail*, August 17, 1968.
2 Henderson, Stuart, "Toronto's Hippie Disease: End Days in the Yorkville Scene, August 1968." *Journal of the Canadian Historical Association* (January 17, 2006). Accessed October 16, 2022 at https://www.erudit.org/fr/revues/jcha/2006-v17-n1-jcha1776/016108ar.pdf, p. 208ff.
3 "Yorkville's Hepatitis Hits Police," *Toronto Daily Star*, August 8, 1968.
4 "Dirty Needles Blamed in Yorkville Hepatitis," *Toronto Daily Star,* February 12, 1969.
5 Reid, John, *The Faithless Mirror* (Darkwood Press, 1974), p. 11.
6 Since his descendants sometimes spelled the family name as Bloore, some controversy exists among local historians about the proper spelling. I use the spelling Bloor himself used in his signature.
7 Arthur, Eric, *No Mean City* (University of Toronto Press, 1964), p. 56.
8 Noakes, C. Taylor, "Joseph Bloor," *The Canadian Encyclopedia*. Accessed January 14, 2023 at https://www.thecanadianencyclopedia.ca/en/article/joseph-bloor.
9 "Billy Saunders Recalls Big Blaze at the Globe," *Globe*, January 8, 1934. The nickname might also have referred to the slaughterhouse on Sydenham.
10 Tiel, Jane, "The Changing Face of Cumberland Street," *Globe and Mail*, March 8, 1958.
11 Wise, Leonard, and Allan Gould, *Toronto Street Names: An Illustrated Guide to their Origins* (Firefly, 2024), p. 86.
12 Toronto city council minutes, Appendix A, Committee on Property Report No. 7 (1956), p. 1405.
13 Tiel, "The Changing Face of Cumberland Street."
14 Toronto city council minutes, Appendix A, Committee on Property Report No. 12 (1956), p. 2081.

15 Bylaw 17544: "A bylaw to restrict to use for certain residential purposes lands, buildings and structures within the area bounded by the rear limits of Avenue Road, Davenport Road, Bay Street and Bloor Street properties and to use for certain commercial purposes lands, buildings and structures on the said streets."

16 "Housing Study Approved: Bylaw Vote Reversed in '56 Council Windup," *Globe and Mail*, November 6, 1956.

17 Horne, Alistair, *But What Do You Actually Do?: A Literary Vagabondage* (Weidenfeld and Nicholson, 2011). Accessed August 3, 2021 at https://books.google.ca/books?id=ZNE9CQAAQBAJ.

18 Lewis, Wyndham, "On Toronto," *Routledge Library Editions: Wyndham Lewis* (Routledge, 2021), p. 327.

19 Jukes, Mary, "New Coffeehouse Avoids Ham Sandwich, Chrome," *Globe and Mail*, July 7, 1955.

20 No title, *Vancouver News-Herald*, April 30, 1955.

21 The Concerto was closed on Sundays, like almost every other non-essential business as required by the Lord's Day Act, a federal statute in effect in Canada from 1906 to 1985.

22 I believe that Greg Curtis was the first folk musician to have steady employment in a Toronto venue. One possible antecedent is Merrick Jarrett (1924–2005), who had been singing folk music on various Toronto radio stations since 1946, though there don't seem to have been any dedicated folk music venues for him to play. His name does not appear in the listings for any of the Yorkville coffeehouses.

23 Greg's professional theatrical debut was in the fall of 1948, in the New Play Society's production of *You Never Can Tell*. In August 1949, he appeared with the Midland Players, a semiprofessional theatre group, in *Arsenic and Old Lace* at the Brant Inn in Burlington.

24 "Former Cariboo Boy With Midland Players," *Quesnel Cariboo Observer*, October 20, 1949.

25 Whittaker, Herbert, "Show Business," *Globe and Mail*, October 4, 1951.

26 Whelan, Barbara, "Sing a Song of Folk-Singing," *Toronto Telegram*, April 26, 1957.

27 For conversions into 2025 dollar amounts, I've relied on the Bank of Canada's Inflation Calculator at https://www.bankofcanada.ca/rates/related/inflation-calculator/.

28 The live music business of the 1950s and '60s was inextricably linked to the American Federation of Musicians, or AF of M, represented in Toronto by the Toronto Musicians' Association, or TMA. Founded in 1887 as the Toronto Orchestral Association, the TMA by the 1950s was ubiquitous in the local music industry, controlling wages and contracting from Massey Hall to the smallest clubs.

29 "A Bylaw to amend Bylaw no. 17544 so as to permit the use of premises Avenue Road 32 as a coffee shop" (June 5, 1955).

30 Bob Sterio's father, Steve, ran Sterio's Tavern at 431 College Street, later the site of the long-running music venue and bar Sneaky Dee's.

31 Jukes, "New Coffeehouse Avoids Ham Sandwich, Chrome"

32 Jukes, Mary, "Recipes for Continental Gateaux Offered in Time for Your Christmas Baking," *Globe and Mail*, December 8, 1955.

33 Cristall, Gary, "Folk Music In Canada," unpublished manuscript.

34 "Two Firemen Fire Casualties," *Toronto Daily Star*, December 14, 1959.

35 In July 2020, after two years of research into Greg Curtis's life, I unexpectedly reached his ninety-one-year-old twin brother, Allan, by telephone, living in Quesnel, British Columbia, not far from their hometown of Barkerville. My inquiries were unwelcome; Allan declined to speak with me at all. In a subsequent email, his daughter Eddy Curtis filled me in on some details of Greg's early life and wrote, "It's because my uncle was gay is why my dad had nothing to do with him," a brief synopsis summing up an undoubtedly painful story.

36 Koch, Eric, *The Brothers Hambourg* (Robin Brass, 1997), p. 145.

37 See, for example, classified ad, *Toronto Daily Star*, August 24, 1946.

38 Koch, *The Brothers Hambourg*, p. 213.

39 "Clem Hambourg Guests on PM Party," *Ottawa Citizen*, December 5, 1959.

40 Koch, *The Brothers Hambourg*, p. 211.

41 French, William, "Cool Music and Hot Coffee Go Down Well after Hours," *Globe and Mail*, June 11, 1960.

42 Ibid.

43 Ibid.

44 Ibid.

45 Hambourg, Ruth-Nadine, "One Night at the House of Hambourg," Hambourg Family Papers. Fonds 2, Series 1243, File 5. City of Toronto Archives. This account of the capacity of the Cumberland location is contradicted in the June 11, 1960 William French *Globe* article, which claims a total capacity of 150.

46 Rantin, Stan, "Play Jazz 'Till 3 A.M. in Sound-proof Room of Classical Pianist," *Toronto Daily Star*, May 17, 1956. This description is also informed by observation of the House of Hambourg scenes in Sidney J. Furie's 1959 film *A Cool Sound from Hell*. https://vimeo.com/98585363

47 "The House That Jazz Built," *Ottawa Citizen*, November 16, 1957.

48 Rantin. As pointed out to me by Mark Miller, the House of Hambourg co-existed with a few other clubs: Melody Mill (mid-'50s), George's Spaghetti House (1956–1984), and the MINC Club (1959–1960) all offered modern, largely improvised small-group jazz to Toronto audiences in this period.

49 "The House That Jazz Built"

50 "House of Hambourg Balance Sheet," Stern, Sanders and Company, April 18, 1955. Clement Hambourg Papers, Library and Archives Canada MUS 25, Box: 1, Folder 1, Page 2.

51 "Jazz Club for Sale - But Not to Anyone," *Globe and Mail*, June 2, 1962.

52 "Hambourg House Healthier After Jazzmen's Concert," *Globe and Mail,* July 25, 1962.

CHAPTER TWO

1 Schafer, Ted, "Schafer Says: Folknicks Arise," *The Varsity*, November 11, 1960.

2 Brawley, Peter, "Critic in the Dark," *The Varsity*, March 7, 1960.

3 Adilman, Sid, "Folk-Song-Till-Dawn Clubs Booming: 3,500 Are Members" *Toronto Daily Star*, August 20, 1960.

4 Display ad, *The Varsity*, March 11, 1960.

5 Toronto city council minutes, Appendix "A," Committee on Property Report, No. 2, p. 663.

6 Bylaw No. 20623, "To regulate the use of land and the erection, use, bulk, height, spacing of and other matters relating to buildings and structures and to prohibit certain uses of lands and the erection and use of certain buildings and structures in various areas of the City of Toronto."

7 Berton, Pierre, "With Notebook and Pencil Through the Land of the Folkniks," *Toronto Daily Star*, November 23, 1960.

8 Dobson performed "Sing Like a Swallow," as opposed to most other versions of the same song titled "She's Like the Swallow."

9 Adilman, "Folk-Song-Till-Dawn Clubs Booming: 3,500 Are Members."

10 Jennings, Nicholas, *Before the Gold Rush* (Toronto: Viking, 1997), p. 23.

11 The Clef Club's name referred to an element of musical notation, but just as likely, it recalled the Clef Club of Harlem, an important musicians' association founded by James Reese Europe in 1912.

12 Adilman, "Folk-Song-Till-Dawn Clubs Booming: 3,500 Are Members."

13 Ibid.

14 Schafer, "Schafer Says: Folknicks Arise."

15 Berton, "With Notebook and Pencil Through the Land of the Folkniks." Berton was darkly alluding to the Springhill (Nova Scotia) Mine Disasters of 1891, 1956, and 1958. The last of these killed seventy-five miners.

16 Larry Dolgay is the brother of Sid Dolgay of the Travellers; Adam Timoon later appeared at the Concerto Café as a solo act, and continued to perform in the Toronto area into the 2010s.

17 The Farnham folk club appears to have been a private hootenanny on Farnham Avenue in the Summerhill area of Toronto in the '50s.

18 Tyson, Sylvia, "Mariposa Full of Bittersweet Memories for Sylvia," *Toronto Star*, July 26, 1985.

19 Berton, "With Notebook and Pencil Through the Land of the Folkniks."

20 The single microphone that connected to the Onion's sound system was a high-quality but already-antique Shure 730b, a "crystal" type of unidirectional microphone first introduced in 1939.

21 McHarg, Jim, liner notes to Jim McHarg's Metro Stompers featuring Lonnie Johnson, *Stompin' at the Penny*, Columbia CK 57829 (1965).

22 Adilman, Sid, "Sweet Song of Success," *Toronto Telegram*, December 7, 1964.

23 Giacomo Zuccarini imported the first Gaggia machine to Toronto, and his namesake company is still the Italian company's premier Canadian importer.

24 Adilman, "Sweet Song of Success."

25 Duff, Morris, "Jazz Declines and Folk Music Soars," *Toronto Daily Star*, December 30, 1961.

26 Adilman, "Sweet Song of Success."

27 Ibid.

CHAPTER THREE

1 Berton, Pierre with Henri Rossier. *The New City: A Prejudiced View of Toronto* (Toronto: Macmillan, 1961), pp. 27–28.

2 Jahner, Harald, *Aftermath: Life in the Fallout of the Third Reich, 1945–1955* (Knopf, 2019), p. 56.

3 "Africa, Asia and Europe, Passenger Lists of Displaced Persons, 1946–1971" Ancestry.ca, Accessed April 1, 2021 at https://www.ancestry.ca/search/collections/61704/.

4 In B. C. Fiedler's remembrance.

5 "Charge Two Servants in Jewel Theft," *Toronto Daily Star*, June 24, 1961.

6 "Commission Raps Methods: Order More Restraint in House Party Raids," *Toronto Daily Star*, August 18, 1961.

7 Berton, Pierre, "The Unexpected Aftermath of a Typical Toronto House Party," *Toronto Daily Star*, July 31, 1961.

8 "Commission Raps Methods: Order More Restraint in House Party Raids," *Toronto Daily Star*, August 18, 1961.

9 Duff, Morris, "Jazz Declines and Folk Music Soars" *Toronto Daily Star*, December 30, 1961.

10 Though "71 Coffee House" appears to have been the actual name of the club, some sources refer to it as the 71 Club or even Club 71, as the venue is remembered on the *Yorkville Music Scene* historical plaque erected by Heritage Toronto and installed on Cumberland Street. The plaque also cites 1959 as the 71's opening, but this appears to be based on B. C. Fiedler's faulty remembrance and is not supported by documentary evidence.

11 Berton, Pierre, "How Did Those Reefers Get in That Yorkville Coffeehouse?," *Toronto Daily Star*, May 1, 1962.

12 No one I've spoken to who went to the 71 remembers Graeber himself selling cannabis, though others may have been plying their trade discreetly in dark corners of the club. David DePoe remembered buying his first joint there, for a dollar. Others remembered buying pot from Graeber in the 1970s.

13 "Mingled with Patrons: Coffee Cops Had Eye on House," *Globe and Mail*, November 2, 1961.

14 "Claim Lie Detector Supported Graebers," *Globe and Mail*, April 27, 1962.

15 Ibid.

16 Duff, "Jazz Declines and Folk Music Soars."

17 "Folk Guild Now in Toronto," *The Mariposa Folk Festival Gazette* 1/1.

18 Thomas, Ralph, "Let's Meet at a Sidewalk Café," *Toronto Daily Star*, July 27, 1963.

19 Adilman, "Sweet Song of Success," *Toronto Telegram*, December 7, 1964.

20 Duff, "Jazz Declines and Folk Music Soars."

21 Adilman, "Sweet Song of Success."

22 Chapman, Carol, "Coffee-House Art Is Haphazard," *Globe and Mail*, November 10, 1962.

23 Berton, Pierre, "Potpourri: The Canadian Way of Life," *Toronto Daily Star*, June 8, 1962.

24 Adilman, "Sweet Song of Success."

25 Carson, Jo, "Today Is Freer: Teachers Tell of Projects," *Globe and Mail*, December 3, 1962.

26 Duff, "Jazz Declines and Folk Music Soars."

27 Display ad, *Toronto Daily Star*, December 8, 1961.

28 Carson, "Today Is Freer: Teachers Tell of Projects."

29 Adams, James, "Art Dealer Walter Moos, 'The father of Yorkville,'" *Globe and Mail*, July 5, 2013. Accessed August 2, 2022 at https://www.theglobeandmail.com/news/toronto/art-dealer-walter-moos-the-father-of-yorkville/article13050074/.

30 Dubro, James, *Mob Rule: Inside the Canadian Mafia* (Macmillan, 1985), p. 69.

31 Boxer, Rosemary, "Toronto's Rollicking New Night Life," *Toronto Telegram*, April 21, 1963.

32 Batten, Jack, "Jazz: Young man with a big future and a pleasant drinking problem," *Maclean's*, April 4, 1964.

33 Hedy appears prominently in *The Accountant of Auschwitz*, a 2018 documentary film.

34 Display ad, *Toronto Daily Star*, December 9, 1961.

35 "Toronto This Week," *Toronto Daily Star*, July 28, 1962.

36 Caplan, Dave, "Man About Jazz: Don't Have to Dig Deep to Dig the 'Cavemen'" *Toronto Daily Star*, September 8, 1962.

37 "Toronto This Week," *Toronto Daily Star*, September 8, 1962.

38 The Village Vanguard live recording was released on the Kapp LP *Jackie Gleason Says No One in This World Is Like Don Francks* (Kapp, KRL 4501, 1963); the latter was released on CD as *Live at The Purple Onion* (Art of Life Records AL1009-2, 2004).

39 "Folk Song 'Hootenany'[sic] to Reopen Village Corner," *Toronto Daily Star*, June 22, 1962.

40 Ibid.

CHAPTER FOUR

1 Thomas, Ralph, "'Let's Meet at a Sidewalk Café,'" *Toronto Daily Star*, July 27, 1963.

2 "Coffee-House Man Fined for 3 a.m. Noises," *Globe and Mail*, September 22, 1962.

3 Berton, Pierre. "Let's All Give a Lusty Cheer for the Good Old Morality Squad," *Toronto Daily Star*, September 27, 1962.

4 Mariposa Festival programme (1963). Accessed July 26, 2025 at https://digital.library.yorku.ca/node/687900.

5 Klapa is the name given to male quintets or larger who sing traditional Dalmatian songs, often on seafaring themes, with strong belting voices and resonant block harmonies.

6 Sloan, Kathleen, "Joso Špralja: A Passionate Voice of Creativity and Song," *Toronto Star*, March 27, 1994.

7 Streaming at the Spielberg Jewish Film Archive https://www.youtube.com/watch?v=B8ETNGEqvYQ.

8 Kassner, Eli, *Allegro vivace con brio: The Life of Eli Kassner*, privately published, 2016.

9 Malka remembers the pay as $500 ($5,101) a week for the pair.

10 Marom, Malka, liner notes, *Malka & Joso Forever* (EMI Music Canada, 2000).

11 Ibid.

12 Schafer, Ted, "Mariposa: A Review, a Symposium, a Workshop," *Hoot*, No. 2 (1963).

13 Townson, Don, "Coffeehouses Dent Teen Budget," *Toronto Daily Star*, May 22, 1964.

14 Barker, Gerry, "In Town and Out," *Toronto Daily Star*, February 7, 1963.

15 Wordsworth, Simon, *Zal! An Oral History of Zalman Yanovsky* (self-published, 2022) loc 859 of 1272 (Kindle edition).

16 CTV News segment, May 7, 2016. Accessed September 17, 2025 at https://youtu.be/LHlZU3pMnlI?si=y5AmXHKEQnsTHaj4.

17 Ibid. Contradicting Lightfoot's story, John Court told writer Nicholas Jennings in 1996 that it was Steele's Tavern where he first heard Lightfoot: *Lightfoot* (Viking, 2017), p. 48.

18 Rockman, Arnold, "Coffeehouses for Hipsters, Squares," *Toronto Daily Star*, August 1, 1964.

19 Letter to the editor, *Globe and Mail*, February 12, 1969.

20 "Yorkville Association Underlines Sophistication, Rejects Bohemia," *Globe and Mail*, March 3, 1964.

21 Bylaw 22200, "To amend bylaw no. 20623 respecting certain lands abutting Avenue Road, Yorkville Avenue and Cumberland Street" (June 20, 1954).

22 "Or how to murder Yorkville," *Globe and Mail*, February 8, 1969.

23 Luke Gibson among many others I interviewed attended the Concord Tavern matinees. He likens the experience to "getting hit with a baseball bat."

CHAPTER FIVE

1 Thanks to Mark Miller for this information from *Coda Magazine* issues of the time.

2 Facebook comment, *Yorkville Music Scene 1955-1968* group, June 18, 2021.

3 The Black Eagle Jazz Band album can be heard at https://www.youtube.com/watch?v=Tdhpm6tTzhQ.

4 Reguly, Robert, "Yorkville: Hopes Are High for the Future," *Toronto Daily Star*, May 14, 1964.

5 Ibid.

6 "Youth Run Wild, Rock Yorkville Cars," *Toronto Daily Star*, May 11, 1964.

7 Henderson, Stuart, *Making the Scene: Yorkville and Hip Toronto in the 1960s* (University of Toronto Press, 2011), p. 78.

8 Duff, Morris, "Yorkville: The Sad Village," *Toronto Daily Star*, May 30, 1964, p. 26.

9 Lou Curtiss's historical account of the San Diego folk music coffeehouses has them virtually disappearing by the mid-'60s. Accessed July 18, 2025 at https://sandiegotroubadour.com/the-local-coffeehouse-scene-back-in-the-day/.

10 Thomas, Ralph, "Joe, Eddie Light up the Onion," *Toronto Daily Star*, November 12, 1964.

11 Hesse, Jurgen, "Coffeehouses: Has the Zest Gone Out of Yorkville Village?" *Globe and Mail*, June 27, 1964.

12 Barker, Gerry, "In Town & Out," *Toronto Daily Star*, April 3, 1963.

13 Caplan, Dave, "Man About Jazz: Your Guide to After-Hour Coffeehouse Goings-On," *Toronto Daily Star*, April 27, 1963.

14 Duff, Morris, "You Wouldn't Recognize First Folksong Club," *Toronto Daily Star*, July 20, 1963.

15 Barker, Gerry, "In Town & Out," *Toronto Daily Star*, April 17, 1963.

16 Duff, "You Wouldn't Recognize First Folksong Club."

17 Abrams would go on to manage the careers of magician Doug Henning and folk musician Rick Fielding until her death around 2002.

18 Hanlon, Michael, "Smoking Researcher Seeks Volunteers," *Globe and Mail*, January 27, 1965.

19 Duff, Morris, "Teeny Boppers Are C-o-o-ling Yorkville," *Toronto Daily Star*, May 21, 1966.

20 Barker, "In Town & Out," *Toronto Daily Star*, September 24, 1963.

21 Caplan, Dave, "Hymn to Freedom Tops for Oscar Peterson," *Toronto Daily Star*, December 14, 1963.

22 Hanlon, Michael, "Mariposa Festival (Winter Version)," *Globe and Mail*, January 23, 1965.

23 Schiff, Marvin, "Enjoyment Infectious: Flamboyance Shown by Greenbriar Boys," *Globe and Mail*, January 28, 1965.

24 This was confirmed by the late Doug Chappell, bassist with Richie Knight and the Mid-Knights, a popular local rock and roll band at the time with a #1 hit on CHUM radio, "Charlena." He recalled a commonplace situation where a band would finish the last night of their contract. They would then be given a cheque for the contracted amount, which they would then endorse for cash. This cash amount was always lower than the cheque amount—the real price was negotiated separately—and the union was none the wiser.

25 Thody, Ron, "A Peek through the Mousehole," *Satyrday*, Fall 1966.

26 While various art studios did occupy 113 Yorkville at the same time as the Mousehole, none of them can be definitively connected to Albert Volpe. For a time, 113 was occupied in the late 1960s by the studio of Norman Elder, a well-known art collector and Toronto eccentric.

27 The Toronto property assessment rolls for 1965 list Shirley and Albert Volpe as tenants of 134 Yorkville Avenue, the Riverboat's address.

28 "Memorandum: La Cosa Nostra." Accessed July 21, 2025 at https://www.archives.gov/files/research/jfk/releases/docid-32576140.pdf.

CHAPTER SIX

1 Barker, Gerry, "In Town & Out," *Toronto Daily Star*, April 16, 1964.

2 "And *The Star*'s own opinionated guide to where they dance," *Toronto Daily Star*, July 23, 1966.

3 "Yorkville," *Toronto Daily Star*, May 21, 1966.

4 Thomas, Ralph, "Yorkville? Squaresville!" *Toronto Daily Star*, January 23, 1965.

5 "And *The Star*'s own opinionated guide to where they dance."

6 Marom, Malka, *Joni Mitchell: In Her Own Words*, (ECW Press, 2014), p. 76.

7 *The Complete Geffen Recordings* (Geffen, 2003).

8 Goddard, John, and Richard Crouse, *Rock 'n' Roll Toronto* (Doubleday, 1997), p. 41.

9 Crowe, Cameron, "A conversation with Joni Mitchell" *Archives Vol. 1* booklet, p. 27.

10 Marom, Malka, *Joni Mitchell: In Her Own Words*, p. 39.

11 As announced in December 1963 issue of the Toronto Musicians Association journal *Crescendo*.

12 Based on quotes in David Yaffe's *Reckless Daughter* (HarperCollins, 2017), p. 33; Mark Bego's *Joni Mitchell* (Taylor Trade Publishing, 2005), p. 31.

13 Bego, Mark, *Joni Mitchell*, p. 31.

14 Cohen, Nathan, "A costly production," *Toronto Daily Star*, October 14, 1964.

15 The list of early live appearance listings on jonimitchell.com are informed in part by scrapbooks kept by Joni's mother, Myrtle, and Joni's letters to her at the time, sources that are not available for examination by researchers.

16 Joni may have been alluding to this situation when she told journalist Pamela Wallin, "I was dirt poor. I mean I was on-the-street poor, I didn't have a penny . . . so I became the housekeeper for these two guys."(Quoted in Goddard and Crouse, *Rock 'n' Roll Toronto*, p. 46.)

17 That Joni lived with John Soules, a story that has never been told in any of the Joni biographies, has been independently corroborated by friends of his from the time, Kig Vanderleck (letter to David Reville, September 13, 1994) and Alison Reid (email to author, December 6, 2021).

18 Marom, Malka, *Joni Mitchell: In Her Own Words*, p. 66.

19 Carol Robinson was a British-born actress and singer best known for her stint in the Yorkville jug band supergroup the Dirty Shames, also featuring multi-instrumentalist and veteran folksinger Chick Roberts, ace guitarist and bass singer Amos Garrett, and the guitarist-singer Jim McCarthy. In 1966, they shared a manager, Toronto-born Mary Martin, with Leonard Cohen. After a personnel shakeup, the band recorded a few songs, including a mesmerizing Carol lead vocal on John Sebastian and Zal Yanovsky's "Coconut Grove." Carol went on to appear on Wayne and Shuster TV specials and in a widely seen series of Lottario commercials. She died of cancer in 1990. Jim McCarthy, like Carol Robinson, grew up in Birkenhead, across the River Mersey from Liverpool. A traditional folksinger, he emigrated to Canada in 1956 and was a fixture at Yorkville folk clubs. After leaving the Dirty Shames, he went into the film business as a soundman and married actress Elizabeth Ashley in the 1980s. Al Cromwell (1938–1995) was an African-Canadian singer-guitarist from Nova Scotia, where he learned a repertoire of folk, blues, and spirituals from his father. He was active in folk clubs and taverns around Toronto through the early 1990s.

20 Comment in the Facebook group *Yorkville Music Scene 1955-1968*, April 29, 2023.

21 Richter, Volkmar, "A New Girl," *The Varsity*, October 2, 1964. Accessed July 22, 2025 at https://jonimitchell.com/library/view.cfm?id=1445.

22 Posen, Shelley, "Correspondence with Buffy Sainte-Marie and Joni Mitchell," Toronto Archives, Fonds 477, File 15.

23 Joni's timeline on her website has her "sitting in" at the New Gate of Cleve when Tom Paxton didn't show up on March 19. This is confirmed by a mention in the *Globe:* Hanlon, Michael, "Police Cars Cheaper Than Motorcycles" *Globe and Mail,* March 23, 1965.

24 The first recorded version of "Both Sides, Now" was captured live at the Second Fret club in Philadelphia on November 17, 1966. Her Riverboat appearance was the week before, November 8-13.

25 "Woman Struck, Toronto Man Faces Charge," *Globe and Mail*, February 22, 1965.
26 Barker, Gerry, "Tear gas siege ousts armed man," *Toronto Daily Star*, March 4, 1965.
27 Ibid.
28 "'Passion crime' sends man to jail," *Toronto Daily Star*, April 8, 1965.

CHAPTER SEVEN

1 Klein, Estelle, "Coffeehouses: A Review," *Hoot* No. 3 (1963).
2 Schiff, Marvin, "Lightfoot Appealing with Guileless Air," *Globe and Mail*, March 10, 1965.
3 Jennings, Nicholas, *Before the Gold Rush*, p. 86.
4 Dafoe, John, "Good Songs and Voice Are in Lightfoot's Art," *Globe and Mail*, January 19, 1966.
5 Ibid.
6 There was an earlier Left Bank club in Toronto, far west and south of Yorkville at 1263 Queen St. W. It was billed as opening on May 12, 1961. Whether the two Left Bank clubs were related is not known.
7 Mulroney, Catherine, "Team Strategy Reaches for 'Houses in the Sky,'" *Globe and Mail*, September 3, 1999.
8 Hanlon, Michael, "Complete Program for Royal Ballet," *Globe and Mail*, March 30, 1965.
9 Miller, Mark, *Way Down That Lonesome Road: Lonnie Johnson in Toronto 1965-1970* (The Mercury Press, 2012), p. 12.
10 Miller, *Way Down That Lonesome Road*, p. 15.
11 Cohen, Nathan, "Rain Falls on Critics," *Toronto Daily Star*, June 7, 1965.
12 Richter, Volkmar, "A Gentle, Dignified Performance," *The Varsity*, October 1, 1965.
13 Miller, *Way Down That Lonesome Road*, p. 15.
14 Thomas, Ralph, "Dancers of the Roaring 60s," *Toronto Daily Star*, July 23, 1966.
15 "And the Star's Own Opinionated Guide to Where They Dance," *Toronto Daily Star*, July 23, 1966.
16 "Marijuana Grown in Yorkville Patches Lawyer Tells Court," *Toronto Daily Star*, July 2, 1965.
17 Thomas, "Dancers of the Roaring 60s."
18 Quoted in Nick Warburton, "Luke and the Apostles" canadianbands.com. Accessed July 22, 2025 at https://canadianbands.com/luke-the-apostles/.
19 Gray, Walter, "Newcomers Turn to Own Kind," *Globe and Mail*, September 7, 1956.

CHAPTER EIGHT

1 Cohen, Nathan, "A Tear for Cindy-Ella," *Toronto Daily Star*, December 11, 1964. When I spoke with John Soules in 2022, he was grieving the recent death of his wife but otherwise enjoying retirement and writing haiku poetry in rural Wingham, Ontario. After leaving the Half Beat he drove taxi in Toronto for a while, then worked as an elementary school teacher for a few years before moving to Thunder Bay and becoming a logger and miner. Dave Pirie has eluded my research.

2 "What's Going On," *Toronto Telegram*, January 9, 1965.

3 Thomas, Ralph, "Yorkville? Squaresville!," *Toronto Daily Star*, January 23, 1965.

4 "Things to Do and See During the Weekend," *Globe and Mail*, June 25, 1965.

5 Kay, John, with John Einarson, *Magic Carpet Ride* (Quarry Press, 1994), p. 124.

6 Located at 20 Richmond Street East in that era, the Saphire Tavern (the misspelling was intentional; the legend goes that a signpainter made the mistake and the owner went with it to get a discount) was later the site of a classic live recording by R&B singer Jackie Shane.

7 Richter, Volkter, "Yorkville/Teenville Pt. 2," *The Varsity*, March 5, 1965.

8 Letter to David Reville, September 13, 1994.

9 Kirby, Blaik, "A Guide for Swinging Boulevardiers," *Globe and Mail*, March 30, 1968.

10 Cohen, Nathan, "A Costly Production," *Toronto Daily Star*, October 14, 1964.

11 Cohen, "A Tear for Cindy-Ella."

12 Scott, Patrick, "Jazz Scene: Coffee with Varnish and a Band without," *Globe and Mail*, April 28, 1965.

13 "Police Raid Coffeehouse, Charge 28," *Toronto Daily Star*, December 26, 1964.

14 "2,000 Throng Yorkville Area; Youths Seized," *Globe and Mail*, April 10, 1965.

15 Hanlon, Michael, "Talking with the Penny Farthing's Boss," *Globe and Mail*, May 14, 1965.

16 Ibid.

17 Cohen, Nathan, "Budding Tycoon," *Toronto Daily Star*, May 10, 1965.

18 Miller, *Way Down That Lonesome Road*, p. 43.

19 quoted in Miller, *Way Down That Lonesome Road*, p. 45.

20 Cohen, Nathan, "Youth Orchestra Rehearses," *Toronto Daily Star*, July 5, 1965.

21 Scott, Patrick, "A Metamorphosis in Yorkville," *Globe and Mail*, September 18, 1965.

22 "Action by City Urged against the Swinging Clubs in Yorkville," *Globe and Mail*, May 14, 1965.

23 Young, Scott, "Shh! The Mayor Was There," *Globe and Mail*, June 11, 1965.

24 Ibid.

25 Haggart, Ron, "Two Freshmen Lead the 'Prejudiced Poll,'" *Globe and Mail*, June 9, 1965.

26 Haggart, Ron, "A Current Report on the Yorkville War," *Globe and Mail*, October 25, 1965.

27 Haggart, Ron, "Bill Archer's Fight for Yorkville's Kids," *Globe and Mail*, October 27, 1965.

28 Ibid.

29 Ibid.

30 Barker, Gerry, "In Town and Out," *Toronto Daily Star*, March 6, 1964.

31 "And *The Star*'s own opinionated guide to where they dance."

32 "Dee and the Yeomen" *RPM* 4/14, November 29, 1965.

33 Dunnet, Graham, *Life and Musical Legacy* (self-published, 2018).

34 Lawson, Bruce, "The Image Makers: 'Hey kid . . . I can make you a star,'" *Globe and Mail*, October 8, 1966.

35 Ibid.

36 "3 Yorkville Coffeehouses Licensed, Despite City Ban," *Toronto Daily Star*, June 10, 1965.

37 "Yorkville Businesses Have Mixed Feelings about Limiting Licenses for Coffeehouses," *Globe and Mail*, May 28, 1965.

38 "And the Star's own opinionated guide to where they dance."

39 "3 Yorkville Coffeehouses Licensed, Despite City Ban."

40 Bingham, Dave, *Noise from the North End: The Amazing Story of the Ugly Ducklings* (Friesen Press, 2015), p. 31.

41 "And the Star's own opinionated guide to where they dance."

42 According to a band financial ledger book in Shays drummer John Wetherell's collection.

CHAPTER NINE

1 Prokop, Skip, with Jaimie Vernon, *Sunny Days: The Skip Prokop Story* (Bullseye Canada/ The Record Vault, 2021), p 54.

2 "The Paupers," https://citizenfreak.com/artists/100957-paupers.

3 Finkelstein, Bernie, *True North: A Life in the Music Business* (McClelland and Stewart, 2017), p. 45.

4 Named, he told me, "sort of as a tribute to both [record producer] Phil Spector, who was a huge hero, and SPECTRE from James Bond films."

5 Prokop and Vernon, Sunny Days, p. 64.

6 See Prokop and Vernon, *Sunny Days*, p. 66 and https://garagehangover.com/Paupers/ for more context. Bill Marion would go on record one solo single and then join the Last Words, another Yorkville band. Later, he wrote jingles, did voice-over work and released albums under his real name, Bill Misener. He died in 2014.

7 Beal, Chuck, "Goin' to New York," November 13, 2019. Accessed July 24, 2025 at https://chuckbealbubblingundder.wordpress.com/blog-feed/.

8 Ibid.

9 "The Mynah Bird: Topless Dancer a Possibility at Yorkville Coffeehouse," *Toronto Daily Star*, August 10, 1966.

10 Bradburn, Jamie, "Past Pieces of Toronto: the Mynah Bird." Accessed July 25, 2025 at http://jbwarehouse.blogspot.com/2013/07/past-pieces-of-toronto-mynah-bird.html.

11 "The Mynah Bird: Topless Dancer a Possibility at Yorkville Coffeehouse."

12 Reeves, John A., "REVIEW - 4 minutes - The Mynah Bird" radio script, c.1969.

13 Kerr, Colin, narration in a 1970s re-recording of "The Mynah Bird Song," and from the liner notes.

14 "Bobbi Lee Discusses Yorkville Village and the Mynah Birds on Kitchener Daytime TV Show." Accessed June 9, 2025. https://youtu.be/dUnPK8pQRss?si=lq_L2TGqdWLDppMo.

15 James, Rick with David Ritz, *Glow: The Autobiography of Rick James* (Atria Books, 2015), p. 60–61.

16 Ibid., p. 64.

17 Ibid., p. 65.

18 Ibid.

19 Warburton, Nick. 2022. "Mynah Birds." Accessed June 9, 2025 at https://canadianbands.com/mynah-byrds/.

CHAPTER TEN

1 McDonough, Jimmy, *Shakey: Neil Young's Biography* (Anchor Books, 2002), p. 121.

2 Young, Neil, *Waging Heavy Peace* (Blue Rider Press, 2012), p. 69.

3 Ibid., p. 70.

4 Jennings, Nicholas, "Toronto Songs: Neil Young's 'Ambulance Blues'" (March 21, 2019). Accessed July 25, 2025 at https://www.nicholasjennings.com/toronto-songs.

5 McDonough, *Shakey: Neil Young's Biography*, p. 121.

6 Ibid., p. 122.

7 Einarson, John, *Neil Young: Don't Be Denied* (Quarry Press, 1992), p. 165.

8 McDonough, *Shakey: Neil Young's Biography*, p. 72.

9 James, *Glow*, p. 74.

10 Young, *Waging Heavy Peace*, p. 73.

11 Lawson, Bruce, "Yorkville: Money in the Coffee Beans," *Globe and Mail*, May 14, 1966.

12 Young, *Waging Heavy Peace*, p. 125.

13 Jennings, *Before the Gold Rush*, p. 121.

14 Scott, Patrick, "Jazz Scene: Ellington at O'Keefe Hits the Bottom of Star Rating," *Globe and Mail*, July 2, 1966.

15 Display ad, *Toronto Daily Star*, April 22, 1966.

16 "In and about Town: Hesitant Toronto Awaits a Leader in Topless Dancing," *Toronto Daily Star,* July 30, 1966.

17 "Belated Tax to Boost Yorkville Prices," *Toronto Daily Star*, August 10, 1966.

18 Bylaw 22972, "To amend bylaw no. 20623 so as to prohibit private clubs within certain areas north of Bloor Street West between Huron and Bay Streets." (September 9, 1966).

19 Goddard and Kamin, *Shakin' All Over*, p. 59.

20 Miller, *Way Down That Lonesome Road*, p. 74.

21 Ibid.

22 Ibid., p. 76.

23 Ibid.

24 Ibid., p. 100.

25 Duff, Morris, "Bailiff Closes Door of the Village Corner," *Toronto Daily Star*, June 21, 1966.

26 Lewis, Joe, "Folk Music," *Toronto Telegram*, March 9, 1967.

27 Sherman, Michael, "Tom Rush - Sincerity in Action," *Toronto Daily Star*, February 24, 1966.

28 Duff, Morris, "Trouble at the Gate of Cleve," *Toronto Daily Star,* March 7, 1966.

29 Lawson, Bruce, "Yorkville: Money in the Coffee Beans," *Globe and Mail*, May 14, 1966.

30 "And *The Star*'s own opinionated guide to where they dance."

31 Richter, Volkmar, "Folk Music," *The Varsity*, September 23, 1966.

32 Clayton-Thomas, David, *Blood, Sweat and Tears* (Penguin Canada, 2011): p. 94.

33 Online obituary, 2014.

34 Clayton-Thomas, *Blood, Sweat and Tears*, p. 70.

35 "DCT To Go West," *RPM Music Weekly*, Vol. 5/No. 10 (May 2, 1966).

36 Clayton-Thomas, *Blood, Sweat and Tears,* p. 70.

37 Ibid., p. 75.

CHAPTER ELEVEN

1 Barris, Alex, *The Pierce-Arrow Showroom is Leaking: An Insider's View of the CBC* (Ryerson Press, 1969), pp. 80–81.

2 Ibid., p. 83.

3 Ibid., p. 85.

4 Marom, Malka, *Joni Mitchell in Her Own Words* (ECW Press, 2014), pp 7–8.

5 In a 2021 Zoom conversation, Elena Saldini (Joso's daughter) told me that Malka and Joso were in fact romantically involved, and that this was a major factor in the breakup of the duo.

6 Cohen, Nathan, "Malka and Joso Breaking Up," *Toronto Star* (May 4, 1967).

7 Barris, *The Pierce-Arrow Showroom is Leaking*, p. 87.

8 "Martin Robertson Obituary," Accessed September 24, 2025 at https://www.legacy.com/ca/obituaries/thestar/name/martin-robertson-obituary?id=45137986.

9 Norris, John, "Sunshine in the Strawberry Patch," *Globe and Mail*, August 1, 1967.

10 McAdorey, Bob, untitled column, *Toronto Telegram*, February 2, 1967.

11 Goddard and Kamin, *Shakin' All Over*, p. 70.

12 Beal, Chuck, "Bright Lights, Big City," (November 26, 2019), Accessed September 10, 2025 at https://chuckbealbubblingundder.wordpress.com/blog-feed/.

13 Prokop and Vernon, *Sunny Days*, p. 94–5.

14 Beal, "Bright Lights, Big City."

15 Ibid.

16 Ibid.

17 Fronted by singer Bob Burrows, Bobby Kris and the Imperials played the local dance circuit and had a moderate local hit with their soulful Stan Klees-produced 1966 version on Red Leaf Records of Bacharach and David's "Walk On By."

18 Peter Jermyn, comment on *The Toronto Sound 1955-1968* Facebook group, March 10, 2021.

19 Warburton, Nick, "Kensington Market," Accessed September 29, 2025 at http://nickwarburton.com/wordpress/?cat=5.

CHAPTER TWELVE

1 Pat's claim is not borne out by the usual musician credits for the album, and he may not have played on the released versions of the songs. *RPM* magazine mentioned his involvement in a brief 1973 item: Peter Taylor, "Nuts and Bolts," *RPM*, October 27, 1973.

2 Gerein, Charles "The Somewhat Enigmatic Yorkville Paint-in," *Toronto Daily Star*, April 26, 1967.

3 "Youth Charged after Death in Yorkville," *Globe and Mail*, May 12, 1967.

4 "Jailed 4 Years for Fight Death in Yorkville," *Globe and Mail*, October 28, 1967.

5 "12 Yorkville Night Spots Face Licensing Charges," *Globe and Mail*, July 19, 1967.

6 "Coffeehouse Freed Despite Split-Image," *Toronto Daily Star*, November 30, 1967.

7 Owram, Doug, *Born at the Right Time* (University of Toronto Press, 1996), p. 62.

8 Haggart, Ron, "A Current Report on the Yorkville War," *Globe and Mail*, October 25, 1965.

CHAPTER THIRTEEN

1 "Circus," *A Spoonful of Cathy Young*, reprinted with permission.

2 Goddard and Kamin, *Shakin' All Over*, p. 59.

3 "Curtis Knight Live Dates" earlyhendrix.com, Accessed June 13, 2025 at http://www.earlyhendrix.com/curtis-knight-live-dates.

4 According to Facebook comments on a thread about the incident in the group *Yorkville Music Scene 1955-1968* (January 21, 2022).

5 Henderson, *Making the Scene*, p. 217.

6 Kirby, Blaik, "Yorkville: the in-ghetto enters phase IV," *Globe and Mail*, July 13, 1968.

7 McDonald, Marci, "The Other Underground," *Toronto Daily Star*, September 14, 1968.

8 Kirby, "Yorkville: the in-ghetto enters phase IV."

9 In 2025, Susan Fiedler is a successful jewellery designer and the founder of F Cancer Embrace Life, a fundraising company. She is also the sales and marketing director for Sola's textile art studio.

10 McDonald, "The Other Underground."

11 Kirby, "Yorkville: the in-ghetto enters phase IV."

12 A light organ is a series of lights that flash on and off in response to the beat of the music. Linda Buttrey e-mail correspondence via Yedi Zak, October 5, 2025.

13 Korducki, Kelli, "Remembering Rochdale College, Toronto's Hippie Heart," *Globe and Mail*, November 8, 2013. Accessed October 1, 2025 at https://www.theglobeandmail.com/news/toronto/remembering-rochdale-college-torontos-hippie-heart/article15357582/.

14 Wookey, Richard, *Fortuna* (Macfarlane Walter and Ross, 1998), p. 273.

15 Ibid., p. 275–279.

16 Ibid., p. 282.

17 Ibid., p. 283.

18 Veillette, Eric, "A Drink with Founder of Penny Farthing Coffeehouse," *Toronto Star*, April 18, 2014. Accessed October 16, 2022 at https://www.thestar.com/life/2014/04/18/a_drink_with_founder_of_penny_farthing_coffee_house.html?rf.

19 Yorke, Ritchie, "Pop Scene: Rhinoceros Substitutes Competence for True Excitement," *Globe and Mail*, January 27, 1969.

20 Goddard, John, "Neil Young: The T.O. Years," *Toronto Star*, November 12, 2005.

21 Bradburn, Jamie, "Past Pieces of Toronto: The Mynah Bird," Accessed October 1, 2025 at https://jamiebradburnwriting.wordpress.com/2021/09/22/past-pieces-of-toronto-the-mynah-bird/.

22 In Rheta Maroosis' memory. Toronto City Directories for 1968 and 1969 show both 116 Yorkville (the Upper Crust) and 120 Yorkville (the ice cream shop) as "vacant."

23 "Shopping with Liz," *Toronto Daily Star*, December 17, 1970.

24 O'Malley, Martin, "Remember the Good Old Days of Yorkville?" *Globe and Mail*, November 21, 1973.

25 Kelly, Caitlin, "Over the Counter: The Street Charm of the Bourgeoisie," *Globe and Mail*, June 16, 1979.

26 "Your Cafe Table Awaits You, Toronto," *Toronto Star*, July 13, 1980.

27 "Acta de Defuncion de Werner Graeber" (death certificate).

28 "Yorkville Founder: Mexico Police Probe Torontonian's Death," *Globe and Mail*, November 3, 1978.

29 Daniels, Steve, "Refusal Report - Zoning Bylaw Amendment Application - 175 Avenue Road (Toronto Centre-Rosedale, Ward 27)" City of Toronto, 2004.

Index

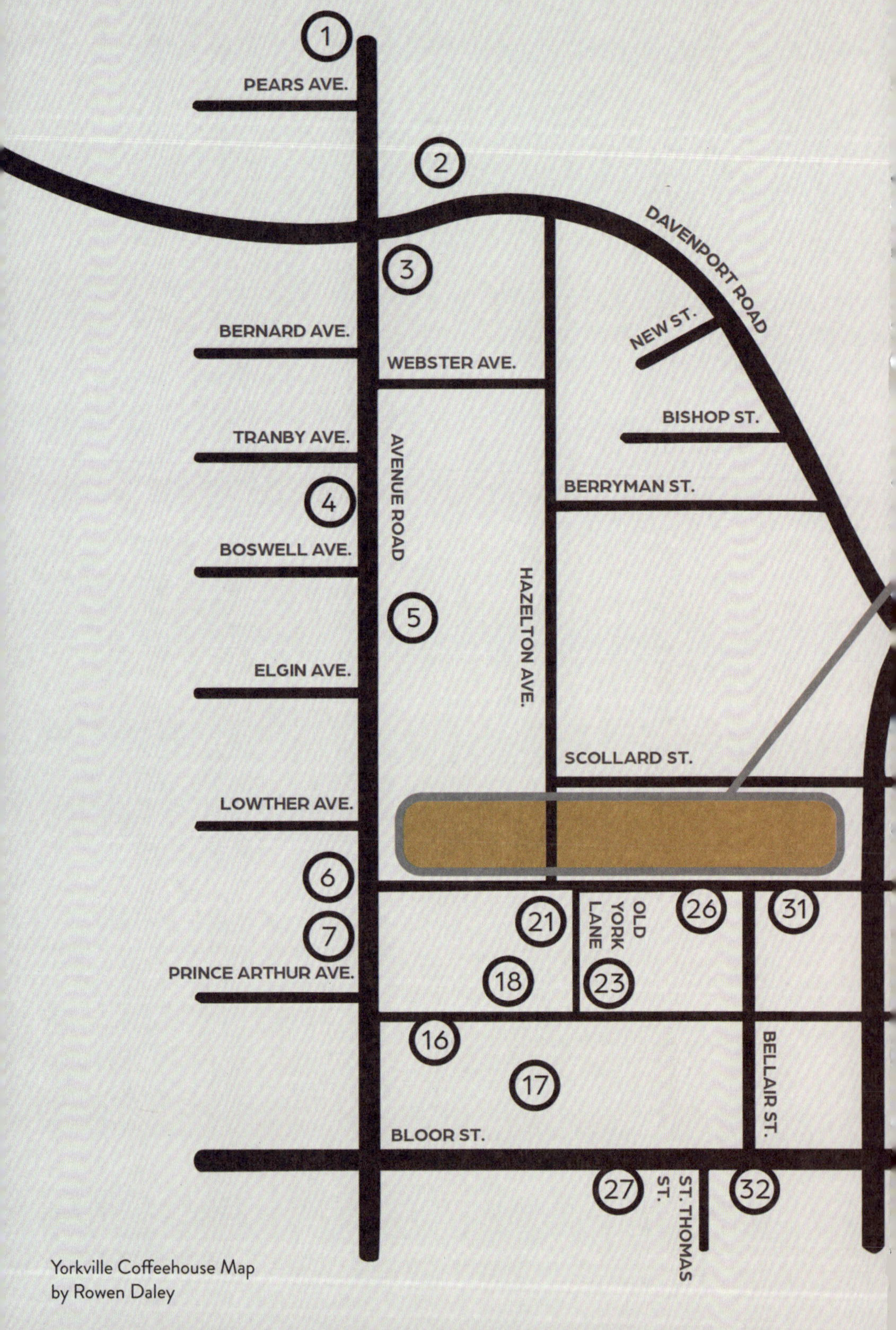

Yorkville Coffeehouse Map
by Rowen Daley